PROFILES
IN INJUSTICE

PROFILES IN INJUSTICE

Why Racial Profiling Cannot Work

David A. Harris

THE NEW PRESS

New York

Published in the United States by The New Press, New York, 2002
Distributed by W. W. Norton & Company, Inc., New York

LIBRARY OF CONGRESS CATALOGING-IN-PUBLICATION DATA
Harris, David A.
Profiles in injustice : why racial profiling cannot work / David A. Harris.
p.   cm.
Includes bibliographical references and index.
ISBN 1-56584-696-6 (hc.)
ISBN 1-56584-818-7 (pbk.)
1. Racial profiling in law enforcement—United States.
2. Law enforcement—United States.   I. Title.
HV8141.H298   2002
363.2'3'08900973—dc21   2001044177

The New Press was established in 1990 as a not-for-profit alternative to
the large, commercial publishing houses currently dominating the book
publishing industry. The New Press operates in the public interest rather
than for private gain, and is committed to publishing, in innovative ways,
works of educational, cultural, and community value that are often
deemed insufficiently profitable.

The New Press, 450 West 41st Street, 6th floor, New York, NY 10036
www.thenewpress.com

Printed in the United States of America

2   4   6   8   10   9   7   5   3   1

www.profilesininjustice.com

For Rebecca, Alicia, and Sam
Your love has meant everything to me

"Our Government is the potent, the omnipresent teacher. For good or for ill, it teaches the whole people by its example. . . . To declare that in the administration of the criminal law the end justifies the means—to declare that the Government may commit crimes in order to secure the conviction of a private criminal—would bring terrible retribution."
—JUSTICE LOUIS BRANDEIS, OLMSTEAD V. U.S. (1928)

"Law enforcement is not automatic. It isn't blind. . . . We know that no local police force can strictly enforce the traffic laws, or it would arrest half the driving population on any given morning."
—ATTORNEY GENERAL ROBERT JACKSON,
"THE FEDERAL PROSECUTOR" (1940)

"I feel like I'm a guy who's pretty much walked the straight line and that's respecting people and everything. But if the cops will even bother me . . . it just makes you wonder—was it just because I'm black?"
—JAMES BANKS, SALES EXECUTIVE, TOLEDO, OHIO (1998)

CONTENTS

ACKNOWLEDGMENTS

When I began this project, I wondered whether people who felt that they had been subjected to racial profiling would be willing to share their stories with me. I quickly discovered that I need not have worried. Almost every African American or Latino I talked to had either had this experience personally or had a family member or close friend who had. And every person I asked, without exception, was willing to talk to me, explain what had happened to them, and to tell me what it felt like. I am deeply grateful to all of those who opened their lives and their hearts to me. Many of their stories appear in this book; others do not, but every story I heard helped me write this book.

I owe a great debt to John Lamberth, Joseph Jacoby, and Mathew Zingraff, all of whom helped me to understand the many statistical issues that surround racial profiling. These three men gave me their time and attention again and again, and I found their help invaluable.

Robert Wasserman, William Bratton, Dean Esserman, Bob Stewart, Charles Moose, John Crew, and Samuel Walker all helped me to understand the law enforcement context in which racial profiling has emerged. Without this perspective, there is little chance that any attempt at reform, no matter how well intentioned, could succeed.

I am grateful to all of my colleagues at the University of Toledo College of Law, particularly Daniel Steinbock, who has read almost everything I've written, and Dean Phillip Closius, who has supported and encouraged my work. Early versions of this work benefited from the careful consideration and helpful comments received at the University of Michigan Law School Faculty Workshop, the University of Toledo College of Law Faculty Colloquium, the University of Toledo Humanities Institute, and the Wayne State University Faculty Forum.

I owe a great deal to Ellen Blum Barish and Hope Viner Samborn, who encouraged my writing, helped me improve it, and always pushed me forward. Their advice and support was more valuable than I can explain. Zick Rubin provided sound advice. He was a font of solid and practical wisdom on the world of publishing. Nancy Mahon and Gil Kline understood this project and gave it the kind of support that is rare in today's world. And Marcia Minnick and Jan Hendrickson both supplied invaluable help.

My editors at The New Press were tremendously important to the success of this book. Few novice writers realize that producing a book takes a team effort, and I would venture to say that even fewer are as lucky as I was in the editing help they receive. My thanks to Andy Hsiao, Marc Favreau, and Diane Wachtell, all of whom did a tremendous job in shaping this book and helping me make it as good as it could be. Special thanks to Diane Wachtell, who believed in the project from the beginning, helped me as I worked, and whose editing skills, nimble mind, and sense of humor are all beyond compare. Diane was, quite simply, the best editor one could hope to have. Making the manuscript into a book with all of them was a genuine pleasure.

Most of all, I wouldn't have been able to do any of this without the help, love, and support over many years from my wife, Rebecca Harris. For everything she's done for so long, I am appreciative beyond words.

Finally, I have learned many things in the course of writing this book, not least that finding the right place to write is an absolute necessity. For this I thank all of the wonderful people at the Sufficient Grounds Coffee House. They allowed me to take over the booth in the back corner on the second floor and kept me going with their dark, delicious brews. For me, this was a place where the words just flowed.

This project was supported by a Soros Senior Justice Fellowship from the Center on Crime, Communities & Culture of the Open Society Institute, and by grants from the University of Toledo College of Law.

Chapter One

PROFILES IN INJUSTICE: AMERICAN LIFE UNDER THE REGIME OF RACIAL PROFILING

SERGEANT ROSSANO GERALD

Sergeant First Class Rossano Gerald, a black man, had made the United States Army his life.[1] He served in Operation Desert Storm in Iraq, winning the Bronze Star, and in Operation United Shield in Somalia. His nineteen-year military career has included postings both in the United States and overseas. Military service runs deep in Sergeant Gerald's family; he describes himself as an "army brat" who grew up on military bases.

One blazing hot August day in 1998, Sergeant Gerald and his twelve-year-old son, Gregory, were on their way to a big family reunion in Oklahoma. Almost as soon as they crossed into Oklahoma from Arkansas, an Oklahoma Highway Patrol officer stopped their car. He questioned them, warning Sergeant Gerald not to follow cars in front of him too closely, then allowed him to leave. (Gerald denies following any other cars too closely; because he had noticed several highway patrol cars as he entered the state, he had been driving with extra caution.) But less than half an hour farther into Oklahoma, another highway patrol officer stopped Sergeant Gerald again, this time accusing him of changing lanes without signaling. Sergeant Gerald denied this, and he told the officer that another officer had just stopped him.

Despite Sergeant Gerald's having produced a valid driver's license, proof of insurance, and army identification, the troopers—several squad cars had arrived by now—asked to search his car. Sergeant Gerald politely refused; after answering numerous questions, Sergeant Gerald asked many times that the officer in charge call his commanding officer at his base. The highway patrol officers refused each request. Instead, the police put Sergeant Gerald and Gregory into a squad car, turned off the air conditioning, and turned on the car's fan, which blew suffocatingly hot air into the vehicle; they warned Sergeant Gerald and Gregory that the police dogs present would attack them if they tried to escape.

When Sergeant Gerald still refused to allow them to search his car, the troopers told him that Oklahoma statutes allowed them to search (a blatant misstatement of the law), and they had a drug-sniffing dog search the vehicle. Sergeant Gerald knew something about these animals; as part of his army duties, he'd worked with military police officers using drug-detection dogs. The dog never gave any signal that it smelled drugs, but the troopers told Sergeant Gerald that the dog had "alerted" to the presence of narcotics and that they were going to search his car.

For what seemed like hours in the oppressive heat, Sergeant Gerald—now in handcuffs in the backseat of a patrol car—watched as officers used a variety of tools to take apart door panels, consoles, even the inside of the car's roof; at one point they announced that they had found a "secret compartment" in the car's floor. (It was actually a factory-installed footrest.) The troopers attempted to block his view of the search by raising the hoods on their vehicles, and one of them deactivated a patrol car video-evidence camera. They went through every item in the luggage, questioning Sergeant Gerald about Gregory's plane tickets home, which they found in one of the suitcases. (Gregory lived with his mother in northern Indiana, and Sergeant Gerald planned to put him on a plane home after the reunion.) Meanwhile, Gregory was moved to another police car against his father's express wishes; he was made to sit in the front while a dog barked and growled at him from the backseat and a police officer asked him about his father's "involvement" in drug trafficking.

After two and a half hours—and no recovery of any drugs—the police released Sergeant Gerald with a warning ticket. When he asked them what they planned to do about the mess they had made of his car and his personal belongings, they gave him a screwdriver. Their parting words to him: "We ain't good at repacking." Damage to the car amounted to more than a thousand dollars.

Sergeant Gerald filed a lawsuit to contest his mistreatment. Although he has little taste or desire for litigation, he felt he owed it to his son, Gregory, to show that people who have power cannot abuse others with impunity. "I'm an authority figure myself," Sergeant Gerald says. "I don't want my son thinking for one minute that this kind of behavior by anyone in uniform is acceptable." The lawsuit ended with a settlement of seventy-five thousand dollars paid to Sergeant Gerald and Gregory, even as state officials still denied any wrongdoing. "I think I serve my country well," Sergeant Gerald said. "I never want my son to see racism like this happen." Gregory, he said, remains "scarred" by the experience.[2]

JUDGE FILEMON VELA

In 1980, President Carter appointed Filemon Vela United States District Judge for the Southern District of Texas.[3] Vela had been an elected state judge for six years before that, following a career in private practice. Judge Vela's chambers are in Brownsville, Texas, just across the Rio Grande from Matamoros, Mexico. Brownsville has a long history of connection with Mexico; many of its 130,000 citizens are of Mexican descent. Judge Vela's own great-grandfather came to Texas from Mexico in the 1860s. People know Judge Vela not only for what he does in his courtroom, but also for his activities in the community. His bedrock beliefs in education and straight talk led him to help organize and direct a program in which young male and female convicts serving drug sentences come to local high schools to tell the students how involvement with drugs and violence stole their futures. Judge Vela plays the Ted Koppel role in these sessions, asking the inmates about everything from their fear of prison rape to their shame at having embarrassed their families. Judge Vela's wife, Blanca Vela, is the mayor of Brownsville; between their friends, families, and their many personal and professional acquaintances, they know almost everyone in the city who is involved in politics and civic life.

In 1997, the area around Brownsville became the focus of intense immigration enforcement.[4] "Operation Rio Grande" increased the number of agents in the area from seven hundred to twelve hundred by the end of 1999 and poured sophisticated equipment and resources into the effort. The stepped-up activity paralleled similar operations in California, West Texas, and other illegal immigration hot spots. The result was a strong, proactive Border Patrol presence, enough to affect almost everyone of Mexican descent.

During the summer of 1999, Judge Vela and three members of his staff drove to Laredo, one of the cities in south Texas where Judge Vela holds court on a regular basis. The four rode in a Ford Explorer. A Border Patrol agent, who'd been sitting in a vehicle parked next to the side of the road, pulled them over. The agent asked Judge Vela and the others in the car about their citizenship. After they had answered, Judge Vela asked the agent why he had stopped the car. "He said he stopped us because there were too many people in the vehicle," Vela says, though the Explorer could certainly have held more passengers. Only then did Judge Vela tell the agent who he was; he also said that he felt that the agent did not have legal grounds to stop them. Though the agent quickly ended the encounter, telling Judge Vela and his staff they could go, Vela made a complaint to the officer's superiors—not so much about the conduct of the particular officer involved but rather about the practices and policies that led him to make an unjustified stop. As a judge, he was keenly aware that for any search that uncovers contraband to "stand up in court," the stop of the car that led to the search had to be legal. If the stop was illegal, a judge would have to throw out the evidence—and a criminal would go free. It's not at all surprising that Judge Vela's complaint was taken seriously by the Border Patrol; he received assurances that Border Patrol agents would get more training and education to teach them to stop motorists only with a legal basis.

Almost exactly a year after his first encounter with the Border Patrol, Judge Vela was again on his way to Laredo to preside in court, driving on the same road, this time as the passenger of an assistant U.S. attorney. His staff was riding in another vehicle, traveling along with them. Again, a Border Patrol agent pulled the car over; again, Judge Vela—an American citizen, an attorney, and a federal judge—had to answer questions about his citizenship. Once again, Judge Vela asked why the agent stopped them. The answer this time: the car had tinted windows. Judge Vela filed another complaint, but he was not surprised that a second incident had occurred.

Judge Vela talks about these experiences with candor and a touch of humor. He feels that although it is important to speak out, he cannot allow himself to be defined or embittered by what has happened. "If I ever catch myself being affected by these kinds of things, I should not allow myself to sit [as a judge]," he says. Yet it is clear that these experiences have confirmed for him that everyone in the Hispanic community is a target of immigration enforcement, regardless of whether they are citizens, or of their status or station in life. "If they stop us . . . we who are attorneys, we who study law . . . then my goodness, what will they do to persons who do not have our place?" he wonders. "If they can do it to you and me," he says, referring to himself, his staff, and the assistant U.S. attorney who were with him, "who won't they do it to?" Vela has taught American law and constitutionalism on behalf of the Unites States government to attorneys, judges, and other officials all over the world, particularly in Latin America, and he believes with all his heart that the United States and its Constitution are something special, something unique—something worth preserving. "But if you let these things happen, it will deteriorate." He worries that something is badly out of balance. Another Hispanic judge in Brownsville, who has also experienced the Border Patrol's tactics firsthand, puts it this way: "It feels like occupied territory. It does not feel like we're in the United States of America."[5]

MINHTRAN TRAN AND QUYEN PHAM

With school out for the year, Minhtran Tran and Quyen Pham went shopping one morning at a strip of stores in Garden Grove, a city of approximately 150,000 in Orange County, California. Neither girl, both fifteen-year-old honor students, had a police record or had had any contact at all with law enforcement. When they decided to leave and went to a pay phone outside the stores, police from Garden Grove's gang suppression unit drove up, got out of their cars, and confronted them and a third young Asian girl. The police accused them of making trouble and asked them whether they belonged to a gang, allegedly because they were wearing gang clothing. Officers then put the three girls up against a wall and took photographs of them with a Polaroid camera. None of the girls consented; in fact, the police never asked for their permission, let alone the permission of their parents. The "gang attire" they were alleged to have been wearing could have described the clothing of a million other teenagers that day: form-fitting shirts and oversized baggy pants. The police also took down information from the girls, including height, weight, age, hair and eye color, their home addresses, and the names of the schools they attended.[6]

Minhtran Tran and Quyen Pham may have felt disturbed by their treatment that day, but they received a worse shock later.

Other kids they knew who went to the Garden Grove Police Station later that day told the girls that they saw the Polaroid pictures the police had taken of them pinned up on a prominent bulletin board. The girls found this hard to understand; police had not charged or cited them, and they hadn't done anything. They felt that the police had labeled them criminals and treated them as gang members because they were Asians dressed in a certain way. Eventually, along with other young Asian Americans, the two girls became the plaintiffs in a lawsuit against the Garden Grove Police Department.

The photographing of the high school honor students by police did not happen by accident. Rather, it came about as part of a set of practices put in place as a deliberate effort to fight gangs in California. With an influx of Asian immigrants to the West Coast over the last twenty-five years, including refugees from Southeast Asia, the region's Asian population has surged. The growth of any immigrant population typically contributes to the problems one customarily finds in any city or suburban area, including crime and gangs. The Asian population is no different, despite the model minority stereotype, and in the early 1990s southern California communities began to make a concerted effort to combat what they saw as a rising menace.

One of the first examples of the effort came in a thirty-page report, entitled "Asian Gangs in Little Saigon: Identification and Methods of Operation."[7] The document, written by Detective Mark Nye of the Westminster Police Department, explored many aspects of Orange County's Asian youth gangs, from what they did to how they dressed to which cars they drove. The report discussed many different demographic groups, including female gang members. Nye warned that "female gang members in some cases dress very similar to male gang members. They will wear baggy, loose fitting clothing, baggy pants, oversized shirts, usually untucked, and in some cases baseball caps." (Parents will recognize this description of clothing as the nearly ubiquitous uniform of the American teenager—Asian, African American, Hispanic, or white.) Female members of Asian gangs, Nye said, looked enough like their male counterparts that they "can be mistakenly identified as males." And in a catch-22 that makes it difficult to see how any young Asian woman could avoid being labeled as a gang member, Nye said that Asian girls who did not dress in typical gang attire were really just in "disguise."

ROBERT WILKINS

In the early morning hours of a Monday in May 1992, Robert Wilkins and three members of his extended family were driving to Washington, D.C., from Chicago.[8] The four, all African Americans, had traveled together to Chicago a few days before for the funeral of Wilkins's grandfather, the family patriarch. As they drove along an interstate highway outside of Cumberland, Maryland, a Maryland State Police car pulled them over. Wilkins's cousin had been at the wheel; when Wilkins noticed that the stop had lasted some time and that the trooper had brought his cousin to the rear of their rental car, where he could not be seen, Wilkins and his uncle got out to see what was happening.

Wilkins's decision to get out of the car and investigate made perfect sense. He had exactly the right training to deal with a situation like this. A graduate of Harvard Law School, Wilkins was himself a criminal defense lawyer. He practiced with Washington, D.C.'s Public Defender Service, one of the most highly regarded public defender offices in the nation. Wilkins had considerable seasoning not only in the ins and outs of criminal and constitutional law, but also in the nuances of police tactics and street stops. He was a skilled trial lawyer, accustomed to speaking his mind in court crisply, authoritatively, and carefully, even though he was a soft-spoken person. He also had considerable experience dealing with police officers.

Wilkins's cousin, who had been driving, told him that the trooper wanted consent to search the car. It was true; the trooper showed Wilkins a consent-to-search form—a piece of paper that, if signed, would indicate that the trooper had obtained voluntary consent to a search of the car. "I explained to him who I was and that I was a public defender in Washington, D.C.," Wilkins said, "and I understood clearly what our rights were and what his rights were, and that we didn't want to have the car searched." The trooper's reply, though perhaps showing a lack of understanding of the law, was just as clear as Wilkins's statement had been. "He looked at me," Wilkins said, "and he said, 'Well, if you don't have anything to hide, then what's the problem?' "

Undoubtedly, most ordinary people would have given in to the officer's demand at this point, but Wilkins was not so easily intimidated. "I thought to myself that this is the exact, most inappropriate response that the law enforcement officer can give," he said. Just asserting your rights "shouldn't make you suspicious." Wilkins held firm; he told the officer that he and his family wanted to be left alone.

The trooper seemed genuinely puzzled and surprised. Giving the trooper credit for frankness, Wilkins remembers his explanation. "He said, 'Well, this is routine, no one ever objects.' I said I don't know what other people do and that may be the case that nobody else does, but we object." The trooper, perhaps sensing that he was not going to get to search the car the easy way, began to play hardball. He told Wilkins that he and his family would have to wait for a drug-sniffing dog. Wilkins continued to stand his ground, calmly but firmly. He told the trooper that *United States* v. *Sharpe,* a U.S. Supreme Court decision, said that he could not detain Wilkins and his family without some fact-based suspicion, and he asserted that there was nothing even remotely suspicious about the family. Though Wilkins clearly had the law on his side, the trooper didn't care to debate the issue. He told Wilkins that these searches were "just routine procedure" because the police had been having "problems with rental cars and drugs." (Wilkins and his family were driving a Virginia-registered rental car; the license plate, with its first letter *R*, showed this.) "He wasn't rude, he was firm," Wilkins recalls. "He just made clear, 'Look, you know, this is procedure. . . .

You're gonna have to wait here for this dog.' " Even offering to show the trooper the program from his grandfather's funeral did not change anything. By this time, other troopers had arrived. Though they saw Wilkins begin to write down names and badge numbers on a pad, the troopers were undeterred; in fact, Wilkins remembers that at least one seemed quite amused by his insistence on his rights.

And the way the trooper wanted it was, in the end, the way it went. The family was held until the dog arrived. Despite their strenuous objections, all of them were forced to get out of the car and stand in the dark and the rain by the side of the road as the dog—so reminiscent to Wilkins and his family of the dogs turned loose on blacks in the South by police in civil rights confrontations—sniffed every inch of the exterior of the car. And only after this careful search turned up nothing were they allowed to leave—with a $105 ticket, though the trooper had originally told them they would receive only a warning. It was only later that Wilkins learned he'd been stopped because of a written profile (prepared by the Maryland State Police) that described him perfectly—a black male in a rental car.

All four of these stories may sound like egregious examples of police run amok, the work of rogue officers. But the truth is that these situations were the result of a well-known, well-used law enforcement technique that has spread all over the country. It has become known as "racial profiling"—and it describes life for millions of Americans who happen to be black, brown, or Asian. What happened to Sergeant Gerald, Judge Vela, Minhtran Tran and Quyen Pham, and Robert Wilkins is not uncommon at all among people like them. They have lived with these practices for many years—even if the rest of the nation has become aware of racial profiling only recently.

Racial profiling grew out of a law enforcement tactic called *criminal* profiling. *Criminal* profiling has come into increasing use over the last twenty years, not just as a way to solve particular crimes police know about but also as a way to predict who may be involved in as-yet-undiscovered crimes, especially drug offenses. *Criminal* profiling is designed to help police spot criminals by developing sets of personal and behavioral characteristics associated with particular offenses. By comparing individuals they observe with profiles, officers should have a better basis for deciding which people to treat as suspects. Officers may see no direct evidence of crime, but they can rely on noncriminal but observable characteristics associated with crime to decide whether someone seems suspicious and therefore deserving of greater police scrutiny.

When these characteristics include race or ethnicity as a factor in predicting crimes, *criminal* profiling can become *racial* profiling. Racial profiling is a crime-fighting strategy—a government policy that treats African Americans, Latinos, and members of other minority groups as criminal suspects on the assumption that doing so will increase the odds of catching criminals. Many in law enforcement argue that it makes sense to use race or ethnicity in criminal profiles because there is a strong statistical association between membership in minority groups and involvement in crime. Having black or brown skin elevates the chances that any given person may be engaged in crime, especially drug crime, the thinking of police and many members of the public goes. The disproportionately large number of minorities reflected in arrest and incarceration statistics is further proof, the argument continues, that skin color is a valid indicator of a greater propensity to commit crime. Supporters of racial profiling arrive, therefore, at the conclusion that focusing police suspicion on blacks, Latinos, Asians, and other minorities makes perfect sense. Racial profiling is nothing more than rational law enforcement.

If racial profiling is what directs police suspicion at minorities, it is high-discretion police tactics that put these suspicions into action, turning profiles into police investigations. These high-discretion methods allow police to detain, question, and search people who have exhibited no concrete evidence of wrongdoing—something the law would almost never otherwise allow. But thanks to the U.S. Supreme Court, which has widened the permissible scope of police discretion and vastly increased law enforcement power at the same time that profiling has come into wide use, these tactics are all perfectly legal. For example, police officers can use traffic enforcement as a legal excuse to "fish" for evidence, even though officers have observed no criminal conduct. Officers can also ask for "voluntary" consent to search, without even a whisper of a reason to think the citizen asked has done anything wrong. And officers can also "stop and frisk" pedestrians without the probable cause they need in other circumstances.

Taken at face value, we could say that racial profiling is morally and ethically wrong. It is clearly unconscionable to treat an individual as a criminal suspect simply because a small number of individuals from the same racial or ethnic group are criminals. But in a society dedicated to equal justice under law, such a practice also undermines our commitment to individual civil rights. Enforcing the law on the basis of racial and ethnic calculations therefore also offends the Constitution. All Americans are guaranteed "the equal protection of the law"; there are few values closer to the core of our political culture. Enforcing the law in a racially or ethnically biased way violates this central principle.

Racial profiling also damages the relationship between police departments and the communities they serve. Almost all police departments today describe themselves as service oriented; community policing, a philosophy of law enforcement that features partnerships between police and the citizens they serve, has become the accepted and applauded orthodoxy everywhere. Yet profiling, which treats all citizens of particular racial and ethnic groups as potential criminals, can do nothing but alienate these same citizens from their police. It breaks down the trust that must be at the heart of any true partnership, and it threatens to defeat community policing's best efforts to fight crime and disorder. Racial profiling reinforces the preexisting fissures of race in our society. By putting citizens in categories by race and ethnicity to determine which ones should be regarded as suspicious and therefore worthy of greater police scrutiny, we divide ourselves into "the good" and "the bad," the citizen and the criminal.

But, as this book will show, apart from the moral, ethical, and constitutional arguments against racial profiling, which have increasingly been embraced by Americans of all colors in recent years, new data now offer an irrefutable statistical argument against the practice. Despite the widespread belief that racial profiling, reprehensible though it may be, is an effective and efficient way of catching criminals—a "rational" approach to law enforcement—newly collected information about "hit rates" gives the lie to this assumption: the numbers just don't add up. Data emerging from studies done over the last few years demonstrate conclusively that hit rates—the rates at which police actually find contraband on people they stop—run contrary to long-held "commonsense" beliefs about the effectiveness of racial profiling. The rate at which officers uncover contraband in stops and searches is *not* higher for blacks than for whites, as most people believe. Contrary to what the "rational" law enforcement justification for racial profiling would predict, *the hit rate for drugs and weapons in police searches of African Americans is the same as or lower than the rate for whites.* Comparing Latinos and whites yields even more surprising results. Police catch criminals among Latinos at *far lower rates* than among whites. These results hold true in studies done in New York, Maryland, New Jersey, and other places. We see the same results in data collected by the U.S. Customs Service, concerning the searches it does of people entering the country at airports: the hit rate is lower for blacks than it is for whites, and the hit rate for Latinos is lower still.

Other data also yield startling surprises. For example, while it is true that automobile stops sometimes result in large seizures of drugs, this rarely happens. In fact, police usually find nothing at all; when they do find drugs, it is almost always very small amounts. The quantities discovered seldom exceed enough for personal use and often amount to even less—so-called trace amounts that can be detected but not used. Of course, what we see on the evening news are the big seizures; we seldom hear about the small ones and never about the far more numerous times that officers come up empty-handed. We come away with the mistaken impression that these tactics are not only rational and fair but successful—when nothing could be further from the truth. All of this exposes the rational law enforcement argument as, at best, the product of a set of mistaken assumptions. If blacks and Latinos who are stopped as a result of racial profiling are no more likely or are even less likely to be in possession of drugs or other contraband than whites, it simply doesn't make sense to enforce the law in this way. And if the net results are not a constant parade of big-time seizures of contraband but mostly "dry holes" and tiny amounts, there's no real payoff. If "rational" law enforcement seems to make sense, that is only because we are selective in our interpretations of facts and limited in our vision of what police do and in the effects these actions have.

Even if we were to overlook racial profiling's moral, legal, and social flaws, it simply does not work as a law enforcement tactic. And it is a way of enforcing the law that we almost surely would not accept in other circumstances. Suppose, for example, that profiles focused not on race and ethnicity but on poverty. We can imagine appearance characteristics for poverty that would prove almost as easy to observe as skin color: clothing and personal appearance, the physical condition and age of vehicles, and the neighborhood in which a person lives. Yet we would almost certainly object if police consistently stopped, questioned, and searched almost everyone who looked poor. The assumption that police should treat *all* poor people as criminal suspects because *some* poor people commit crimes would—and should—outrage us. Yet this is precisely what is happening when we police with racial profiles—except, of course, that the burden is likely to be distributed not by poverty but by race and ethnicity.

It would be easy to assume that racial profiling has its roots only in the racism of individual racist police officers—that the officers who engage in this practice are bigots whom we should simply root out of the police force. Surely there are bigots among police officers, but there are also bigots in every other profession. The great majority of police officers are good people who make use of racial profiling unintentionally. They do so not because they are bigoted or bad, but because they think it is the right way to catch criminals. Racial profiling is an institutional practice—a tactic accepted and encouraged by police agencies as a legitimate, effective crime-fighting tool. It is a method full of assumptions that have, for too long, gone untested, unexamined, and unchallenged. And when we do challenge it—push hard on its underlying premises and look at real data—policing with racial profiles cannot be said to be a rational response to crime. It is instead a misdirected attack on a difficult set of problems that causes its own damage to innocent individuals, to policing, to society, and to the law itself. Racial profiling is based not on real evidence but on distorted ideas about crime and an overly narrow view of how to attack it. We can do better; in fact, we must do better. The task of this book is to get us beyond the inaccurate, incorrect, and misleading ways in which we think about crime and how to fight it.

In the aftermath of the terrorist attacks of September 11, 2001, new calls for racial and ethnic profiling arose. Because all of the suicide hijackers came from one narrow group—Muslim Arabs—many Americans have advocated using race or ethnicity as part of a profile to catch potential terrorists in the future. It is, they say, the only course that makes common sense. Some have even gone so far as to argue that those who oppose racial profiling are something-less-than-patriotic Americans, and might be partly to blame for the terrorist attacks. But these arguments share all of the flaws of arguments promoting racial profiling as an effective tactic in the War on Drugs. If we take the time to examine these assertions in light of what we already know about racial profiling—that it does not, in fact, help us catch criminals, and carries very substantial social costs—we can look for more effective and less damaging ways of accomplishing our goals.

Chapter Two

PROFILING PAST AND PRESENT, AND HIGH-DISCRETION POLICE TACTICS

A profile is simply a set of characteristics—physical, behavioral, or psychological. In *criminal profiling,* law enforcement personnel use characteristics associated with either a particular crime or group of crimes to develop a profile of someone likely to engage in illicit behavior. Using these profiles to identify potential criminals is a form of playing the odds. If the characteristics of the profile correlate with criminal behavior, the assumption is that there's a higher probability that someone matching the profile will be engaged in crime. In practical terms, there simply aren't enough police officers or resources to keep every person and every place under surveillance—we probably wouldn't want a society like that, anyway—so officers welcome any tool to help them identify the most likely lawbreakers. Profiles enable the police to create portraits of criminals using facts instead of gut instinct or wishful thinking. Profiles can systematically pool collective police experience into information that is comprehensive, solid, and accurate—something much better than the selectively remembered war stories of individual officers. Compiling this information into a real picture of criminal activity on the street should offer a better basis for suspicion than simple intuition.

THE HIJACKER PROFILE

We've heard more about profiles in the last several years than ever before, but the idea is actually not new. One of the first well-known efforts to use a profile came in the battle against air piracy. This was the so-called hijacker's profile, which was employed as part of a system designed to stop the hijacking of American commercial airliners to Cuba (and a few other countries) in the late 1960s. By the end of that decade, airplane hijackings had reached an unprecedented level. Eighteen American planes were hijacked in 1968; in 1969, hijackers made forty attempts against U.S. aircraft, succeeding thirty-three times. There were even more of these crimes involving planes from other nations.[1] For a brief time, the federal government tried to stem the problem by putting "sky marshals"—specially trained members of the U.S. Marshal Service—on flights deemed at greatest risk. But this proved ineffective; hijackings continued.

To prevent hijackings, the authorities needed to stop the crime on the ground, before it could start. A government task force came up with the idea of a more comprehensive, ground-based hijacker detection system using a profile. The system used a number of steps, each a little more intrusive than the one before, to identify those most likely to hijack a plane on the ground in the airport, before those suspected under the profile could board the aircraft.[2] The system began with public notification at airport entry points that officials might search any bags. Once at the ticket counter, airline ground personnel "screened" each passenger with a behavioral profile. The task force designed the profile based on study of the characteristics of all known hijackers. (While the task force never made the characteristics of the profile public, it apparently includes only the general behaviors of all boarding passengers and not their social, racial, or ethnic identifiers).[3] Those who fit the profile had their boarding cards marked. In the boarding area, officials screened all passengers with magnetometers; while many passengers set off the warning signal—the machines were set to detect guns but would also sound whenever a passenger carried other metal objects—only those who both set off the detector and had a marked boarding card were singled out for further inquiry. These passengers would be asked for identification. If the response to this request was unsatisfactory in some way, these passengers might have to go through further magnetometer screening, questioning, or even a luggage or body search.[4] In 1972, the Federal Aviation Administration (FAA) made use of some or all of the parts of this profile-based system mandatory.[5]

But there was a problem with the hijacker identification system: it didn't work. While it reduced airline highjackings a little, it didn't eliminate them.[6] The FAA scrapped hijacker profiling, and in January of 1973 it adopted a new system: mandatory electronic screening of all passengers, in much the same form we have today. All passengers must pass through metal detectors, removing objects that set the machine off until they can pass through it successfully. Security personnel also x-ray all carry-on baggage and also conduct hand searches of selected bags. Universal screening—not just of those selected by a complicated profile, but of everyone—proved to be the only way to assure safety from air piracy; by 1976, only four hijackings of U.S. airliners took place—a drop of 90 percent from the high water mark of forty in 1969.[7]

THE SERIAL-KILLER PROFILE

Another crime-fighting effort, better known than the unsuccessful hijacker profile, has become part of popular culture: the profiling of serial killers. The FBI generally receives credit for this innovation, and numerous books have been written by, and about, the members of the elite unit within the bureau that did the work.[8] The serial-killer profile relied on a central insight: to find out about serial killers—who they are, how they operate, and what motivates them—talk to the ones who've been caught. By conducting hours of interviews with these criminals, FBI agents constructed a profile designed to assist in apprehending serial killers when evidence of their deeds began to surface. Officers who had worked on these cases were interviewed too, their case records reviewed in detail, and any other available information added to the database. When added to information concerning any new case, these portraits yielded a rich, highly textured picture, something useful to agents in the field who needed to spot and apprehend suspects before they did any more murderous damage. Working with detailed, voluminous data in the context of a set of actual known offenses, and focusing on extremely rare events, it is not surprising that sometimes these profiles helped the authorities find and apprehend these killers. Sometimes they did not. Since we have no data that would tell us how often these profiles resulted in an arrest, we have no way to measure just how effective they were overall. Nevertheless, the FBI profilers have become pop cultural icons. The character Jack Crawford, the supervising FBI agent in the film *Silence of the Lambs,* was supposedly based on John Douglas, one of the best known of those involved in the FBI profiling operation.[9] A current (and entirely forgettable) television series, *Profiler,* uses the idea as a dramatic twist on the usual police-detective drama.[10]

THE DRUG-COURIER PROFILE

But it was not until the 1980s that profiling came into much wider use with the advent of the "drug-courier profile" at airports. The idea was to apply profiling against a much broader category of crime. Drug offenses are not extremely rare or especially heinous crimes occurring in a particular area, as are airline hijackings or serial killings; rather, drug crimes are much more common and quite widespread. Likewise, drug dealing or transportation are generally not sets of similar, related, already-discovered crimes, like a string of similar bank robberies. Rather, use of the drug-courier profile in airports was designed for proactive detection of common drug offenses *as yet unknown to the police.* These profiles were designed to be *predictive* of crime, not *descriptive* of particular criminals; they thus were much closer in theory to the hijacker profile than to serial-killer profiling.

In the late 1970s and early 1980s, federal agents thought they could stop the use of commercial air travel to transport narcotics by devising a set of characteristics for spotting passengers who might be carrying drugs. Former Drug Enforcement Administration agent John Marcello, who now writes crime dramas, says that he and former agent Paul Markonni "are considered the 'Godfathers' of the DEA's airport-interdiction program" because in 1976 they, along with others, identified common characteristics of illegal drug couriers.[11] Lawsuits regarding the use of the profile in airports, which began to be filed in large numbers in the 1980s, showed that those who met the profile were stopped, questioned, and sometimes searched by law enforcement authorities.

In 1989, drug-courier profiles used in airports came before the U.S. Supreme Court. In *U.S. v. Sokolow,* the Court upheld the profile as a constitutionally acceptable basis for the temporary detention of a suspect in an airport to investigate possible drug trafficking.[12] Agents stopped Sokolow at the Honolulu airport because he fit a profile: (1) he paid for his ticket with a large amount of cash; (2) he traveled under a name different from the one under which his telephone was listed; (3) he had made a round-trip to Miami, a so-called drug-source city; (4) though the round-trip took twenty hours, he stayed in Miami only forty-eight hours; (5) he appeared nervous; and (6) he did not check any luggage. The justices had no problem with law enforcement's use of the profile instead of customary, case-by-case police work. The question was whether police had observed enough to give them legal cause to act, the Court said; it didn't matter whether their suspicions had come from a profile or some other method. "[T]he fact that these factors may be set forth in a 'profile' does not somehow detract from their evidentiary significance as seen by a trained agent."[13] In other words, profiles were just another set of tools for doing what police officers had always done.

As with the serial-killer profile, many claim great success for drug-courier profiling. Former DEA agent Marcello is blunt: "Drug-courier profiles work when officers are properly trained, period." And if what Marcello means is that officers using profiles sometimes catch drug couriers, he is undoubtedly right. But his comment certainly tells us nothing about whether the drug-courier profile works better than other enforcement techniques. Just as with the serial-killer profile, no one has any statistics on the success rate of drug-courier profiles that would show us how effective this technique really is.

PROFILING ON THE HIGHWAY

If it was in the relatively rarefied context of the DEA's investigation of narcotics trafficking through airports that the drug-courier profile first emerged, it was on the highway that the idea was spread as law enforcement gospel. And many people say the man responsible for this is Bob Vogel—former Florida State Trooper, former sheriff of Volusia County in central Florida, and surely one of greatest practitioners and proponents of profiling to come out of law enforcement. Bob Vogel wasn't the first to come up with the idea of criminal profiling. But it's probably safe to say that he's the one who brought it to its full potential. Vogel is the man who thought of applying profiling not to rare dangerous criminals like serial killers or even to drug smugglers in airports, but to everyday citizens in their cars, in order to find drugs. When people think of drug-courier profiling on the highways, Vogel is often the one who gets the credit—or the blame.

Bob Vogel joined the Florida Highway Patrol (FHP) in 1972 after returning from Vietnam, where he'd served in the marines.[14] In the early 1980s, he attended training that taught FHP officers that drug distributors were shipping their product into Florida from Central and South America largely by water, and out of Florida to other points in the United States by highway. This focused Vogel on how traffickers used the roads in their business, and he increasingly came to use traffic stops to investigate. By

1984, he'd begun making large numbers of drug busts by stopping drivers on Interstate 95; Vogel says that between February 1984 and March 1985, he made thirty major narcotics arrests, many of them for large quantities of cocaine and marijuana. In the course of these thirty arrests, Vogel noticed that he saw certain things over and over. He began keeping a list of these "cumulative similarities"—Vogel prefers not to use the word *profile*—and he began to refer to them when deciding which drivers he should search. These cumulative similarities included the driver's demeanor, vehicles not registered in the driver's name, driving overcautiously, things that looked out of place (such as a spare tire in the backseat), use of a large late model car or rental car, driving in the early morning hours, and male drivers and occupants who avoided eye contact. According to Vogel, these factors were never meant to be used as a sort of an automated checklist to be followed without thinking about the particular situation; "a lot of it has to do with training and experience." And he says that officers stopping people based on a kind of nonrigorous, seat-of-the-pants approach, instead of Vogel's cautiously constructed "cumulative similarities" based on concrete experience, were making a "fundamental error." When his list of "cumulative similarities" told Vogel a particular driver deserved a closer look, he'd use the pretext of any routine traffic infraction to pull the driver over and begin investigating.

Vogel's achievements began to attract attention. The DEA became aware of his successes and embraced his system wholeheartedly. Vogel says DEA agents rode with him on his patrol shifts to observe him, and he conducted training classes for the DEA's Operation Pipeline—the DEA's effort to convert law enforcement agencies around the country to the gospel of highway drug interdiction. Vogel was there, very much a part of Pipeline, as it was getting started in the mid 1980s; to hear him tell it, his work was very much the inspiration for Pipeline's efforts.[15] In law enforcement circles he became a widely known teacher of his tactics.

Courts at first proved wary of Vogel's "cumulative similarities." One federal appeals court denounced Vogel's method—his "hunch" that the suspects looked like criminals, which, as Vogel testified, justified his stopping the car—as "counter to our Constitution's promise against unreasonable searches and seizures." [16] But Vogel soon discovered a way around these problems. Instead of using the similarities themselves as the legal justification for the stop, Vogel began stating that the traffic offense was the reason he stopped the car. The "cumulative similarities" only came into play later, after the stop. Courts now upheld his work, and the Supreme Court itself later legitimized this approach in a case in 1996. His constant hard work netted him many arrests. It also began to bring him awards and press attention, including a piece on CBS's *60 Minutes*. In 1988 he won election as sheriff of Volusia County, Florida, and immediately set up a drug-interdiction unit patterned on his methods. And his influence outside of Florida has been vast. The DEA eventually got Operation Pipeline up and running nationally; the agency became the great evangelizer of Vogel's methods. A river of federal tax dollars flowed in to spread the highway drug-profiling gospel everywhere. DEA leveraged these federal dollars by training state and local police. By one count, approximately twenty-seven thousand officers have received Operation Pipeline training;[17] they, in turn, trained other officers in their own and other police departments.

PROFILING ON THE STREETS

Law enforcement has also profiled pedestrians on the streets. The chief tactic used in this context is known as "stop and frisk"—a temporary detention of a citizen, often accompanied by a limited search in which officers "pat down" the citizen's outer clothing in an attempt to detect any weapon that might be present. There is nothing new about stops and frisks; police have been doing them for years, and they became the centerpiece of *Terry* v. *Ohio,* one of the most important criminal cases of the 1960s. It is how and why stops and frisks have been used that make them pertinent to profiling. And it was with the aggressive policing in the early 1990s in New York that we began to see how stops and frisks could evolve into a tactic that ultimately became another avenue for racial profiling.

Police have often used stops and frisks in a way that differs fundamentally from other aspects of law enforcement. We often think of crime fighting as reactive: a victim of a crime calls the police, who respond, or the police witness a crime taking place and engage in efforts to apprehend the criminal. In fact, police often look for opportunities to act preemptively. They find themselves in situations in which there has been no reported crime, and they have not witnessed one. Nevertheless, what they have observed makes them suspicious, and they take action to investigate. The action takes the form of confronting the suspect and briefly detaining and questioning him or her in an effort to either confirm or dispel suspicions of potential criminal wrongdoing. The Supreme Court's *Terry* case legalized this approach, adding that a cursory search for weapons—a frisk—could also be part of the scenario. The idea, the Court said, was to allow police officers to take preemptive steps to investigate crime in situations that raised "reasonable suspicion"—not a hunch or a gut-level instinctive response, but a suspicion founded upon the officer's observations and reasonable inferences a trained and experienced police officer would make. The officer could take only limited actions: a temporary detention and a frisk. Nevertheless, police could detain and search preemptively; they did not need to wait until a crime had occurred.

In the 1990s, it was the New York Police Department that showed just how aggressively a law enforcement agency could use stops and frisks to target crime. The NYPD had made a conscious policy decision in 1994 to pursue a crime-fighting strategy that heavily emphasized order-maintenance policing—the so-called broken windows theory of crime control. This idea, first widely articulated in a 1982 magazine article by James Q. Wilson and George L. Kelling,[18] is that police must fight low-level social disorder on the streets—such as graffiti, public drunkenness, and marijuana smoking to set a tone of law and order. Wilson and Kelling argued that these minor crimes break down social controls, cause citizens to become fearful and withdraw from public spaces, ceding them to potential criminals who feel free to perpetrate more serious crime.[19] Wilson and Kelling put it this way: "[I]f [one broken window] is left unrepaired, all the rest of the windows will soon be broken."[20] (The second but equally important part of Wilson and Kelling's theory, that the success of order-maintenance policing required "close collaboration between police and citizens . . . in the development of neighborhood standards"[21] of conduct, seems to have concerned NYPD decision makers a lot less than the first.)

Written NYPD policies adopted in 1994 reflected an aggressive order-maintenance outlook. Police Strategy No. 5, entitled "Reclaiming the Public Spaces of New York," presented the department's approach to fighting low-level street disorder. This aggressive plan for dealing with low-level disorder was "the linchpin of efforts now being undertaken by the New York City Police Department to reduce crime and fear in the city."[22] Police Strategy No. 1, "Getting Guns off the Streets of New York," described the department's offensive against gun violence by increasing efforts to find and confiscate guns.[23] These strategies would work together, the department said, because "[b]y working systematically and assertively to reduce the level of disorder in the city, the NYPD will act to undercut the ground on which more serious crime seems possible and even permissible."[24] The increased enforcement against low-level offenders meant that criminals would run a larger risk by carrying a gun.[25] Police hoped that criminals would respond by not carrying guns, resulting in fewer gun-related crimes and deaths. This strategy would also mean, of course, that the use of stops and frisks would grow substantially. Data on stops and frisks from all twelve months of 1998 and the first three months of 1999 show clear evidence of this. Fully one-third of all stops and frisks during this period involved suspected weapons possession. The NYPD's Street

Crimes Unit, whose mission strongly emphasized recovering illegal guns, made more than 10 percent of all documented stops, though it represented only about one percent of all NYPD officers. Thus the period from the mid-1990s on in New York offered a kind of large-scale experiment in which one could observe the consequences of a strong commitment to the aggressive use of stops and frisks as a way of preempting and predicting crime in order to fight it. The result, as we will see, was the emergence of the use of race as a part of a profile.

THE INHERENT DANGERS OF PROFILING

As discussed previously, criminal profiling seems to be most effective in describing the characteristics of someone likely to have committed a specific, existing crime rather than predicting who might be committing crimes not yet known to the police. Using profiles predictively often results in faulty analysis and enforcement, based more on untested assumption than on facts.

Profiles can be either formal or informal, based on hard data accumulated methodically over time, or more impressionistic, relying on a small number of personal experiences or memories. Informal profiling is a way of looking at crime in which filtered experience and preexisting judgments get shaped into "street sense," and in which the unquestioned folk wisdom of the police squad room substitutes for careful analysis. As with predictive profiles, informal profiles run the risk of reflecting preconceptions in the profiler rather than being accurate representations of who commits crime. A profile is only as good as its components: a profile built on false assumptions and unexamined premises will be no more effective than mere guessing.

Informal Profiling

Most of the profiling we see today is informal, less rigorous, and less structured than formal profiling, less (or not at all) reliant on systematically collected data, and oriented toward the vagaries of human recollection instead of the correlation of acts across multiple cases. Indeed, some informal profiles are profiles in name only; they share little with the meticulous and careful collection of facts and detail that the FBI engaged in to build the serial-killer profile. Much more often, these informal profiles consist of individual officers' own memories of significant experiences, in conjunction with those of their colleagues. The result may be law enforcement based on a kind of folk wisdom—information that has more in common with stories and legends than with well-constructed patterns of data. Drawing on only a small, unrepresentative sample of events, these less formal profiles can easily become dangerously inaccurate.

During the last several decades, social scientists have made great strides in understanding how people think, remember, and process information. Most people do not think cognitively (i.e., figuring out what is happening around them and reasoning their way to a logical conclusion supported by the facts). Rather, most people think affectively.[26] They perceive the world around them selectively and make decisions based on views that they already hold.[27] Most people reason deductively: they start with a few basic opinions about the world, then accept, disbelieve, or even alter new information they receive in order to have it fit conclusions they have already reached.[28] Hindsight bias—"the tendency to overestimate the probability one assigns to an event once the outcome of that event is known, combined with a denial that such a judgment has been affected by knowledge of the outcome"—also plays a role. According to research, once outcome information becomes available, people reinterpret evidence, and information consistent with the outcome becomes "more accessible and inconsistent information becomes less accessible."[29] The result is that people recall and incorporate into their memories items that agree with their preexisting views of the world, and they discount, discard, and distort recollections that conflict with their perspectives.

When informal profiling is the norm, evidence that supports a view other than the prevailing wisdom will not change what an officer thinks, even if, in any fair and objective sense, it strongly contradicts these beliefs. Thus the use of informal profiling presents a stark and real danger. Strongly held beliefs of police officers may not represent the most reliable source of information concerning the proper focus for police suspicion. Rather, these beliefs, however sincere, may simply reflect preexisting views, biases, or stereotypes based on a selective mix of experiences, formed from a limited pool of personal opinion and suspicions instead of hard facts. Profiles such as these don't create good law enforcement; they are more likely to lead law enforcement astray.

A Profile Is Only as Good as Its Elements

Applying a profile involves creating a set of assumptions: given what we know, we assume that persons who [insert a profile characteristic: drive late-model cars, have a Hispanic appearance, get off the plane last, etc.] are more likely to be involved in [insert an offense]. We make assumptions constantly in everyday life; indeed, we can't live without doing this occasionally. We simply don't have the time or energy to collect enough information on everyone and everything around us to base every thought we have and judgment we make on solid facts. At the same time, we know that our assumptions can only be as good as the information on which we base them. If we begin with incorrect premises, our assumptions will likely lead us in wrong directions.

Because profiling involves some basic assumptions—reasoning from what we already know to what we don't—we may do no better than guessing if we don't base these assumptions on solid facts. If we aren't relying on *all* the facts but instead some subset or sample, is the sample large and inclusive enough to give us confidence in what it tells us? (The size of the sample might, for example, be a concern with respect to the "cumulative similarities" put together by Bob Vogel, because he relied on just thirty cases—a relatively small number considered in the context of any statistical investigation, and definitely not a random sample.) Even if a criminal profile is a good idea in the abstract, it cannot be any better in practice than the concrete information from which we construct it.

We see this problem in especially stark terms when we examine court cases that have involved the use of drug-courier profiles. A study of these cases reveals odd and disturbing patterns, which might seem funny if such serious consequences did not turn on them. We find direct 180-degree disagreement over what the correct drug-courier profiling factors are, as well as evidence that these profiles are retroactively constructed—tailored to meet the specifics of each case. In a 1991 case entitled *U.S. v. Hooper*,[30] Federal Court of Appeals Judge George Pratt used a quote from Lewis Carroll's *Through the Looking Glass* in his dissenting opinion to explain his view of the drug-courier profiles.

> "When I use a word," Humpty Dumpty said, in rather a scornful tone, "it means just what I choose it to mean—neither more nor less."
>
> "The question is," said Alice, "whether you can make words mean so many different things."
>
> "The question is," said Humpty Dumpty, "which is to be master—that's all."[31]

Pratt explained that the drug-courier profile had a "chameleon-like" ability to become whatever it needed to be in any particular case.[32] One specific fact in the *Hooper* case drew Judge Pratt's pointed contempt: "To justify their seizure of Hooper's bag the agents testified he had come from a 'source city' and [that he] fit the DEA's 'drug courier profile.' Yet the government conceded at oral argument that a 'source city' for drug traffic was virtually any city with a major airport, a concession that was met with deserved laughter in the courtroom." Judge Pratt called the drug-courier profile "similarly laughable, because it is so fluid that it can be used to justify designating anyone a potential drug courier if the DEA agents so choose."[33] Pratt then produced a list of profile "factors" that had been culled from many published cases from across the country and that covered the gamut of possibili-

ties for anyone traveling by air. Many of these factors were oppo-
sites—"arrived late at night . . . arrived early in the morning,"
"one of the first to deplane . . . one of the last to deplane . . . de-
planed in the middle," "traveled alone . . . traveled with a com-
panion," "acted too nervous . . . acted too calm."[34] Professor
David Cole's research produced a similar long list of drug-
courier profile factors used by law enforcement agents, many
characterizing opposite behaviors as suspicious, just as those
listed by Judge Pratt had.[35]

FROM PROFILE TO INVESTIGATION: THE LEAP FROM SUSPICION TO ACTION WITH HIGH-DISCRETION POLICE TACTICS

Profiling tells police officers whom to focus on—whom to regard
as suspects. Once profiling helps officers make that determination, they put it into action by using a variety of high-discretion
tactics—such as traffic stops, consent searches, and stops and
frisks—to act on their suspicions. All of these tactics are methods
that officers can employ virtually at whim whenever a person
seems suspicious for any reason at all, no matter how thin the
reason might be. And traffic stops have always been the proto-
typical example.

Traffic Stops

Well before Bob Vogel, traffic stops were the most potent
high-discretion police tactic. In the last fifteen years, police have
raised traffic stops to an art form. They use traffic enforcement
as a pretext to stop drivers they want to question and even to
search them. These stops have nothing to do with the rules of
the road—and everything to do with "fishing" for evidence of
crimes.

To understand how this works, start by looking at the traffic
and vehicle codes of any state in the country. Contrary to what
most of us think, traffic regulation does not begin and end with
exceeding speed limits and running stoplights. These "moving vi-

olations" are only the most visible and well known of a huge number of rules that govern driving. Add to this just as large a number of regulations governing both the required equipment any car must have and the car's condition. The bottom line: hundreds of pages of laws about even the most minute aspects of driving, combined with an incredibly detailed array of standards for cars and trucks themselves—many almost wildly hypertechnical.

For example, in any number of jurisdictions, police can stop drivers not only for driving too fast, but for driving too slow.[36] In Utah, drivers must signal for at least three seconds before changing lanes; a two-second signal would violate the law.[37] Many states require that drivers signal for at least one hundred feet before turning right; anything less makes the driver an offender.[38] And the driver making that right turn should not slow down "suddenly" (undefined) without signaling.[39] In most states, it's a crime to drive with a malfunctioning taillight,[40] a rear license plate illumination bulb that does not work,[41] windows that are too darkly tinted,[42] or tires without sufficient tread.[43] Drivers must also display not only license plates, but yearly validation stickers, pollution-control stickers, and safety-inspection stickers, and they must display them in the proper place.[44] And there are also catchall provisions: regulations that allow police to stop drivers for conduct that complies with all of the rules on the books as written, but that the officer on the scene considers "imprudent" or "unreasonable" under the circumstances, or that describe offenses in language so broad that, for all practical purposes, they mean whatever the officer thinks they do.[45] The upshot: *no* driver can go for even a short drive without violating *some* aspect of the traffic code. And since there are no perfect drivers, everyone's a violator.

Once an officer observes a traffic offense—*any* traffic offense, no matter how trivial—he or she has full probable cause to make a stop of the vehicle and begin investigating. The point is not that all police officers are looking for the tiniest infraction so they can conduct a traffic stop; rather, if police officers *want* to, they *can* stop any driver, whenever they like, simply by following the car for a short distance.[46] A traffic offense is not a chance occurrence but an inevitability. A 1967 book discussing police techniques contains these statements by police officers:

> You can always get a guy legitimately on a traffic violation if you tail him for a while, and then a search can be made.

> You don't have to follow a driver very long before he will move to the other side of the yellow line and then you can arrest and search him for driving on the wrong side of the highway.

> In the event that we see a suspicious automobile or occupant and wish to search the person or the car, or both, we will usually follow the vehicle until the driver makes a technical violation of a traffic law. Then we have a means of making a legitimate search.[47]

Even if these officers do not fully understand important nuances of search and seizure law—for example, traffic stops are not now and were not then a sufficient basis for a "legitimate search"—they understand one thing perfectly: the traffic code is the police officer's best friend. Police discretion over traffic stops is, for all practical purposes, unlimited.

Once an officer makes a stop, the law allows officers to question the driver and passengers on matters having nothing to do with traffic enforcement—destination, reason for the trip, whom they plan to see and why, or anything else. They may also question them about possession of or involvement with drugs or weapons, and even order the driver and passengers out of the car, regardless of whether the officer has any safety concerns. Police can search the car if they observe some evidence of crime; even if they see no such evidence, they can ask for consent to search. And if that doesn't work, officers can call in a drug-sniffing dog. The point is not that police do this every time they see a traffic violation, or that they always question and search everyone they stop, but they can if they want to. They have almost complete discretion to do these things—and it all starts with a traffic stop. As long as Americans continue to prefer automobile travel to any other mode of transportation, traffic stops offer a convenient way for police officers to sidestep restrictions on whom they may detain and serve as a powerful tool for putting criminal profiling into action.

Consent Searches

Most automobile searches (and many other types of searches) take place because a police officer has a suspicion that a person may have committed a crime, even though the officer may not have any evidence or "probable cause" that the law requires for a search. When officers have no evidence of crime, they can search only if they ask drivers for permission to search their vehicles. Drivers have a right to refuse these requests, but police need not tell drivers that they can say no. As long as drivers give permission voluntarily—without coercion, either overt or implied— a search is perfectly legal. Consent searches have become an indispensable part of law enforcement's arsenal, especially when police suspect a drug-related crime or the presence of weapons.

Twice over the past twenty-five years,[48] the Supreme Court has confronted the validity of a defendant's consent for a search. In both cases, the police could not have conducted a valid search without consent; there was no evidence of any crime. But in both cases, officers asked for permission to search.[49] In both cases, the U.S. Supreme Court found the police actions constitutional, emphasizing the importance of consent searches to police work.[50] The Court refused to require police to tell suspects the truth about these searches: that the suspects could refuse to consent[51] and leave[52] if police had no evidence against them.

The Supreme Court's reasoning contains two important assumptions. First, the Court assumed that if police tell people what their rights are, individuals will be more likely to exercise these rights, perhaps foiling efforts to investigate crime. Second, the Court assumed that if a citizen does refuse to consent to a search, that will end the matter. The officer seeking consent will respect the refusal, and the citizen will be allowed to leave. Both of these assumptions have been proved wrong, despite the certainty with which the Court presents them. They are premised on the letter of the law and on the assumption that people will behave accordingly, even though all available evidence supports different conclusions.

First, the "voluntary" consent people give for these searches is not in fact voluntary in any real sense. New research shows that consent searches have nothing to do with exercising free choice and everything to do with yielding to authority. And few figures in modern society represent authority more strongly than the police officer.

In recently completed doctoral work, Illya Lichtenberg of Rutgers University tested the idea of the voluntariness of consent to search.[53] Using data from Ohio and Maryland,[54] which together included more than nine thousand consent searches,[55] Lichtenberg's findings directly contradict the Supreme Court's assumptions. Lichtenberg found that about 90 percent of drivers who were asked for consent gave it[56]—rates far higher than in any of the classic psychology experiments on compliance with authority.[57] There were no significant differences in the rates of consent when the data were broken down by sex,[58] by age,[59] or by race.[60] Basically, almost everyone consents; few people—just one out of ten—refuse. Even the use of a warning—telling the suspect that he or she was free to go before asking for consent—made no difference.[61] All in all, Lichtenberg's work raises considerable doubt that these interactions can ever be considered voluntary. People who agree to searches do not make a free choice to grant consent. Rather, they consent because that is how people respond to authority. Calling such an interaction voluntary is at best misleading and at worst completely wrong.

The Supreme Court's second assumption—that if a citizen refuses to consent and wants to leave, the officer will respect his wishes—is equally inaccurate. The Court clearly assumes as much. Otherwise, there would be no reason for the justices to fear that warning the defendant that he has the right to refuse or is free to go would hinder law enforcement. To test this assumption at its limits, we return to the story of Robert Wilkins, the criminal defense attorney searched by the Maryland State Police while on his way back from a family funeral. Recall that Wilkins refused to give consent, though the officer insisted that these searches were "just routine" and implied that withholding consent meant that Wilkins was guilty. Wilkins still refused, politely but firmly explaining the law to the trooper, and even recording names and badge numbers. Nothing he did mattered in the end. The police brought a drug-sniffing dog to the scene and did the search that way.

Wilkins's experience was no accident. Rather, it directly reflects the U.S. Supreme Court's decisions. Even when a driver refuses to consent to a search of his car, and an officer has observed nothing that would give her probable cause or reasonable suspicion to conduct a search, the law still gives the officers a range of options. In *U.S. v. Sharpe*[62] the Supreme Court said that any detention of a driver must be reasonable, depending on the circumstances. Police could not extend the detention beyond what would be reasonably necessary to carry out the purpose of the stop. If the detention continued past this (rather indefinite) point, any evidence gathered as a result of the illegal detention would be thrown out.[63] The *Sharpe* case leaves considerable room for police investigation during the detention, such as observation of the interior of the car from the outside,[64] questioning of the occupants,[65] removing the driver[66] and passengers[67] from the vehicle, and even something more sophisticated: a search of the exterior of the vehicle with a dog trained to detect drugs. In *U.S. v. Place*,[68] the Supreme Court decided that canine sniffs of objects (in the *Place* case, luggage) were unlike any other types of searches,[69] given their singularly unintrusive nature (dogs detect contraband from outside containers, with no need to open them)[70] and the limited amount of information they supply (only whether or not contraband is present, and no other information on the contents).[71] Given their unintrusive nature and the limited amount of information they produce, the Court said, the use of these trained dogs could take place without a warrant, probable cause, reasonable suspicion, or any evidence of crime at all.

Using these cases, a police officer in a reasonably well trained and equipped police department need only apply legal, efficient, and logical tactics to be able to conduct almost any search within the bounds of the law, even if the suspect refuses to consent. Once the officer makes the initial stop of the vehicle, the officer typically talks to the driver. These driver's-side-window questions are allowed, without the need for Miranda warnings.[72] If anything in the driver's answers, manner, or possessions the officer sees through the car window makes the officer want to search the car for any reason,[73] the officer should proceed as in any normal case: she should take the driver's license and registration back to the squad car. While the officer calls the police dispatcher for the customary computer checks on those documents, she should also call for the nearest drug-sniffing canine unit to come to the scene. Assuming that the dog is available within the time it will take to resolve the computer record checks and complete any citation-related paperwork,[74] the officer will have two options. First, she can ask the driver for consent to search; she need not give any warnings of any kind. In the unlikely event that the driver refuses, the officer can move briskly—and legally—to her second option: she will ask the canine officer to use the trained dog on the car. If the dog "alerts" to the presence of contraband, that provides the necessary probable cause for a full-scale search. Even if the dog does not alert, the officer has already accomplished the primary goal: the vehicle has been searched, regardless of the citizen's refusal. And the officer has also shown the suspect the futility of refusing to consent. The law and the availability of the drug-sniffing dog make the search possible and legal regardless of consent, as long as it is performed within a reasonable time.

Robert Wilkins's experience captures the essence of how obtaining consent actually works. If you don't give consent, the officer will push you. If you persist, the officer will imply that you have something to hide, that there could be no other reason for your refusal to follow procedures that are "just routine." And if you still refuse, the officer will still get his way, by using a dog. So you might as well give up. And if you tell the officer that you understand the law, that you know he can't do this, even cite to him the cases you learned in law school and use every day in a court of law, so what? Police officers will not take no for an answer. When they want to search, they will search. And nothing the Supreme Court or you or anyone else says will stop them.

This brings us back to Lichtenberg's research. Lichtenberg followed his study of the Ohio and Maryland data with surveys of about fifty of the individuals who had been searched in Ohio. Why had they consented? What were they asked? Had they tried to refuse? If so, what happened?

Lichtenberg's data from these interviews shed some light on Wilkins's experience. Most of the respondents who consented did so because, whether out of ignorance, experience, or instinct, they already believed what Robert Wilkins learned: that the police were not actually *asking* to search. They intended to search regardless. As Lichtenberg put it, "[the subjects] stated time and time again that they had no doubt the police would search their car [*sic*], regardless of non-consent."[75] They consented because they thought that refusals were futile and because they feared reprisal in one form or another. Asked outright, almost none felt the police would honor the refusal; the search would be conducted no matter what they said.[76]

Stops and Frisks

A stop is a detention of a person by the police. It differs from a seizure or an arrest in that it is presumed to be temporary. A frisk is a search, but like a stop it is a limited type of police action that, according to the Supreme Court, can include only a "pat down" of the suspect's outer clothing. No further search—no reaching into a pocket or under a shirt—can take place. Nevertheless, a frisk can be quite thorough. According to one description, "the officer must feel with sensitive fingers every portion of the suspect's body. A thorough search must be made of the suspect's arms and armpits, waistline and back, the groin and area about the testicles, and the entire surface of the legs down to the feet." [77]

What traffic stops are to profiling on the highway, stops and frisks are to profiling on the streets. Stops and frisks have evolved into a well-honed high-discretion tactic for sidestepping civil rights in police pursuit of crime. Stops and frisks are one of the most common kinds of encounters police officers may have with citizens. For example, in one fifteen-month period in the late 1990s, police officers in New York City recorded 175,000 stops and frisks—a number that may actually underreport these incidents. [78]

The story of Detective Remo Franceschini's many years on the streets of New York gives us unusually sharp insight into this particular high-discretion police tactic. Franceschini spent more than thirty years in police work. [79] For much of that time, he carried the gold shield of a New York Police Department detective. He worked every type of crime in those years, and he capped his career by landing the biggest of fish: John Gotti, the organized crime boss dubbed "the Teflon Don" by the media. When Franceschini became a detective in 1961, his superiors assigned him to a precinct in Harlem. Although the law said that police had to have probable cause to search a suspect, officers would stop and frisk anyone they suspected, whether they had observed the commission of a crime or not. Because the probable cause rule was not enforced by the courts, officers ignored it. Instead, they simply relied on instincts to tell them who was "dirty." Then they put the person up against a wall and searched him. Franceschini says that police even had a name for this kind of search: they called it giving a guy "a toss." [80] Police used this tactic aggressively, along with others, to control the streets and assert their authority, as well as to catch criminals. As Franceschini says, "They knew we were detectives, and they didn't give us a hard time. That's the kind of fear and respect we commanded; they knew we controlled the streets." [81]

By the mid-1960s, stops and frisks had become an important enough part of police activity and public policy that the state of New York had enacted laws to govern their use.[82] The Supreme Court used its 1968 decision in *Terry* v. *Ohio*[83] to give its legal blessing to stops and frisks. *Terry* set out a new, lower standard for brief street-level encounters. From *Terry* onward, officers would not need probable cause. The bottom line was a new set of rules that regulated but also legitimized a high-discretion police practice, giving police much more formal latitude than they had ever had in these situations under the law.

According to the Court, police could briefly detain and question a citizen on the street relying on a "reasonable suspicion"—something less than "probable cause," the standard then in use—that the suspect was involved in criminal activity, based on the facts officers had observed and the reasonable inferences they drew from those facts. Further, if an officer had reasonable suspicion that the detained defendant might be armed and dangerous—either because the officer observed a weapon or its telltale bulge under clothing, or because the officer suspected involvement in a violent crime—the officer could perform a frisk: a search limited to a pat down of the suspect's outer clothing to feel for weapons. Reasonable suspicion under the *Terry* decision meant more than just a hunch or a feeling that a suspect seemed suspicious or was up to no good; an officer had to have some reasons he or she could articulate for thinking the person was involved in crime.

In the thirty years that followed *Terry,* the Supreme Court addressed stops and frisks just a handful of times, in almost every case broadening the scope of police discretion. A 1981 case entitled *U.S.* v. *Cortez*[84] emerges as perhaps the most important of these few cases. On the one hand, *Cortez* seemed to limit police discretion by making clear that the police officer's "reasonable suspicion" meant "particularized suspicion." "Particularized," the Court explained, means that all of the evidence—the facts officers observe, police intelligence, and any "inferences and deductions that might well elude an untrained person"—must show specifically that a *particular individual* may be involved in the crime afoot, not just that *someone* may be involved. All of the circumstances together must yield a reasonable suspicion that *this person* is involved in a crime.[85] On the other hand, the justices used the *Cortez* case to order judges in stop-and-frisk cases across the country to show the utmost deference to police judgment and actions, thereby setting an extremely indulgent standard of police behavior that has been in effect ever since. *Terry* stops were, by their nature, educated guesswork, the Court reasoned. Its opinion made clear the Court's conclusion that the judgment of police officers in the field should not be second-guessed in courtrooms:

> Long before the law of probabilities was articulated as such, practical people formulated certain commonsense conclusions about human behavior; jurors as fact finders are permitted to do the same—and so are law enforcement officers. Finally, the evidence thus collected must be seen and weighed not in terms of library analysis by scholars, but as understood by those versed in the field of law enforcement.[86]

The message is simple. Courts hearing challenges to *Terry* stops should view the facts with a strong presumption that officers acted properly. Judges presiding over these cases should look at them through the eyes of the officers involved, since they are presumed to be the best positioned to understand the facts and interpret them for the court. The hypertechnical analysis of academic criticism has no place in the discussion; in any close case, give the police the benefit of the doubt.

The *Cortez* case seems uncontroversial at first glance. Why wouldn't we want judges to defer to the police, since they have the most experience with crime and criminals? But this aspect of *Cortez* has turned out to have less to do with the law in the books and more to do with the law of unintended consequences. Its effect, over the years, has been to allow lower courts—federal trial and appellate courts and state courts—to create end runs around the Supreme Court's strict *Terry* rules. These lower courts have decided a great many *Terry* cases, and their opinions have become the dominant body of specific rules governing stop-and-frisk procedures. With the Supreme Court seldom paying attention to those lower-court opinions and speaking only in broad generalities when it decided cases, these lower courts filled the vacuum. If the Supreme Court seemed concerned with the principle of particularized suspicion in *Cortez,* lower courts seemed oblivious to the idea. In fact, if members of the Supreme Court read lower-court *Terry* decisions on stops and frisks in the middle to late 1990s, they would find a body of law strikingly at odds with their own rulings.

Automatic Frisks   The *Terry* case gave officers the power to conduct stops and frisks whenever they had reasonable suspicion. But it also limited how and when stops and frisks can take place. Officers can use frisks only to assure their safety by searching for weapons, and they may not use frisks unless there is, in fact, some reason to believe that their safety is in question. Barring either a violent crime or the suspected presence of a weapon, officers cannot frisk, and certainly they cannot do so as a routine matter every time they stop a citizen.

As recently as 1993, the Supreme Court reaffirmed this aspect of the *Terry* case, making clear that the threat of real danger was still a prerequisite to a frisk.[87] But in case after case, lower courts at both the federal and state level have effectively washed the requirement of danger out of the law. In its place they have constructed a system of broad categories to decide the question of whether or not someone might be dangerous enough to frisk. Instead of asking about the individual facts of each case—Did police suspect a violent crime? Did they see a bulge that might have been a weapon?—these courts ask whether *all suspects in a particular category of crimes* should be considered dangerous. In other words, they judge the propriety of the frisk not by what actually happened on a case-by-case basis, as the *Terry* and *Cortez* cases clearly command, but on a broad categorical basis. This might seem a small point, but its impact on police discretion in areas involving profiling has been enormous.

Cases having to do with drugs illustrate this trend best. Cases decided in the first years after *Terry* showed that police made widespread use of the stops and frisks on suspected drug dealers. Many of these cases involved large-scale trafficking. Judges reasoned that major drug sellers were so likely to be armed that police could frisk automatically, any time they legitimately stopped a person suspected of being a major dealer, without regard to the particular facts.[88] Weapons, especially guns, are the "tools of the trade" for big-time dealers, one court said,[89] and police should protect themselves from these dangerous people by frisking as soon as they stop them, without regard to other circumstances.

Standing alone, this does not seem objectionable. Large-scale trafficking in illegal drugs—or substantial quantities of any black market commodity, for that matter—involves the possession of valuable contraband, and of large—sometimes extremely large—quantities of illicitly obtained cash. Traffickers must rely on themselves for protection of their goods and money, as well as for "justice" in the event of a theft or a robbery; they obviously can't call the police. The presence of weapons in these cases would make perfect sense. But subsequent cases carried this "automatic-frisk" rule further. In these cases, courts began to say that dealers in narcotics—not only large-scale traffickers but also low-level distributors and the smallest of small-time street corner sellers—likely carried weapons.[90] They, too, could be frisked automatically when stopped, regardless of whether they exhibited any sign of being armed. These cases authorizing automatic frisks for any drug dealer were then followed by a third group, which did not involve suspicion of trafficking or sales of drugs at all. In this most recent wave of decisions, the courts have said that police could automatically frisk anyone involved in a drug transaction in any way—including purchasers and users—because of the violent nature of drug crime. Indeed, some courts now say that the dangerous nature of all drug offenses always supports an automatic frisk, without reference to any trafficking, major or minor, or any transaction of any size. Thus, we now have an entire category of automatic-frisk crimes—drug offenses, which make up a huge proportion of all arrests and jailings today—to which the Supreme Court's rules routinely do not apply. There are other automatic-frisk crimes too, including burglary and gambling, which some courts have said are so dangerous that police can frisk any suspect of these crimes for weapons.[91] Though it may be uncomfortable with this system of categories, the Supreme Court has not stopped this fundamental erosion of the *Terry* frisk rules despite having had opportunities to do so.[92]

Location Plus Evasion If we look back over the years of *Terry* cases decided by lower federal and state courts, certain factors continually emerge as justifications for officers' stopping of pedestrians as evidence that "crime was afoot." Two of these factors—the location in which the police see the suspect and whether the suspect takes any evasive action when he sees the police—come up again and again. Like the automatic frisk decisions, decisions that rely on location plus evasion have created a whole new category of high-discretion police tactics allowable under the law.

In almost any stop-and-frisk case, courts mention the location of the encounter as a key reason for the stop. And these references almost always have one thing in common: they describe these locations as hotbeds of crime. Phrases such as "high-crime area" and "drug location" recur with remarkable frequency in these opinions. The judges who write these opinions do not, of course, make up this information. Rather, it comes directly from the police officer's testimony explaining why he performed the stop and frisk at issue. The danger of crime occurring in particular hot spots is, in effect, imputed to everyone seen there. Surely, not everyone walking past a particular street corner known for drug sales is a buyer or seller; they may only have the misfortune to live or work in the area. Yet being in these places makes them more likely candidates for criminal behavior in the eyes of police officers than someone walking by a "clean" corner.

If judges do not bring the ubiquitous high-crime area label to courts, neither do they exhibit much skepticism about it. They simply accept what officers tell them. For example, in an electronic search of every reported court decision in Ohio between January 1995 and November 2000, in which a court reported that a law enforcement officer described a location in which a suspect had been stopped or apprehended using a phrase such as "high-crime area" or "drug-trafficking location," only a handful of judges expressed any doubt about this designation. On the contrary, the overwhelming majority counted it as a factor that legitimately bolstered police suspicion. To be fair, the cases judges hear in court, day after day, seem to confirm the impression that judges should not challenge police designation of a place as a high-crime location. Since in any court case police have made an arrest—otherwise, there would be no case for the judge to hear—police do, in fact, find criminals at these places. This reinforces the value of the high-crime location designation, making judicial skepticism that much less likely. Of course, judges never hear about the cases in which officers stop and frisk people without finding anything. There is no reason they would, since stops and frisks that produce nothing generate no cases for them to hear.

Many stop-and-frisk cases also describe evasive behavior on the part of suspects. Although not quite as common as cases mentioning a high-crime area, descriptions of evasive suspect behavior still appear frequently in court opinions. These cases often seem to follow a script: an officer drives through an area on patrol, and when a man on a particular corner sees the squad car approaching, he walks away, walks away rapidly, or runs. In another common scenario, a person in a suspicious location sees a police officer and makes an abrupt turn away from the police. Here's an example from *Minnesota* v. *Dickerson*,[93] one of the Supreme Court's own cases.

On the evening of November 9, 1989, two Minneapolis police officers were patrolling an area on the city's north side in a marked squad car. At about 8:15 P.M., one of the officers observed respondent leaving a 12-unit apartment building on Morgan Avenue North. The officer, having previously re-

sponded to complaints of drug sales in the building's hall-
ways and having executed several search warrants on the
premises, considered the building to be a notorious "crack
house." According to testimony credited by the trial court,
respondent began walking toward the police but, upon spotting the squad car and making eye contact with one of the officers, abruptly halted and began walking in the opposite
direction. His suspicion aroused, this officer watched as respondent turned and entered an alley on the other side of the
apartment building. Based upon respondent's seemingly evasive actions and the fact that he had just left a building
known for cocaine traffic, the officers decided to stop respondent and investigate further.[94]

The assumption is that evading police officers shows some consciousness of guilt or wrongdoing. After all, police officers may
think, we know nothing about this person; why is he making an
effort to avoid us? In another Supreme Court case in which a
young man fled from police, Justice Antonin Scalia captured
these thoughts neatly by quoting from Proverbs: "The wicked
flee when no man pursueth." [95]

Of course, pedestrians may have many reasons to want to
avoid police that have nothing to do with criminal conduct, and
their reasons may have everything to do with a perfectly natural
desire to avoid trouble—which is perfectly legal, of course. They
may not want to take the time to speak to the police. They may
fear getting blamed for something they did not do, or simply do
not want to get involved in any police business, even if only as a
potential witness. They may also have experienced abuse or harassment by the police in the past. In fact, evasion of potential
difficulties with the police finds support in another quote from
Proverbs: "A shrewd man sees trouble coming and lies low; the
simple walk into it and pay the penalty." [96]

All of this makes cases concerning high-crime locations and
evasion of police troubling. For example, some state courts have
decided that unprovoked flight from the police, alone, is enough
to constitute the. reasonable suspicion necessary for a *Terry*

stop.[97] This makes the citizen into a suspect on the basis of just one ambiguous action. But the potential for making *Terry* into one of the most pointed weapons in the arsenal of high-discretion police tactics only emerges when we begin to view cases that use the location and evasion factors together. Many courts have found that even if either presence in a high-crime location or evasion of the police, alone, would not supply reasonable suspicion, any situation involving both factors will suffice. In other words, just being in a "drug area" might not be enough evidence to show reasonable suspicion for a *Terry* stop, but walking quickly away from a police officer in this same area surely is. High-crime location plus evasion equals reasonable suspicion.[98] For example, in *Harris* v. *State of Georgia*,[99] officers on "routine patrol" in an area known for drug activity saw a group of individuals. When these people saw the police car, they began running. When the officers caught defendant Harris, they stopped and frisked him. The arresting officer told the court that "it had been his experience that when police patrol 'high-drug areas,' individuals with drugs on their person usually run upon the arrival of the police."[100] Of course, this does not mean that *everyone* who runs from the police has drugs. Nevertheless, the Georgia Court of Appeals said that under these circumstances, the suspect's flight after seeing a police car in this location gave officers reasonable suspicion to stop and frisk him.[101]

Cases such as *Harris* may seem perfectly commonsensical. After all, the "reasonable suspicion" requirement means that officers do not need to have evidence that someone is committing a crime. Wouldn't people in drug areas generally run from the police if they have drugs and fear getting caught? Even if we agree, it is the implications of the "location plus evasion" cases that ought to give us pause. There are many people who have nothing to do with crime whom we might expect to be in these places and want to avoid the police. Many innocent people will exhibit the twin characteristics of presence in a high-crime or drug-involved location and evasion of police—and they are likely to be African Americans, Latinos, and other minorities.

Often obliged to live and work in high-crime areas for economic and social reasons beyond their control, minorities become caught up in a vicious cycle. The experience of being stopped and frisked in these areas is nearly universal among blacks and Latinos. They know that these encounters with the police can be unpleasant, upsetting, embarrassing, and sometimes even physically dangerous. Their response is to avoid such encounters whenever possible. In turn, this evasive (though perfectly legal) behavior in high-crime neighborhoods serves as a legal basis for further stops and frisks. And as this continues, year in and year out, each of these stops and frisks is done at a cost—a cost paid in anger, in fear, in resentment, and in distrust and dislike of the police.

The Supreme Court exacerbated this problem as recently as 2000 in *Illinois* v. *Wardlow* [102] by endorsing at the national level what had been commonly accepted at the state level for decades. "Headlong flight—wherever it occurs—is the consummate act of evasion," the justices said. And while neither location nor evasion would be enough for reasonable suspicion alone, together they supported the officers' "commonsense judgments."

Wardlow confers the Supreme Court's blessing on a tactic that boils down to racial profiling. In short, *Wardlow* declares open season in the inner city.

The evolution of stop-and-frisk law into a regime that allows automatic searches on the street of anyone the police feel they have reasonable suspicion to stop has become a powerful tool for criminal profiling. In this respect, the importance of this tactic parallels that of the two other high-discretion police tactics: traffic stops, used as pretexts to stop drivers for investigation having nothing to do with enforcement of traffic safety laws, and the use of consent to search in situations in which the law would not otherwise allow a search. Each of these tactics allows police officers enormous discretion in how they decide to enforce the law and against whom they decide to enforce it. Police discretion could not be eliminated, and it should not be. But, as the next chapter will show, when the nearly unlimited discretion implicit in all of these tactics is combined with profiling that may include race or ethnic appearance, a new set of problems emerges.

Chapter Three

PROFILING UNMASKED: FROM CRIMINAL PROFILING TO RACIAL PROFILING

Former sheriff Bob Vogel, who first employed profiling as a means of identifying drug couriers on the highways in the 1980s, says that race was never part of his method; it was never a factor. In fact, he says, it would have made no sense for him to focus on either African Americans or Latinos; the greatest number of "upper-level dealers" that he arrested as a result of his stops were white men. Yet something strange happened to his work as the DEA began to use his methods throughout the country in Operation Pipeline. Whatever the training was designed to identify, many officers and agencies seemed to emerge from it focused on particular groups of people—races, ethnic groups, and subgroups—who were considered most likely to be involved with the drug trade.

Some of the Operation Pipeline training materials suggest how this program eventually became focused on minority racial and ethnic groups. One video, put together by the New Mexico State Police, lays out a number of indicators to spot potential highway drug couriers and presents several mock traffic stops designed to demonstrate the dos and don'ts of the method. In all of the mock stops, the driver has an Hispanic surname.[1] William

Buckman, an attorney who has handled profiling cases in New Jersey, describes another training video in which an off-screen voice tells trainees that Jamaicans dominate certain aspects of the drug trade. A picture shows a black man in informal dress and dreadlocks. The image then changes, showing a similar black man wearing a business suit with short hair. The voice admonishes trainees that they should not be fooled; these drug dealers can look like anything at all.[2]

The DEA denies that race had any role in the Pipeline program or training, either now or in the past.[3] A spokesman said that the DEA actually trained police not to consider race when deciding whether to pull over a car.[4] The use of profiles—"indicators," Pipeline trainers call them[5]—is one thing, they say. We did not then, and do not now, train anyone to use race or ethnicity as part of these profiles. In the most literal sense, this may be true—the DEA may actually instruct trainees that using race as a factor in profiles is illegal and unconstitutional. But some training stressed the ethnic and racial characteristics of narcotics organizations, and state and local police officers have been trained to look for, among other characteristics, "people wearing dreadlocks and cars with two Latino males traveling together."[6] At the same time that the DEA says it continued to train officers not to use race to stop people, the agency and other federal law enforcement units involved in drug interdiction circulated intelligence to police departments around the country emphasizing racial and ethnic characteristics of drug-trafficking organizations. In 1999, a DEA intelligence report identified those it suspected of involvement in the heroin trade. "Predominant wholesale traffickers are Colombian, followed by Dominicans, Chinese, West African/ Nigerian, Pakistani, Hispanic, and Indian. Midlevels are dominated by Dominicans, Colombians, Puerto Ricans, African Americans and Nigerians."[7] And surprisingly, the DEA still admits that it in fact trained local police to use race—as "one of many factors" when considering whether to conduct a search of a vehicle.[8] In other words, the cops on the street received a mixed message. John J. Farmer, New Jersey's current attorney general, says that officers got two sets of signals. "On one hand, we were training them not to take race into account. On the other hand, all the intelligence featured race and ethnicity prominently. So what is your average trooper to make of all this?" [9] Even if federal agents said "race has nothing to do with our mission," the officers they trained could connect the dots—and every indication is that these lessons, whether implicit or explicit, "took" very well. For example, a 1987 New Jersey State Police training memorandum discussed indicators of drug involvement, including "Colombian males, Hispanic males, a Hispanic male and a black male together, or a Hispanic male and female posing as a couple." [10] Debra L. Stone, Deputy Director of the New Jersey Department of Law and Public Safety, wrote in a February 1999 memorandum that racial profiling was a deeply rooted part of state police culture—a tactic taught to rookies by their field trainers, who are referred to within the department as coaches. "Trooper after trooper has testified that coach taught them how to profile minorities," Stone said. "The coaches also teach this to minority troopers." [11] In short, whatever the explicit message was, police officers in the field understood the real, implicit message.

In 1999—years after Operation Pipeline methods had begun to generate complaints—the California legislature's Task Force on Government Oversight issued a report on Pipeline operations in California. [12] The report, which focused on the California Highway Patrol (CHP), drew on interviews with CHP officials, attorneys, and DEA officials, extensive CHP records of field officers and canine units, trial transcripts from civil and criminal cases, and videotapes of hours of Pipeline stops by CHP. A task force consultant also underwent two days of actual Pipeline training, along with about two dozen police officers from northern California police departments. The result was the most comprehensive, detailed portrait of Pipeline activity anywhere, and it showed that Pipeline's roots had grown very deeply into CHP; "California had become one of the states most actively involved in the Pipeline program." [13] CHP officers trained by the DEA were spreading the gospel of profiling, or "indicators," through local law enforcement agencies around the state. The report says that in 1999 there were more than forty canine units on the road in California as part of Pipeline operations, and "Pipeline teams are running formal operations on all of California's major highways." [14] The report also makes clear that Pipeline's tactics make extensive, primary use of profiling and that, despite denials that race is part of this, these profiles result in stops and searches that disproportionately affect minorities, especially Latinos. Sworn testimony from officers involved in these stops indicated that Latinos made up two-thirds or more of all those stopped and searched, a share "far out of proportion to the number of Latino drivers" in California. [15] And this was not the result of the actions of a few "bad apples" breaking CHP rules or policy to target minorities. Rather,

> [i]t should be emphasized that this program has been conducted with the support of CHP management. Individual officers involved in these operations and training programs have been carrying out what they perceived to be the policy of the CHP, the Department of Justice, and the Deukmejian and Wilson Administrations. Thus we are not faced with "rogue" officers or individual, isolated instances of wrongdoing. The officers involved in these operations have been told repeatedly by their supervisors that they were doing their jobs exactly right. [16]

Operation Pipeline was not the first time that race had been identified as a factor in policing and in how police actions caused great irritation and anger in minority communities. In 1967, the President's Commission on Law Enforcement and the Administration of Justice found that stops and frisks—the primary tools of criminal profiling on the streets—were not being used evenhandedly, concluding that stops and frisks "are a major source of friction between the police and minority groups." This tension would increase, the commission predicted, "as more police departments adopt 'aggressive patrol' in which officers are encouraged routinely to stop and question persons on the street who are unknown to them, who are suspicious, or whose purpose for being abroad is not readily evident." [17]

Civil rights activists increasingly came to see the issues of race and criminal justice as intertwined, and they regarded stops and frisks as a major source of tension between police and minorities in inner cities. And, although the fact is typically overlooked, the Supreme Court explicitly discussed the racial ramifications of stops and frisks in the *Terry* case in 1968. Although *Terry* did not involve racial discrimination as such, and the races of the suspects did not even merit a mention in the Court's opinion, the racial subtext of the case bubbled to the surface. The justices felt compelled to note the long-standing tensions that aggressive use of stops and frisks had aroused in black and other minority communities, even quoting directly from the President's Commission report. On the one hand, the Court seemed to discount the role of race, noting that if the police seemed intent on using stops and frisks and similar tactics to suppress, harass, and control minority populations, a rule requiring judges to throw out evidence in such cases would do nothing to stop these practices, since they were not really aimed at gathering evidence. On the other hand, the justices noted that minorities, particularly blacks, frequently complained that "wholesale harassment" by police had sharpened the already tense relationship between police and these communities. Yet even in the wake of all the urban unrest at the time, few people paid attention to the racial dimension of the problem that the Court sketched out.

Twenty-five years later, the racial aspect of profile-based policing was incontrovertible in the eyes of people of color. Slowly, and without any coordinated strategy, legal actions were mounted to challenge these practices. Key cases illustrate how and why the nation's thinking on racial profiling changed—in large measure because of these cases.

NEW JERSEY

In the late 1980s and early 1990s, African Americans com-plained that state troopers on the New Jersey Turnpike made a regular practice of stopping and searching them. This had hap-pened to many of them several times. One man—an African American dentist who drove a gold BMW—said that he had been stopped approximately fifty times, was never given a ticket, and was always asked whether he had drugs or guns in the car.[18] Such plentiful anecdotal evidence led observers to suspect strongly that troopers targeted and stopped blacks in numbers far out of proportion to their presence on the road. Criminal defense lawyers had long observed the effects of these tactics as they de-fended case after case based on these traffic stops. They saw first-hand that "a strikingly high proportion of cases arising from stops and searches on the New Jersey Turnpike involved black persons."[19] In 1990, a group of these lawyers mounted a chal-lenge to this practice. The case, State v. Pedro Soto,[20] trans-formed the idea of criminal profiling by showing how it became racial profiling.

From the start, the state fought the allegations in Soto with a sharp-edged bitterness, denying at every turn the existence of any racial profiling. William Buckman, one of the attorneys who rep-resented the defendants claiming profiling, remembers the con-stant, scathing denials, both in court proceedings and in the press. "Certainly in the courts, the state's response was a com-plete denial of any wrongdoing," Buckman says. Proceedings in the case began in November 1994, before the Honorable Robert Francis of the New Jersey Superior Court. Both sides presented statistical experts, but it was the analysis of Dr. John Lamberth of Temple University that mattered most.[21]

Lamberth, who was retained by the defendants as an expert to study the problem, set out to measure whether, in fact, New Jersey State Troopers were stopping and investigating African Americans in numbers significantly higher than the number of blacks in the traveling population on the turnpike.[22] To do this,

Lamberth used a research methodology designed to determine two things: first, the rate at which troopers stopped, ticketed, and arrested blacks on the relevant portion of the highway and, second, the percentage of blacks among all travelers on the same stretch of road. Data concerning the rate at which blacks were stopped, ticketed, and arrested came from reports of all arrests resulting from stops on the turnpike from April 1988 through May 1991, patrol activity logs from randomly selected days from 1988 through 1991, and police radio logs from randomly selected days from 1988 through 1991.[23] Lamberth then measured the racial composition of the population of drivers on the road with a roadway census—direct observation by teams of researchers in randomly distributed blocks of time on different days. He also conducted a violator census—a rolling survey in which teams of observers in cars driving down the turnpike observed all the cars that passed them violating the speed limit, and noted the race of the drivers. Lamberth's surveys of the driving and violating population of the turnpike included observations of more than forty-two thousand cars.[24]

Lamberth's analysis of the data began by addressing an alternative hypothesis: even if blacks do get stopped by police in higher percentages, perhaps this happens because blacks violate the traffic laws at higher rates. In other words, maybe police stop more black drivers not because of their skin color but because of their driving behavior. The violator survey Lamberth performed yielded a direct answer: absolutely not. The data showed unequivocally that blacks and whites violate some aspect of the traffic laws at almost exactly the same, very high rate. There was no statistical difference in driving behavior between the two groups.[25] The testimony of several New Jersey State Police supervisors and troopers bolstered Lamberth's conclusion. All of them testified in the *Soto* case that they had never observed any difference in black and white driving behavior.[26] Gil Gallegos, the national president of the Fraternal Order of Police and a veteran police officer, put it this way: "I think [all racial and ethnic groups] drive the same. Terrible." Most people commit traffic violations every time they drive, he says, "including police officers in their driving." [27] Gallegos confirms what police officers everywhere say: no driver anywhere can drive for more than a few blocks without committing some type of traffic offense. Both the violator census results and the police testimony dovetail perfectly with what police officers everywhere have said for years: everyone breaks one or more traffic laws during any drive.

Lamberth's analysis then moved on to the key question of whether the New Jersey State Police had targeted blacks for disproportionate enforcement. To obtain the answer, Lamberth compared data on state police stops, citations, and arrests to the black driving population. He found that although blacks made up 73.2 percent of those arrested, only 13.5 percent of the cars on the turnpike had a black occupant—a difference Lamberth described as "statistically vast." [28] To understand how large the difference is, it is useful to consider the statistical measuring tool known as standard deviation. Statisticians calculate the standard deviation to decide whether a difference between two numbers is real—statistically significant—or is the result of pure chance. Statisticians agree that a difference is real—not the result of chance—at approximately two standard deviations. According to Lamberth, there were 54.27 standard deviations in the comparison between the arrest figure for blacks and the turnpike's population of blacks. According to Lamberth, this meant that the probability that the difference between these two numbers is the result of chance is "infinitesimally small." [29] Records of stops in state police radio and patrol logs were also quite different than the percentage of blacks on the highway. Blacks were approximately 35 percent of those stopped, and 13.5 percent of those on the road—19.45 standard deviations. Taking into account all the records of police activity and observations in the data, the chance that 35 percent of the cars of those who were stopped, ticketed, and arrested would have black occupants is, in Lamberth's words, "substantially less than one in one billion." [30] Lamberth concluded that, all in all, the data allowed a dispassionate observer to come to only one possible explanation:

Absent some other explanation for the dramatically disproportionate number of stops of blacks, it would appear that
the race of the occupants and/or drivers of the cars is a deci-
sive factor or a factor with great explanatory power. I can say
to a reasonable degree of statistical probability that the disparity outlined here is strongly consistent with the existence
of a discriminatory policy, official or de facto, of targeting
blacks for stops and investigation. . . . Put bluntly, the statistics demonstrate that in a population of blacks and whites
which is (legally) virtually universally subject to police stops
for traffic law violation (cf. the turnpike violator census),
blacks in general are several times more likely to be stopped
than non-blacks.[31]

Judge Francis evaluated both Lamberth's analysis and the statistical work of the state's expert and came to the devastating
conclusion in his 1996 decision that the state police had, indeed,
been targeting African Americans on the turnpike for years. No
other explanation, the judge said, could account for the large disparities between whom police stopped, ticketed, and arrested
and the much smaller population of black drivers on the road.
Lamberth's data were simply too powerful to ignore. His analysis showed that, contrary to the assertions of the state officials,
blacks and other minorities had not been imagining things or exhibiting some kind of group persecution complex. Racial profiling was real.

Lamberth's statistics alone would have been enough to prove
the case, but Judge Francis did not stop there. He based his decision not only on the data, but also on a completely independent
source—evidence that the state police hierarchy, from the superintendent on down, had long known about these practices but at
best failed to do anything about them and at worst even con-
doned them. Troopers at every level got the message in myriad
ways: keep on doing what you're doing, and we'll take the heat
and back you up.[32] Looked at together, Judge Francis said, the
statistics and the actions of the state police showed beyond a

doubt that African Americans and other minorities had been right all along.

The New Jersey Attorney General's Office, which defended the state police in court, appealed Judge Francis's decision, denying that there had been any racial profiling. But documents released in late 2000 reveal that officials within both the attorney general's office and the state police seem to have known at least since 1996 that there was, in fact, clear evidence of racial profiling. Internal state police documents show that officials at the highest level had evidence that a problem of racial targeting existed. In a memorandum dated October 4, 1996, Captain Ron Touw, Bureau Chief of State Police Internal Affairs, says that an examination of data from the Moorestown station showed that "the percentage of minorities stopped by both minority and non-minority troopers was dramatically higher than the 'expert' testified to in [the *Soto* case]." In other words, the situation was even worse than John Lamberth had said. Another memorandum, this one from Sergeant Thomas Gilbert to Carl Williams, who was then superintendent of the state police, examines numbers from the Moorestown and Cranbury stations from 1994 and 1996. These were the same two state police stations than had been at the center of the allegations of profiling in the *Soto* case. The memorandum reports that the motorists searched by troopers were overwhelmingly minorities, most of them black. Records of some of the individual troopers showed that they searched mostly minority citizens; some of them searched no one else. Sergeant Gilbert concluded from this that "at this point, we are in a very bad spot . . . the [U.S.] Justice Department"—which was by then beginning its investigation into the New Jersey State Police—"has a very good understanding of how we operate and what type of numbers they can get their hands on to prove their position." [33]

An event in the spring of 1998 eventually became the catalyst for real public attention to the issue of racial profiling. Two troopers on the New Jersey Turnpike stopped a van carrying four young black men. According to the troopers, the van attempted to back into them after the stop, and they reacted with a volley of gunshots. The van ended up in a ditch, and so did the four occupants, three of them bleeding from gunshot wounds. Miraculously, none of the men died. The men said later that police refused to allow them to have medical attention until the police had pulled apart their clothes and searched them. Investigations into the shootings began, and it quickly emerged that the young men had been headed to a basketball tryout at North Carolina Central University. No weapons or drugs—only basketball equipment and a Bible—were found in the van.

The controversy continued to bubble, with a U.S. Justice Department investigation into the shooting intertwining with the department's existing investigation into the allegations of profiling. On February 10, 1999, the Newark *Star-Ledger,* the state's largest circulation daily, said that police records indicated that 75 percent of those arrested on the turnpike were minorities.[34] As tensions continued to mount, New Jersey Attorney General Peter Verniero appointed a task force to put together a comprehensive report on the state police, including the issue of profiling. On February 26, Governor Christie Whitman nominated Verniero— who, as attorney general, had ultimate official responsibility for the state police—to a seat on the New Jersey Supreme Court. Then, on February 28, 1999, another article in the *Star-Ledger* brought the ongoing profiling controversy to a fever pitch: Carl Williams, the superintendent of the state police, told the newspaper that minorities perpetrated most of the drug and drug-trafficking in his state. "The drug problem is mostly cocaine and marijuana. It is most likely a minority group that's involved with that." When the president of the United States wanted to discuss international drug trafficking, Williams said, he went to Mexico, not Ireland or England.[35] Williams's comments seemed to confirm the worst suspicions about the state police. They also seemed likely to imperil Verniero's nomination. Whitman fired Williams the next day, but she still refused to admit that the problem existed.[36]

Shortly afterward, the attorney general's task force issued its report. Few expected anything like what it contained. Despite numerous strong statements to the contrary by state officials over the years, the report said that the evidence left little room for doubt that "minority motorists have been treated differently than non-minority motorists in the course of traffic stops on the New Jersey Turnpike. . . . [T]he problem of disparate treatment is real—not imagined."[37] Examining statistics on traffic stops from 1997 and 1998, a period that *followed* the damning verdict in *Soto* as well as intense media coverage of the allegations of profiling by the state police, the task force reported that more than 40 percent of all traffic stops involved a racial minority, and that blacks made up more than one in four of all persons stopped.[38] All of this was "consistent with the data developed during the course of the Soto litigation."[39]

Data on searches of drivers—drawn from a larger stretch of time than the data on stops—showed even larger biases: almost 80 percent of these searches involved either a black or Hispanic driver.[40] With remarkable understatement, the report said this meant that "race and ethnicity may have influenced the exercise of discretion by some officers" performing searches. The report also broke down citations issued by type of enforcement unit. Radar units, which used radar to track speed, exercised relatively little discretion in whom they stopped. Tactical patrol units focused on vehicle law enforcement with particular objectives in particular locations—they exercised somewhat more discretion. General patrol units exercised the most discretion. The more discretion a unit exercised, the task force reported, the greater the proportion of its tickets went to African American drivers: radar, 18 percent; tactical patrol, 23.8 percent; and general patrol, 34.2 percent. For tickets issued south of turnpike exit 3 the disproportion was even greater, with the general patrol unit issuing 43.8 percent of its tickets to African Americans. This meant that "officers who had more time to devote to drug interdiction may have been more likely to rely upon racial or ethnic stereotypes" than others.[41] All of this, the report said, generated fear, anger, and resentment among minorities; made law enforcement's job more difficult by eroding public confidence in police; and divided black and white citizens on questions of race, criminal justice, and public safety. For all of these reasons, the report concluded, the New Jersey State Police had to make a number of crucial changes, including the way in which they conducted traffic stops and their techniques of supervision, training, discipline, and information management.

The New Jersey Task Force report represents one of the most far-reaching statements on profiling and traffic stops any government at any level has ever made. New Jersey's struggle with profiling illustrates many of the problems found in the use of traffic stops as a high-discretion enforcement tool: lack of accountability, denial, a failure to face facts, defensiveness, and an utter disregard for the implications of policing policies, no matter how loudly some members of the public cry out.

MARYLAND

Recall the story of Robert Wilkins, the African American Harvard law graduate whose rental car was stopped and searched as he and his family were returning to the Washington, D.C., area from a family funeral in Chicago. Civil rights lawyers sometimes say that despite the volume of complaints they receive about racially biased traffic stops, victims usually feel reluctant to come forward and sue. Some may fear retaliation. Others may not want to get involved in complex, politically charged, protracted, and very public litigation charging a police department with racial bias. To get involved in a case like this, one must have an absolutely squeaky clean personal history, the knowledge and personal resources to access the legal system, and the moxie to take on the task. Most people would simply rather forget these unpleasant experiences.[42]

As an attorney with substantial experience in search and seizure law, Robert Wilkins knew exactly what his rights were and how the Maryland State Police had violated them. And he was unafraid of the legal system—working within it was his daily bread and butter. Wilkins and his family members contacted the American Civil Liberties Union (ACLU), which filed suit on behalf of the four of them and all other motorists whom police had treated the same way. The suit alleged that the police had violated civil rights laws and other statutes by illegally stopping and detaining them on the basis of a racial profile.[43] The state police vigorously denied Wilkins's allegations. A spokesman said the practice of stopping a disproportionate number of blacks represented not racism but "an unfortunate byproduct of sound police policies."[44] Despite this and other race-neutral explanations, the turning point in the lawsuit came when a document entitled "Criminal Intelligence Report" came to light. This document contained an explicit profile targeting African Americans and was dated just days before the state police stopped Wilkins and his family. A settlement followed soon after. Wilkins and his family received small amounts of monetary damages, and the state police agreed to change their policies, practices, and training. But the real meat of the agreement was the settlement's requirement that the state police keep data on every traffic stop that resulted in a search, and submit the data to the court for a period of three years so that it could monitor whether the state police had in fact changed their ways.[45]

It was these data that emerged as the key contribution of Wilkins's suit. When they became available, the ACLU retained John Lamberth to perform the same kind of analysis he had done in the New Jersey case. Lamberth took the data from the state police concerning the number of stops broken down by race, and he compared these data to road population surveys and violator surveys he and his research associates conducted on I-95, the main location of Maryland State Police drug interdiction.[46] What he found was that blacks and whites drove no differently; every racial and ethnic group violated the traffic laws at the same very high rate.[47] But more important, he found that although 17 percent of the driving population on that road was black, African Americans were a full *72 percent* of all those stopped and searched.[48] In more than 80 percent of the cases, the person stopped and searched was a member of a racial minority.[49] The numbers were also broken down by individual officer: half of the officers stopped more than 80 percent African Americans, one officer stopped more than 95 percent African Americans; and two officers stopped *only* African Americans.[50] The disparity between 17 percent (the black driving population) and 72 percent (percentage of drivers stopped and searched who were black) includes 34.6 standard deviations, a level of statistical significance that Lamberth described as "literally off the charts."[51] In careful, temperate language, Lamberth came to a devastating conclusion:

> While no one can know the motivation of each individual trooper in conducting a traffic stop, the statistics presented herein, representing a broad and detailed sample of highly appropriate data, show without question a racially discriminatory impact on blacks. . . . The disparities are sufficiently great that taken as a whole, they are consistent and strongly support the assertion that the state police targeted the community of black motorists for stop, detention and investigation within the Interstate 95 corridor.[52]

FLORIDA

Located in central Florida, Volusia County surrounds a busy stretch of Interstate 95 several hundred miles south of Maryland. In the mid- to late 1980s, this portion of highway became the focus of the same Sheriff Vogel who had developed the concept of a drug-courier profile for highway drug interdiction and whose methods had been spread around the country by the Drug Enforcement Administration. Using a group of officers called the Selective Enforcement Team, Vogel operated a major drug interdiction effort against drivers moving narcotics by car through his jurisdiction.[53] The deputies aimed not only to make arrests but also to make seizures of cash and vehicles, which their agency would keep under the asset forfeiture laws.[54]

As with most police agencies, the Volusia County Sheriff's Department kept no records of stops and searches in which no arrests or seizures occurred in the three years that the Selective Enforcement Team operated.[55] Thus no one might ever have learned about the Selective Enforcement Team's practices had it not been for one unusual fact: Volusia County had had deputies' cars fitted with video cameras.[56] Deputies had taped many of the I-95 stops, and when this practice came to light, the Orlando *Sentinel Tribune* used Florida's public records law to obtain 148 hours of the videotapes documenting almost eleven hundred stops.

Although African Americans and Hispanics made up only about 5 percent of the drivers on the county's stretch of I-95 during the time period,[57] the tapes show that more than 70 percent of all drivers stopped were either African American or Hispanic.[58] One African American man tells the officer who stops him that he has been stopped seven times by police; another says that he has been stopped twice *within minutes*. Examining the figures for all of Florida, 70 percent is vastly out of proportion not only to the 5 percent of black drivers on the road, but even to the percentage of blacks among Floridians of driving age (11.7 percent), the percentage of blacks among all Florida drivers convicted of traffic offenses in 1991 (15.1 percent), and the percentage of blacks in the nation's population as a whole (12 percent).[59] (Hispanics make up about 9 percent of the population.)[60] The deputies not only stopped black and Hispanic drivers more often than whites, they also stopped them *for longer periods of time*. According to the videotapes, deputies detained blacks and Hispanics for twice as long as they detained whites.[61] And the tapes showed that although police followed a stop with a search only half the time, 80 percent of the cars searched belonged to black or Hispanic drivers.[62]

It should surprise no one that Sheriff Vogel's deputies stated that they based these nearly eleven hundred stops on "legitimate traffic violations." [63] Infractions ranged from "swerving" (243), to exceeding the speed limit by up to ten miles per hour (128), burned-out license tag lights (71), improper license tags (46), failure to signal before a lane change (45), to a smattering of others.[64] Even so, only *nine* of the nearly eleven hundred drivers stopped—considerably less than 1 percent—received tickets.[65] Deputies even released several drivers who *admitted to crimes*, including drunk driving, without any charges.[66] These stops weren't about traffic enforcement at all. The tapes also showed that the seizure of cash remained an important goal of the stops, with deputies seizing money almost three times as often as they arrested anyone for drugs.[67] Race clearly played a role in these seizures of cash: 90 percent of the drivers from whom cash was taken, but who were not arrested, were black or Hispanic.[68]

Notwithstanding these numbers, Sheriff Vogel denied the presence of any racial component in his department's work. Prior to the release of the tapes, he stated that the stops were not based on skin color and that deputies stopped "a broad spectrum of people."[69] He still strongly denies that his deputies were using race as part of the "cumulative similarities" used to spot potential drug couriers. The release of the tapes eventually led to two lawsuits in federal court in which plaintiffs alleged violations of their civil rights because they were targeted for stops on the basis of their race.[70] In both cases, a judge refused to certify a class of all minority citizens illegally stopped, making it virtually impossible for the plaintiffs to win. Sheriff Vogel proclaimed victory. The plaintiffs appealed, but they lost in the United States Court of Appeals for the Eleventh Circuit.[71]

ILLINOIS

As in many other states, African Americans and Hispanics in Illinois had made hundreds of complaints alleging that the Illinois State Police targeted them for pretextual traffic stops.[72] The ACLU eventually filed suit, and a man named Peso Chavez who had been stopped and searched by the Illinois State Police became the lead plaintiff. But Mr. Chavez's encounter with the Illinois State Police did not happen by chance.

Chavez was a private investigator, with twenty years of experience. He was also a former city councilman in Santa Fe, New Mexico, where he had served for eight years. A lawyer for an Hispanic man who alleged racial profiling by the Illinois State Police hired Chavez, himself an Hispanic, to drive across areas of Illinois that had been the source of complaints.[73] Chavez would drive cautiously, and a paralegal in another car would follow at a distance to observe his driving. The idea was a "reverse sting"[74]—an attempt to catch police in the act of making illegal stops and searches.

On February 18, 1993, Officer Thomas of the Illinois State Police began to follow Chavez. He tailed Chavez for twenty miles, through two downstate counties.[75] Thomas eventually pulled Chavez over,[76] and was soon joined at the scene by another officer. Officer Thomas told Chavez that he had stopped him for a traffic violation, and demanded Chavez's license.[77] After questioning Chavez, Thomas gave him a warning for failing to signal when changing lanes. (The paralegal following Chavez saw no violation.)[78] The other officer then asked Chavez if he could search his car. When Chavez asked whether he had to allow the search, the officer said that he wanted a drug-sniffing dog to walk around Chavez's car. Chavez unequivocally refused and asked to be allowed to leave, but the officers would not let him go.[79] Instead, an officer led a dog around Chavez's car. To his astonishment, the police told Chavez that the dog had "alerted" to the presence of narcotics, and they ordered him into the backseat of a patrol car.[80]

For the next hour, Chavez watched from the back of the police car as the police conducted a thorough search of the interior, trunk, and engine compartment of his car. Officers opened his luggage and searched through his clothes, toiletries, and personal possessions.[81] Meanwhile, an officer sitting in the patrol car with Chavez kept up a steady stream of probing questions about his personal life.[82] The police found nothing, and eventually they allowed Chavez to leave.[83]

Despite his background as an investigator, his government experience, and the knowledge that he was part of a reverse sting, Chavez found the experience more than unnerving. Watching police search his car, after telling him that the dog had detected drugs, Chavez said, "I became very frightened at what was happening. I never had my mouth as dry as it was—it was like cotton." [84]

Chavez became the plaintiff in a federal lawsuit to force the state police to stop racially based searches and seizures. When the suit became public, many other African Americans and Hispanics who were subjected to illegal stops and searches also became plaintiffs.[85] When several rulings by the judge made it all but impossible for the plaintiffs to present a winning case, they withdrew the suit so they could immediately appeal the judge's actions. In 2001, the U.S. Court of Appeals ruled against Chavez and the other plaintiffs on all counts.[86]

COLORADO

In the late 1980s, the Eagle County, Colorado, Sheriff's Department established a highway drug interdiction unit. The High Country Drug Task Force used a drug-courier profile made up of twenty-two indicators to stop cars along Interstate 70. Prominent among these indicators was "race or ethnicity, based on 'intelligence information' from other law agencies." [87] Although the task force used traffic infractions as a pretext to stop many drivers, not one person stopped received a ticket.[88]

On May 3, 1989, Eagle County deputies stopped Jhenita Whitfield as she drove from San Diego to Denver to visit relatives. With her were her sister and their four children.[89] A disabled vehicle in the roadway forced them to move to another lane; soon after, an officer pulled them over for failing to signal before doing so.[90] The deputies told Whitfield straight out that she " 'fit the profile' of a possible drug runner," and asked if they could search her car.[91] Whitfield wanted to refuse, but she didn't feel she could. She thought that if she said no to the officer, she might be "set up" [92]—drugs would be planted on her. She also felt she had no choice because the children were hungry and one needed a bathroom, so she consented.[93] The experience left Whitfield, an African American, shaken, and it has changed her life in a significant way. Despite having family out of town, she does not visit them. "I do not travel anymore," she said.[94]

A group of seven people who, like Jhenita Whitfield, had been stopped by Eagle County deputies filed a class action suit in 1990, asking the court to halt the task force's practice of race-based profile stops.[95] The court eventually certified a class consisting of four hundred individuals who had been stopped.[96] Among them were many African Americans and a large number of Hispanics, who alleged that deputies stopped them because of their ethnicity.[97] In November 1993, a federal court ruled that the task force had violated constitutional protections against unreasonable searches and seizures. With appeals pending, the parties reached a settlement requiring Eagle County to pay damages to each person searched, amounting to a total of $800,000. The county also agreed to abandon the task force and agreed not to stop, search, or seize a person "unless there is some objective reasonable suspicion that the person has done something wrong." [98]

OHIO, MICHIGAN, AND ELSEWHERE

Ohio

In 1999, state legislators in Ohio who were considering offering legislation on racial profiling wanted information that would tell them how widespread the problem was in their state. None was available; no police agency of any size in Ohio kept any data that included the race of drivers subjected to police stops. A study was therefore conducted using ticketing information from the municipal courts—the courts that heard almost all traffic matters in the state—in four metropolitan areas: the cities of Toledo, Dayton, Akron, and Franklin County, which included Columbus and its suburbs.[99] These courts had computerized records of all traffic citations in their jurisdictions, and they also had data that enabled them to break down these cases by race for at least the years 1996 and 1997. In Akron, African Americans received 37.6 percent of all tickets for moving violations; in Toledo, they received 31 percent; in Dayton, the number was 50 percent; and in Franklin County, which includes Columbus and most of its suburbs, the figure was 25.2 percent.[100]

By comparing the ticketing rates for blacks to their numbers among people of driving age in each location, a calculation was made showing whether a black person is more likely to be ticketed than a nonblack person. (The term *nonblack* indicates all others—whites, Latinos, Asians, and everyone else—even though many other minorities, especially Latinos, have also complained of being targeted. This makes the calculation both clearer and more conservative.) For Akron, blacks were 2.04 times as likely to be ticketed as all other drivers. For Toledo, blacks were 2.02 times as likely. In Franklin County (Columbus) and Dayton, blacks were 1.8 times as likely to be ticketed as others.[101]

These numbers can be further refined by factoring in information from the National Personal Transportation Survey, a fifty-state study of transportation patterns conducted by the U.S. Department of Transportation. According to the survey, black households are less likely to own vehicles than white households; fully 21 percent of all black households own no vehicle. Blacks also take fewer vehicle trips on the average day (3.9 versus 4.4 for whites), meaning they are less likely to drive. Factoring in just the numbers on vehicle ownership, the likelihood of blacks receiving tickets in these four cities rises—to 2.4 times as likely in Franklin County (Columbus), to 2.5 times as likely in Dayton, to more than 2.7 times as likely in Akron and Toledo.[102]

No claim was made that these numbers were proof positive that racial profiling was taking place in these four cities. The data available in the state had been quite limited, so no statistically perfect conclusion could be drawn. The conclusions drawn were therefore purposely cautious and carefully stated. The numbers, the study said, showed that there could be a profiling problem in Ohio and that further study was in order—with, of course, more thorough and comprehensive data.[103] Law enforcement agencies and their spokespersons around Ohio attacked the study as statistically flawed and ideologically driven.[104] But none ever presented any evidence to back up these claims, and none ever published any statistics of their own to counter the assertions in the study. Those that commented often simply asserted that their agencies did not have a problem, but they did not provide any basis upon which to make such a statement.

The Mobile Data Terminal Study

Criminologist Jay Meehan and sociologist Michael Ponder of Michigan's Oakland University have taken a different approach to racial profiling. Looking at which drivers are stopped and searched is helpful, they say, but it does not delve deeply enough into the problem. Most important, traffic stops do not capture profiling behavior that happens *before* police conduct a stop and perhaps a search—a level of surveillance behavior that may be masked in many cases in which police do not conduct stops and searches. Thus stop-and-search studies, Meehan and Ponder argue, allow an important issue—perhaps the most important one—to go unrecognized and untested: Are police officers more likely to consider minorities suspicious, and what are the hidden first steps police take to act on these suspicions?

Meehan's earlier work gave him a special insight into the problem and an idea for a previously unused source of data. In the past, he had studied information on the use of mobile data terminals (MDTs)—small built-in computers in squad cars—to study various aspects of police behavior.[105] Meehan knew that officers could, and often did, use their MDTs to "run" the license plates of cars they saw on the road around them. He also knew that this would generate an electronic record. Along with Ponder,

Meehan put these insights to work in a paper entitled "Race and Place: The Ecology of Racial Profiling of African American Motorists." [106]

The MDT data allowed Meehan and Ponder to see a whole level of police activity, such as officers' "queries" of their computer systems about suspicious drivers or vehicles, previously hidden from view; they were not limited to data that police deliberately recorded about stops and searches, such as traffic tickets or racial-profiling data reports, the making of which officers might avoid or manipulate. [107] Meehan and Ponder compared racial patterns in these MDT queries in a suburban area to a Roadway Observation Study (a driving population study similar to what John Lamberth did in Maryland and New Jersey). [108] The analysis of the MDT data revealed "systematic evidence of profiling," which became more pronounced the farther away the officers in this almost entirely white suburb were from the town's border with a largely African American city. That is, the more "white" the expected road population of the area and the more that a black driver would therefore seem "out of place," the more officers used racial profiling when deciding whose license plate to make a query about to check their suspicions.

Interestingly, Meehan and Ponder found that with the exception of a group of officers who made the most frequent use of profiling—about 10 percent of the department's officers made the highest number of MDT queries—the racial pattern in MDT queries *did not* translate into a higher number of stops of African Americans. In other words, this clear pattern of suspicion of blacks would have remained hidden had the researchers looked only at stops or tickets. Data on stops in the jurisdiction—blacks, 11.1 percent and whites, 12.2 percent—were not statistically different, the researchers found, and the same pattern held with ticketing. But MDT queries showed considerable racial differences, meaning that focusing on either stops or tickets "masks important surveillance behavior." [109] Although African Americans made up only 13 percent of the drivers in this community (and less than 1 percent of the population), they were the subject of 27 percent of all MDT queries. Whites, who made up 87 percent of the drivers, were the subject of only 73 percent of queries,[110] meaning blacks were twice as likely as whites to be queried. The farther away officers were from the neighboring, mostly black city, the higher the query rates of blacks. In the two police sectors of the town farthest from the city, blacks were the subject of MDT suspicion queries at rates 325 and 385 percent greater than their numbers in the driving population would have predicted. "To put this in perspective," Meehan and Ponder say, "one must consider that to achieve such high query rates on these particular roadways, where there are fewer African American drivers, officers must be 'hunting' for or clearly noticing black drivers in these sectors."[111] This implies that police seem to be scanning and surveilling African Americans because they are "out of place"—in an area of town in which "they don't belong." The more out of place they are, the more likely they will be regarded with suspicion. And, Meehan and Ponder say, crime rates do not explain the higher query rates for blacks; it happens most in areas of lower, not higher, criminal activity.[112]

In other places, news organizations have conducted their own investigations. In North Carolina, journalists found that special highway patrol units that focused on drug interdiction were ticketing black drivers at twice the rate of white drivers and that officers were twice as likely to search them.[113] The *Detroit Free Press* analyzed all traffic stops and tickets issued in a small white suburban community bordering Detroit. It found blacks composed 42 percent of those ticketed though they made up only 32 percent of the overall driving population in the area. In areas of the community closest to Detroit, blacks were from three times to thirteen times as likely to be ticketed as nonblacks. Blacks were also more likely than whites to receive tickets for minor infractions, such as broken taillights.[114] The Minneapolis *Star-Tribune* found that blacks were many times more likely than whites to be stopped, arrested, and jailed for a variety of crimes, including 42 times more likely to be ticketed for not having a valid driver's license.[115] The *Seattle Times* reported that blacks in that city were twice as likely to be ticketed as whites, and that they received outsized portions of tickets for minor violations.[116]

The data on stops are incontrovertible. The information comes from many cities and involves many different police departments and law enforcement contexts. Data-gathering techniques also differ. Not all courts hearing these cases have come to the same conclusion; the difficulty of proving any case of discrimination by police makes this understandable. Nevertheless, all of the data point in the same direction: minorities are stopped, questioned, and searched in numbers far out of proportion to their presence in the driving population. And it is not their driving behavior or vehicles that account for this. As New Jersey's own police officers said, race and ethnicity have nothing to do with who violates the traffic laws.

Profiling has persisted even though we have now been aware of it for some time. It has also continued in the face of strong assertions by African Americans, Latinos, and others that the experience is dangerous, damaging, and humiliating and that it gives rise to disrespect for police and the entire criminal justice system. So why does this practice continue? The answer, according to many in law enforcement, is that it works: it is an effective way to fight crime and apprehend criminals. It may be distasteful to African Americans, Latinos, and others who are inconvenienced, but, the argument goes, it is the right way to catch criminals. Since, as supporters contend, minorities are disproportionately involved in crime, it makes sense to stop and search more of them.

Is racial profiling effective? Is it successful, in the way serial-killer profiles sometimes are? Does it, in fact, allow us to catch more criminals than we would without it? And if so, doesn't that mean that racial profiling is a rational law enforcement policy, no matter how hard it may be for some to stomach its side effects?

Chapter Four

THE HARD NUMBERS: WHY RACIAL PROFILING DOESN'T ADD UP

Marshall Frank served as a police officer for thirty years. He is a former member of the Miami-Dade Police Department, from which he retired as a captain. Frank's years in law enforcement have left him with clear and definite views about racial profiling. Frank says people can "[l]abel me a racist if you wish, but the cold fact is that African Americans comprise [*sic*] 12 percent of the nation's population, but occupy nearly half the state and federal prison cells. African Americans account for 2,165 inmates per 100,000 population, versus 307 for non-Hispanic whites and 823 for Hispanics." This means, Frank says, that African Americans commit most of the serious crimes, and until that changes, police should continue to do business as they always have.[1]

Frank is not alone. "The hard truth in America today," says Clayton Searle, President of the International Narcotics Interdiction Association, "is that the minorities of any major city commit most of the street drug sales and then get arrested disproportionately."[2] John Marcello, a former Drug Enforcement Administration agent who in the early 1970s helped develop the drug-courier profile, puts it forcefully. "If you work in a city where 99 percent of the crack is controlled by minorities, then inevitably the vast majority of couriers arrested will be minorities. It's called reality, and it still will be true no matter how hard the apologists pretend it isn't." [3] Likewise, according to a sergeant from a small police department in New Jersey: "I think it's obvious if you are arresting and seeing more convictions of—whether they be African Americans or Caucasians—that, yes, that's going to tell a story." [4] Harvard Law School Professor Randall Kennedy defends racial profiling as "statistically based" in his book *Race, Crime, and the Law.*[5] The overrepresentation of blacks among offenders, persons arrested, and prison inmates is not racist propaganda but an unpleasant fact, says Kennedy. Facts like these might upset us, but that does not make them any less true. There is a risk, Kennedy says, in attempting to "prettify ugly realities. Crime and its racial demographics are part of those realities." According to Kennedy, racial profiling gives police officers "a sensible, statistically based tool that enables them to focus their energies efficiently. . . . The empirical claim upon which the practice rests is sound. . . ." [6] Heather Mac Donald of the Manhattan Institute agrees with Kennedy. "Judging by arrest rates, minorities are vastly overrepresented among drug traffickers," she says. She also notes that about 60 percent of drug offenders in state prison are black. Given numbers like these, Mac Donald says, high rates of searches of blacks "look proportionate." [7] Author and academic Amitai Etzioni agrees as well. While he grants that "racial profiling is understandably objectionable to those who are the targets," he argues that the practice is nevertheless defensible because "a statistical case can be made that it . . . is an effective tool that shouldn't be dismissed too quickly." [8]

Are these people right? Are the disproportionate numbers of arrests and the heavily minority prison populations evidence of the effectiveness of racial profiling? Imagine for a moment a state that decides to make stopping rape its top priority. Legislators pass new laws criminalizing rape in new ways, increase sentences for the crime dramatically, and limit or even eliminate parole for all sexual offenses. Prosecutors do their part by vigorously prosecuting all cases and asking for maximum sentences, and police drastically increase their enforcement efforts against rape. If we looked at prisons after ten years of these policies, we would surely find a higher percentage of inmates imprisoned for rape than used to be true. But this would not necessarily mean that rape itself is much more common than it was ten years before. Rather, the numbers would reflect the priorities and actions of actors and institutions within the criminal justice system.

This imagined scenario, of course, is almost exactly what has happened in our society with drugs. Politicians at every level, up to and including the president of the United States, identified drug enforcement as the top law enforcement priority. The U.S. Congress and other legislative bodies increased sentences, sometimes greatly. New laws eliminated judicial discretion over sentences. Congress eliminated parole at the federal level altogether. Some of these new laws targeted crack, a form of cocaine more commonly sold in African American neighborhoods, with special vigor. Law enforcement focused on the most visible aspect of the drug trade—retail selling and use on the streets, almost always in minority neighborhoods. Although many studies have shown drug use to be relatively equal across racial and ethnic groups, these enforcement policies resulted in the very heavily minority jail populations that Marshall Frank and other advocates of profiling point to in order to justify what they do.

ARREST AND INCARCERATION STATISTICS

Arrest and crime statistics are indeed facts, but the way we interpret these facts and the conclusions we draw from them are not. In moving from fact to interpretation to conclusion, those supporting racial profiling have missed something critically important.

Objective statistics do confirm that African Americans, Latinos, and other minorities are disproportionately arrested and incarcerated. In 1990, one out of four black men between the ages of eighteen and twenty-eight were under criminal justice control.[9] By 1995, the number had grown to one in three, with even higher percentages in some cities—for example, up to 60 percent in Baltimore.[10]

The important question, however, is not whether the rate of African American or Latino arrest or incarceration is disproportionately higher, but whether this tells us anything about actual offending behavior. At first blush, this may seem too obvious a question to ask. Assuming police officers act in good faith, why would they arrest someone who has not committed an offense? Arrest statistics should indeed reflect offending behavior; every person arrested for a crime represents one crime committed, and in aggregate these numbers should tell us who the criminals are. But even beyond what the hypothetical example of the state that cracked down on rape shows us, there are important reasons to be suspicious of this theory.

First, police do not get reports on all crimes, and for those not reported police will make no arrests. According to 1999 National Crime Victimization Survey (NCVS) data, victims of violent offenses did not report these crimes to the police *more than half the time—54.3 percent.*[11] Almost three-quarters of all sexual assaults, more than a third of all robberies, and more than 40 percent of all aggravated assaults go unreported; almost 75 percent of all purse snatchings and nearly half of all household burglaries never make it into police files.[12] This makes arrest figures less reliable indicators of who commits crimes *overall.* The percentage of unreported crimes is even higher for drug crimes and crimes involving weapons, in which police reports represent a small percentage of the crimes actually committed. Drugs and weapons possession crimes differ fundamentally from such offenses as homicides, assaults, robberies, rapes, or thefts because they are consensual.[13] In drug offenses everyone involved—buyer or seller, retailer, wholesaler, or mere possessor—wants the crime to happen and has absolutely no reason to want the police involved. This means that, in contrast to robberies or assaults, police do not typically get reports of this kind of crime when it happens. Rather, if officers want to enforce the laws against consensual offenses like drug crime, they have to actively seek out such crimes.[14]

Police do, of course, receive complaints of drug sales on street corners from residents. But the great bulk of drug activity, including the transport of larger quantities of drugs by couriers, goes unreported, unseen, and undetected. Police officers may have *general knowledge* of drug activity, its locations, or the people involved. But this tells them little about any specific patterns or instances of offending. Weapons possession offenses work much the same way. Those who have illegal guns have every intention of concealing them from the police; similarly, anyone who sells illegal weapons does not want this activity reported. So if police want to enforce laws against illegal guns, they must seek out the offenders—that is, they must go find these otherwise hidden activities. This explains why so much profiling and high-discretion police activity is oriented toward the detection of crimes involving drugs and weapons. These crimes are least likely to be fully known and reported, so police use other tactics to find them.

In the case of consensual crimes such as drug activity and weapons offenses, arrest and incarceration rates are particularly poor measures of criminal activity. They are much better measures of *law enforcement activity*. They tell us who police have arrested without necessarily giving us a full and correct portrait of *all* offenders and instances of offending. Criminologists and other researchers on crime have known for a long time that arrest statistics tell us nothing more than who police arrest. As far back as 1963, John Kitsuse and Aaron Cicourel asserted that while records of arrest and court activity give us reasonably reliable information concerning the activity of such criminal justice agencies as police departments and courts, these data present problems when used to describe patterns of criminal behavior and characteristics of offenders.[15] In his 1995 Sutherland Prize Presentation to the American Society of Criminology, Dr. Delbert Elliot of the Center for the Study and Prevention of Violence at the University of Colorado made much the same point. "We have fallen into bad habits," Elliot said, referring to the continuing use of arrest data to support conclusions about offender characteristics and behavior. Using arrest statistics this way will "lead to incorrect conclusions, ineffective policies and practices and ultimately undermine our efforts to understand, prevent, and control criminal behavior."[16] When we look at incarceration rates, we see something similar. Rates at which we imprison people do not necessarily show us anything about who actually commits crime. Just as with arrest statistics, incarceration rates measure not crime but the activity of people and institutions responsible for determining criminal sentences—primarily legislatures (the bodies that make the law that determines sentences) and judges (the people who do the actual sentencing).

When we say that arrest and imprisonment rates measure the activity of police or other actors and institutions in the criminal justice system, there is nothing wrong with this. On the contrary, the data tell us many useful things if we understand it for what it is rather than use it to support conclusions for which it simply isn't appropriate. Arrest statistics tell us that police arrest disproportionate numbers of African American males for drug crimes. This reflects decisions made by someone in the police department—the chief, lieutenants, street-level supervisors, or even by individual officers themselves—to concentrate enforcement activity on these individuals. But drawing further conclusions based on these statistics, or using them to justify racial profiling, as the police and academics cited at the beginning of this chapter do, risks a grave misunderstanding that may impair the criminal justice policy choices that we make.

IRRATIONAL POLICING: HOW THE RELEVANT NUMBERS SHOW THAT PROFILING DOESN'T WORK

If arrest and incarceration statistics do not tell us about the effectiveness of racial profiling in catching criminals, other statistics do. And the story these statistics tell is a very different one than the "rational" law enforcement argument would have us believe.

Hit Rates: The Heart of "Rational" Law Enforcement

James Savage, former acting president of the New York Pa-
trolmen's Benevolent Association, explained racial profiling by
recalling the words of one of the country's most famous criminals, the serial bank robber Willie Sutton. "They once asked
Willie Sutton why he robbed banks," Savage said, "and he said,
'Because that's where the money is.' " For Savage, the analogy
seems obvious. "Why do [police departments] send people into
minority or high-crime neighborhoods to look for guns? Because
that's where the guns are." In other words, NYPD officers don't
stop blacks and Latinos more often out of racism or any other
misguided feeling. Rather, officers stop more blacks and other
minorities because "that's where the guns are." [17]

Until a few years ago, there were no data that gave us any insight into hit rates—the rates at which police actually find contraband or other evidence of crime when they perform stops and
searches. Thus we had no way to judge the claim that racial profiling is a rational form of law enforcement, that is, that profiling
actually works as a crime-fighting strategy. New evidence from a
variety of contexts now allows for a statistical analysis of the effectiveness of racial profiling. And the results of this analysis will
come as a complete shock to Marshall Frank and other public
and private supporters of racial profiling: the numbers don't add
up. Racial profiling is neither an efficient nor an effective tool for
fighting crime.

Hit Rates on the Highway   Statistics from stops and searches by
the Maryland State Police during 1995 and 1996 provided some
of the first comprehensive data on hit rates. In terms of stops, the
data, which came from the state police themselves, showed that
the state police stopped and searched African Americans disproportionately. Although they made up only 17 percent of all
drivers, blacks made up more than 70 percent of all of those
searched. The data were compiled from more than eleven hundred searches. Given the official state police line that what they
had been doing was just sound policing—not racism, just "ra-

tional" law enforcement—the hit rates should clearly have borne out the wisdom of the state police approach. Instead, the hit rates showed something different: the rate at which the police found drugs, guns, or other evidence of crime in these searches was almost exactly the same for blacks and whites.

Troopers found evidence on African Americans they searched 28.4 percent of the time; they found evidence on whites 28.8 percent of the time.[18] John Lamberth, who performed the statistical analysis of the Maryland stop-and-search data, found no statistical significance in the difference between the numbers for blacks and whites, given the number of stops and searches included in the data. If in fact there was any difference between blacks and whites in offending behavior, the data showed clearly that racial profiling and high-discretion police tactics *were not uncovering it*. What the data did show was a flaw in the basic assumption underlying racial profiling.

Some of the most recent statistics from New Jersey provide more information on hit rates. After the attorney general of New Jersey released the explosive task force report in spring 1999, the New Jersey State Police began to record data for all of its traffic stops and searches. Data from 2000 concerning the southern end of the turnpike, the area from which the first allegations of profiling came, show that, despite the progress that the New Jersey State Police have made in many areas, blacks and Latinos remain 78 percent of those searched.[19] And the hit rates absolutely contradict the idea that racial profiling is "just good, rational law enforcement." Troopers found evidence in the searches of whites 25 percent of the time; they found evidence in searches of blacks 13 percent of the time, and in searches of Latinos just 5 percent of the time.[20] Whites were *almost twice* as likely to be found with contraband as blacks, and *five times* as likely to be found with contraband as Latinos—clearly not what the advocates of racial profiling would predict.

New data from North Carolina tell a similar story. In 1999, North Carolina became the first state to pass legislation making it mandatory for some of its police agencies to report basic data on all traffic stops and searches. Professor Matthew Zingraff of the North Carolina Center for Crime and Justice Research at North Carolina State University and his colleagues, the analysts conducting the studies required by the new law, have also looked at hit rates. In 1998, Zingraff and his partners found that African American male drivers were 68 percent more likely than white male drivers to be searched by the North Carolina Highway Patrol. But the hit rates did not support any "rational" argument for racial profiling. The highway patrol found contraband on blacks in 26 percent of searches; for whites, the hit rate was 33 percent.[21]

Hit Rates on the Streets   Hit rates from the New York attorney general's study of stops and frisks in New York City, issued in 1999, also give us new perspective on the idea that stopping more minorities "just makes common sense." The context of the study is somewhat different than either the New Jersey or Maryland studies of traffic stops—the data concern stops and frisks of pedestrians. But the practice—using race to focus police suspicion, combined with high-discretion tactics—is basically the same. In addition, the data are plentiful: 175,000 recorded encounters between officers and citizens over fifteen months. The study tracks hit rates by analyzing the percentage of stops and frisks that ended in an arrest. The data are even more striking than the numbers from Maryland and New Jersey. The attorney general found that police arrested 12.6 percent of the whites they stopped, only 11.5 percent of the Latinos, and only 10.5 percent of the blacks.[22] This is precisely the opposite of what the "rational" law enforcement theory would predict. When New York City police officers used stops and frisks intensively, they found what they ostensibly wanted *less* often on blacks and Latinos than they did on whites.

Hit Rates for Weapons Using Stops and Frisks   What about possession of weapons, the activity other than narcotics offenses against which police use profile-based enforcement tactics most often? Again, the comprehensive study of stop-and-frisk activity in New York City by the New York attorney general's office sup-

plies us with some answers. The data in that study cover almost
sixty thousand stops made on suspicion of weapons offenses.
This allows us to separate out a hit rate for weapons from all of
the hit-rate data in the study. Recall that blacks were more likely
to be stopped and frisked than whites, regardless of crime rate or
neighborhood characteristics. When the data were broken down
by categories of offenses and by the race of the person stopped,
the rates of successful stops and frisks for weapons—that is,
stops and frisks that yielded a weapon, as the officer making the
stop had suspected—were actually *lower* for blacks than for
whites. The researchers discovered this by calculating the ratio of
stops to arrests for weapons offenses. Police made 1 arrest for
every 15 white people they stopped on a suspicion of a weapons
offense. For blacks, police made 1 arrest for every 17.4 persons
stopped for a suspected weapons offense. For Latinos, the number was 1 arrest for every 18 weapons stops.[23] Again, this is the
opposite of what the "rational" law enforcement approach targeting minorities would have predicted.

Mobile Data Terminal (MDT) Data   Criminologist Jay Meehan and sociologist Michael Ponder used data from police in-car
Mobile Data Terminal (MDT) queries on suspicious persons to
test whether officers used profiling.[24] Police officers use MDTs to
"check out" any driver they feel is suspicious by running the car's
license plate through law enforcement computer systems. This
enables the officer to see vehicle violations such as an expired
registration or a suspended license of the car's owner, assuming
the owner is also the driver. According to Meehan and Ponder,
the broader purpose is simply to allow officers to investigate, in a
very preliminary way, anyone who strikes the officer as even remotely suspicious, for any reason or for no articulable reason at
all. This can lead not only to traffic stops but to a further, more
intrusive investigation for drugs, weapons, or other evidence.
Meehan and Ponder found that these queries showed a strong
pattern of treating African American drivers with extra suspicion, because police officers asked their computer system for in-

formation on black drivers in numbers far out of proportion to the presence of blacks on the roadways. Meehan also used the MDT data to study hit rates—in this case, the rates at which MDT queries came back with information on either the car (e.g., license tag invalid or suspended, etc.) or its driver (e.g., suspended driver's license). Officers believe, Meehan says, that querying black drivers more often is productive police work because these queries will result in a higher hit rate than queries on white drivers. (Meehan notes that the police department he studied, like most departments, makes no effort to give officers hit-rate feedback; one officer interviewed said that he thought that he and other officers were "wrong more often than right" when they tested their assumptions concerning who is suspicious via MDT query.)[25] Meehan found that the overall hit rate was extremely low—a mere 0.7 percent. In fact, Meehan and Ponder compared the total hit rate of 0.7 percent to hit rates for queries done completely at random, which came out to 0.6 percent—showing just how weak a predictor of criminality racially based police suspicions actually were. The black hit rate of 1.5 percent was slightly higher than the white hit rate of .5 percent, but as Meehan put it, "the low number of cases precludes us from drawing any meaningful race comparisons. What we can say is that the actual productivity . . . was low and that the crimes that these 'hits' revealed were relatively minor. . . . Only white drivers were involved in a serious offense."[26] To produce the "higher" black hit rate, "black drivers were queried at rates that are two-to-three times higher than their numbers in the driving population." If profiling were indeed an efficient crime-fighting tool, Meehan and Ponder say, black hit rates should not have been just a little higher than white hit rates but at least four to five times higher. The small difference in hit rates their data show hardly justifies the disproportionate attention paid to nonwhite drivers.

Hit Rates on Airline Passengers Reentering the United States

Hit rates from another context reveal similar patterns. The U.S. Customs Service, one of the agencies with the task of stopping drugs at the U.S. border, has faced multiple accusations of misusing strip searches and other highly intrusive tactics against disproportionate numbers of black women reentering the U.S. at airports (see chapter 8). The Customs Service's own numbers can be used to show the hit rates for these searches. During 1998, 43 percent of the passengers on whom Customs performed searches were either black or Latino[27]—a percentage that is likely far out of line with the presence of people of color in the traveling population as a whole.[28] In 1998, Customs agents found drugs on the white passengers they searched at a rate of 6.7 percent. For blacks, the hit rate was lower—6.2 percent—than it was for whites. For Latinos, it was even lower—just 2.8 percent.[29] As in the results of the attorney general's study in New York, this is diametrically opposed to what one would expect if the "rational" law enforcement argument were true.

Overall, the evidence on hit rates could hardly be more striking. And none of it supports racial profiling as an effective tool for catching criminals. The data—from Maryland,[30] New Jersey, North Carolina, and New York, from the MDTs in an American suburb, and from the U.S. Customs Service—all come from different contexts and involve different law enforcement agencies. Three sets of data involved highway drug interdiction, one involved pedestrians, and one involved international air travelers. One of the data sets was collected as a result of litigation; others were not. The startling thing is the consistency across all of these different data sets. All reveal the same thing: racial profiling doesn't help police catch criminals.

RACIAL PROFILING'S ILLUSORY "SUCCESSES"

Anyone who watches television news has seen it. The report begins with a scene of police cars, emergency lights spinning in garish red and blue, surrounding a nondescript vehicle pulled over at the side of a highway or road. The film then cuts to a news conference scene: a bouquet of microphones at a podium or conference table in front of a law enforcement official—perhaps a police chief or sheriff—as a reporter's voice gives us the familiar details. "County police made a major drug bust on Interstate 79 near Johnstown today. According to a spokesman for the department, officers stopped a 1998 Chevrolet for a routine traffic violation, and a search of the vehicle disclosed more than two pounds of cocaine hidden in a secret compartment built into the trunk. They also recovered more than twenty thousand dollars in cash." The video images now focus on a table displaying several large sealed plastic bags containing white powder, each one tagged with a brightly-colored "EVIDENCE" sticker. There are also stacks of bills. Standing in back of the table are three officers in uniform, hands clasped in front of them. The image cuts to another person in uniform in close-up; letters at the bottom of the screen identify him as the police department's spokesman. "This is one of the two biggest busts in the state so far this year," he says. "We're proud of our officers, and proud of our department's successful efforts to keep deadly drugs out of the hands of our children and off our streets. It's a real win." The image then returns to the table full of drugs and cash, as the reporter reads a final voiceover. "The department says that today's bust is only one of many successful efforts by its highway drug-interdiction team, which works twenty-four hours a day, seven days a week, to fight the narcotics trade. The chief says that results like these show why drugs will remain one of the department's top priorities." With that, the reporter signs off.

Is the hit-rate evidence misleading? Even though searches of minorities uncover evidence of crime at rates that are the same as or lower than the rates for whites, when police do make a hit, does the size of the bust justify the means used to achieve it? As the Manhattan Institute's Heather Mac Donald argues, does "the fact that hit rates for contraband tend to be equal across racial groups,[31] even though blacks and Hispanics are searched at higher rates, suggest . . . that the police are successfully targeting dealers, not minorities"?

If seizures of any contraband are rare, seizures of large amounts of drugs are much rarer still. In 1999, the Bureau of Justice Statistics of the U.S. Department of Justice surveyed approximately ninety thousand Americans on their experiences with police.[32] In questions on stops and searches, the survey showed that police officers recovered nothing—no evidence of crime whatsoever—almost 90 percent of the time that they conducted searches.[33] Likewise, the report from then–New Jersey Attorney General Peter Verniero's Task Force indicated that fewer than one in five searches—19 percent—produced any evidence of crime at all.[34] In Illya Lichtenberg's study of nine thousand consent searches of drivers in Ohio and Maryland, the data showed that only one of every eight consent searches produced any evidence.[35] And statistics show that the great bulk of all drug seizures studied are for small amounts of drugs that people might use themselves: most seizures involve not cocaine, heroin, or other so-called hard drugs, but marijuana in small quantities. "It appears that consent searches result in the discovery of small-time marijuana users in most cases," Lichtenberg says. The data Lichtenberg analyzed from Maryland show that when the few unusually large seizures police made are removed from the analysis—a common statistical technique used to prevent the skewing of data by a few outlying pieces of data—the average amount of marijuana seized was just 4.2 grams, enough for several marijuana cigarettes.[36] Seizures of cocaine and crack were about half as common as seizures of marijuana, and seizures of heroin were *un*common. Similarly, in the New Jersey Attorney General's Task Force report, most discoveries of evidence were for "less serious offenses," with seizures of significant drug shipments "rare."[37]

Although stacks of white powder in bags and a pile of cash may make good television news footage, the numbers we have tell a different story. Further research that would give us more information concerning whether profiling helps us target high-level dealers would be welcome, and if it showed that profiling did indeed focus police on the worst drug offenders, we might rethink it. But based on the existing evidence, it is clear that racial profiling is neither a good system for identifying criminals nor a good way to target dealers or other perpetrators of major crimes. Racial profiling simply isn't good policing at all.

COUNTING BENEFITS, BUT NOT COSTS

Profiling's advocates tell us that it accomplishes what any law-abiding person would want: getting criminals off the streets. The police make arrests, confiscate drugs and weapons, and lock up criminals. But this is only half the equation. In what other field of endeavor do we measure success by asking what has gone right without asking about, or keeping track of, costs and failures? Police agencies have become accustomed to operating as if only successes—seizures of guns, drugs, or cash—count, and nothing else matters. Police themselves are not really to blame; after all, the public has rarely asked questions concerning the costs of policing. Except in cases involving misconduct or disaster, public officials give police departments little scrutiny outside the yearly budgeting process. We know that police sometimes find contraband when they stop drivers and search their cars, but most times, nothing is found. We've been told that these stops and searches are an extremely important and effective law enforcement tool. What we don't know, in even the most elementary way, is just how effective it is. How many drivers have to be pulled over, interrogated, and searched in order to catch each criminal apprehended this way?

The surprising answer is that in most places, and for most police forces, no one knows. In fact, until quite recently, when some police departments began to collect this information, police departments themselves did not know how effective their search-and-seizure activities were. With the exception of these relatively few police departments, including the ones that have generated the data that allow us to study hit rates, most law enforcement agencies do not track or count the stops and searches that do not result in finding evidence. This means that we have almost no information about the impact that these police tactics have on innocent citizens. Police departments simply do not collect this data in any kind of a systematic way. Most do not require officers to make any kind of record of encounters with citizens, even those involving stops and searches that do not result in an arrest. New York's requirement that police officers record information on each stop and frisk is the exception, and even so there is some skepticism about whether officers actually do this as regularly as they are supposed to.[38] The bottom line is that if a public official or a member of the public asked most police departments a simple question—how many cars, pedestrians, or the like did you stop and search for each time you recovered drugs or weapons?—the police chief could not provide an answer even if he or she wanted to.

A simple story illustrates the problem. In the case of *Ohio* v. *Robinette*,[39] the U.S. Supreme Court declared that police officers need not tell drivers that they are free to go before they ask the driver for consent to a search. The case originated in Ohio, so the Ohio Attorney General's Office represented the state in the Supreme Court. When the state won the case, Betty Montgomery, the attorney general of Ohio, issued a press release. She applauded the Supreme Court's decision; not having to advise the driver that he or she is free to go meant that officers could continue to do business just as effectively as they always had, unimpeded by new rules. State police had used these tactics with great success to keep drugs off the street, the attorney general said, and the Court's decision meant that they could continue to do so.[40]

A telephone call to the attorney general's office provided an opportunity to ask one of her senior aides about the attorney general's claim of successful and effective policing. Within an hour, a fax arrived: a copy of an internal memorandum from the state police to the attorney general's office listing the number of traffic stops over the past two and one-half years that produced arrests for drugs—a few arrests for sizable quantities, but others for lesser amounts—as well as some seizures of cash alleged to be drug money.[41] Missing from the memorandum was any information concerning the total number of traffic stops during that time period. A second phone call to the attorney general's aide, asking for information to answer this question, produced assurances that it would be sent quickly. When a week passed without any answer, a third call to the aide produced a sheepish and somewhat surprised reply. "You know, we looked everywhere," he said. "As far as I can tell, we don't have any information like that. No one in the state police keeps this information. In fact, I can't find any police agency in Ohio that does."[42]

This is the reply most people would get if they asked any police agency for the same information. Police agencies don't keep track of this information and don't record it. But without this information, police departments simply cannot defend profiling as a successful, effective way of policing.

When we think of street-level drug enforcement, we think of stops and frisks; of police jumping out of squad cars to round up everyone around drug "hot spots"; and stopping, questioning, and searching drivers. We know that the cost of these efforts, whatever they net in terms of criminals apprehended, include the time and labor of the police officers involved, a cost already paid for by the taxpayers. But what about other costs, such as the cost to people walking to work who are "rounded up" because they were in the wrong place at the wrong time? Or the cost to people who do not sell or use drugs but who are approached by undercover police officers in buy-and-bust operations? Such costs and consequences mean little to the police because they do not bear them. They are "borne not by police officers but by innocent citizens of the targeted neighborhoods," according to Professor William Stuntz of the Harvard Law School. Stuntz says police "externalize" the cost of street-level drug enforcement because the tactics they use allow them to take action without bearing any of the cost themselves. People in the neighborhood may experience aggravation, fear, inconvenience, or even physical custody, but officers do not. "Like the rest of us," Stuntz says, "the police tend not to take account of costs they do not bear."[43]

Externalized costs can also help us understand part of the reason that police might prefer street-level law enforcement to the more involved effort that it would take to break up a higher-level drug operation inside a suburban home. Street "sweeps," stops and frisks, and traffic stops are all relatively easy, quick, and inexpensive. They yield results fast and don't require extensive intelligence gathering or other investigation. In contrast, efforts to shut down more upscale drug distribution require police officers to work hard to penetrate these operations, either by going undercover or using informants. This is dangerous and expensive work, consuming considerable police time and energy. Since this activity usually takes place inside homes or other structures, the police bear the additional burden of generating enough evidence through investigation to meet the probable cause standard, and jumping through the hoops necessary to obtain a warrant. The cost structure is reversed from the street-arrest model: the innocent public likely bears little or no cost, and the police must absorb a lot. Little wonder, then, that police officers and agencies prefer enforcement in areas in which drug sales are out in the open.

Chapter Five

THE COSTS OF RACIAL PROFILING: CASUALTIES AND COLLATERAL DAMAGE

In every sense of the word, Larry Sykes is a big man.[1] He's tall—well over six feet—and would seem imposing if not for his friendly, soft-spoken manner. Sykes has headed the board of education in Toledo, Ohio, a city of more than three hundred thousand. With the hiring of superintendents, the negotiation of contracts with teachers unions, and the high priority that politicians at all levels have given to education, Sykes frequently shows up on local news broadcasts. He has also played prominent roles in other public institutions, such as the local housing authority. Add this to Sykes's "day job" as vice president of one of the area's largest banks, and he's certainly one of the most recognizable African Americans in the region in which he lives.

A short time ago, Sykes was named to a delegation of Toledo's civic and business leaders who would visit Cleveland for an economic development conference at the invitation of Cleveland's mayor, Michael White. Toledo chartered two large buses to take its group to the meeting. Because Sykes prefers to travel by car, he drove himself. He attended the meetings in Cleveland all day, and when the event began to wind down in the late afternoon he decided to leave a few minutes early and begin his drive back ahead of the buses. All went uneventfully, until he approached Toledo. On the last stretch of interstate highway on his route, an Ohio Highway Patrol officer pulled Sykes over. This surprised him; he'd seen the trooper far up the road as he approached, and as a result he'd been carefully watching his speed. (At the same time, another vehicle traveling near him—with a white driver, Sykes recalls—seemed not to have seen the police car and sped ahead.) The officer said that he'd pulled Sykes over because his car had no front license plate. Sykes—dressed in the crisp suit characteristic of a banker, a sprinkling of gray in his hair—gave the trooper his license, registration, and insurance papers, all of which were in order. But instead of telling him he'd be right back, the trooper did something unexpected: he told Sykes to get out of his car. Sykes asked why but wasn't given a reason. "He said, 'just get out of the car,' " Sykes recalls. Sykes did as he was told and followed the officer's instructions to walk back toward the patrol car. The officer then did something that shocked Larry Sykes: he began frisking him, patting down his clothes. Sykes asked the officer what he was doing. "He said, 'You can't be too careful. You might have a gun.' I said to him, 'Excuse me, but why would I have a gun?' " Sykes didn't know whether he was more surprised or offended, but the officer brushed his objections aside. "He said to me, 'Look, I'm just trying to get home tonight,' " Sykes said, implying Sykes might pull a gun and kill him. "I told him that that's exactly what I was trying to do: get home." The officer then asked Sykes whether he was carrying any drugs or weapons. Flabbergasted, Sykes asked the officer what made him think he had drugs or guns. Again, instead of an answer, the officer ordered him to get in the patrol car. When Sykes protested that the cramped backseat would not fit his large frame, the trooper ordered him instead to stand next to the patrol car, legs spread, arms out and palms down on the top of the car, and not to move.

Sykes couldn't believe what was happening. He was only minutes from home, standing at the side of the highway with his hands stretched out on the top of a state police car with its lights flashing—all because his car didn't have a front license tag. He felt upset, angry, enraged—but when he looked down the road to the east, the direction from which he had come, he realized the situation was about to get worse. Returning from Cleveland in the lane next to where he stood with his hands on the car, were the two chartered buses full of Sykes's colleagues in business, banking, and municipal government with whom he had attended the economic development meeting in Cleveland. Sykes felt so embarrassed he put his head down between his outstretched arms in the hope that his friends and associates would not recognize him. But they all knew his car and the clothing he'd worn that day at the meeting they'd all attended. "We knew it was [Sykes]. Everyone said, 'Uh-oh, look at that, it's Larry—he must have done something," said an official who was on the bus.[2] Sykes never received a ticket, citation, or warning of any kind, and the officer eventually allowed him to leave—without so much as a sorry-for-the-inconvenience. Sykes tried to file a complaint, but "got such a runaround" that he finally just gave up.

When we talk about fighting crime in the United States, we often find ourselves using military metaphors, as in the "war on drugs." Racial profiling has played a key role in this war, from the DEA's effort to spread profiling across the highways of America, to the "rational" law enforcement arguments of Marshall Frank and John Marcello. In a war, we are prepared to accept a certain number of casualties as the price of victory. And as in any war, we must judge the war on drugs and the racial-profiling tactics used in it not only in terms of their supposed successes but also in terms of their costs—the relative effort expended to achieve these successes, along with the resultant casualties and "collateral damage" (injury, destruction, or death that may be unintended but that come as an inevitable consequence of combat). When we look at the use of racial profiling in the war on drugs and crime in this country, we see casualties and collateral damage that should concern every American of every race, ethnic group, and political or ideological stripe. Personal costs to those who have to bear the burden of these encounters are great. But societal costs may be even greater. And unlike the intense personal degradation and embarrassment suffered primarily by members of racial minorities like Larry Sykes, these societal costs affect every American.

THE PERSONAL COSTS

The use of racial profiling and high-discretion police tactics against people like Larry Sykes illustrates the real cost of these tactics: their profound impact on innocent people. For every person in possession of a small amount of marijuana or a large amount of cocaine that police apprehend through profiling, a much larger number of law-abiding, taxpaying African Americans, Latinos, and other minorities of every class, profession, age, and gender get stopped, searched, and treated as if they were criminals.

It would be difficult to underestimate the emotional distress caused by the types of experiences Larry Sykes has been through. Though his encounter with the state police officer is only one of many times something like this has happened, it left a deep mark on him. Months after the incident, the wound remained fresh, even for a man with a full personal and professional life who had earned the admiration of his community many times over. Sykes says, without any hesitation, "I never felt so degraded, humiliated, and belittled in all my life."

Sykes's repeated experiences with these stops led him to believe that the whole ordeal took place because he is black. His suspicion was reinforced by the fact that the officer chose to stop him for a relatively trivial infraction instead of stopping a white driver who was openly violating the traffic laws by speeding. The encounter began against this background and then continued in ways that, Sykes believes, would not have occurred if he were white. In his mind, it seems extremely unlikely that a white banker in a suit, tie, and topcoat in a well-kept late model upscale vehicle would have been ordered from the car, frisked, and asked if he had weapons or drugs.

Many people believe that only complainers—people inclined to see slights everywhere, especially racial slights—actually harbor any grievances over such police encounters. But nothing could be further from the truth. In fact, nothing—not high personal achievement, not education, not wealth, and not personal appearance—protects a black or Latino citizen from going through what Larry Sykes did.

A handsome, well-spoken man in his early forties, Michael heads a large government agency.[3] He supervises hundreds of employees and has responsibility for some of the most critical services provided in his region. One afternoon, Michael drove to a high school in a white neighborhood to work out. As he approached the parking lot, he saw a police cruiser, so he drove with extra caution. As he pulled up and parked his car, the police car came "screeching up behind me—the lights flashing, the whole deal," blocking him in so he could not drive away. When the officer walked up to the driver's window and noticed Michael's official identification, he immediately got back in his car and drove off, without offering any explanation. Despite having just treated Michael like a dangerous criminal, the officer "just backed away and he was gone. Just disappeared." This was not the first time something like this had happened to Michael. Police had pulled him over many times before for what he jokingly calls "courtesy stops," and in fact the incident outside the high school was less of an inconvenience than most of those. It lasted just a few seconds. The officer didn't even ask him any questions, and he had not been subject to public embarrassment outside of his car, as Larry Sykes had. Yet Michael felt angry and frustrated. And the way he explained the experience showed that he could not help but see it in context. He talked not just about the stop at the high school but about all the times it had happened to him. "Each one of those stops, for me, had nothing to do with breaking the law. It had to do with who I was," he said. He drew an analogy that emphasizes what this feels like. "It's almost like somebody pulls your pants down around your ankles. You're standing there nude, but you've got to act like there's nothing happening." Most people would not compare a traffic stop by a police officer to a kind of sexual assault, yet for Michael, the analogy fairly leaps out.

Anyone who has been stopped by the police, even for a minor traffic infraction, knows that the officer immediately moves to assume control of the situation. This involves every indicator of authority the officer has, from uniform and badge to the lights on top of the squad car, to a commanding manner and tone of voice. The idea is simple: the officer has the power and is in charge; the citizen is under the officer's control until the officer says otherwise. When this common dynamic becomes entangled with the suspicion of racial and ethnic discrimination, the result is a feeling of having one's fate completely in the hands of a potentially hostile and all-powerful stranger. Christopher Darden, the African American prosecutor in the O. J. Simpson trial, explains his reaction to the many times he has been stopped by the police this way. "It is so demeaning. It undermines and calls into question everything you've accomplished in your life, everything you've worked for. No matter how hard you've worked, no matter what you do, no matter how diligently [you've] pursued the American dream, you're treated like a common criminal." [4]

Research shows that the experiences of Larry Sykes, Michael, and Christopher Darden are not isolated incidents. In a study of attitudes among residents of different neighborhoods in Washington, D.C., Professor Ronald Weitzer[5] found "substantial agreement across the communities that police treat whites and blacks differently." Weitzer systematically collected and conducted in-depth interviews produced personal stories exhibiting the same themes of anger, resentment, humiliation, and powerlessness in the face of police authority discussed by Larry Sykes, Michael, and Christopher Darden. "If you're black, there's a presumption of guilt, a presumption of wrongdoing if you're stopped. I think white folks are probably treated with a great deal more respect, a lot more tolerance and patience," said one of

Weitzer's African American interviewees. According to another, "If they stop a white guy at three in the morning, they'll figure he was working late and he's on his way home to see his wife. You stop a black person at three in the morning and figure he was up to no good, or just got through robbing a store, shooting somebody, or whatever. Always assuming the worst when it's someone of color." A black woman told Weitzer, "When the citizen is black, the police tend to treat them in more of a brusque manner, tell them to move along, tell them that they are in danger of violating the law when really in fact they're not." Another said, "You're treated like dirt if you're black. They have their ways of being nasty. 'Well I don't care if you call. I'll lock you up!' You can't say anything to them. They don't care. They don't listen."

The constant exposure to the threat of police intervention, the thought that one runs a risk of an unpleasant, humiliating, even physically dangerous encounter any time one sees a police officer or car, and the repeated, daily requirement of thinking about how society's bearers of authority might choose to render one both helpless and powerless right out in public are all severe psychological stressors. Having to live this way puts one on guard—on "red alert" every time one sees the blue of a police car or uniform. And anyone who lives under this kind of constant stress will likely feel the effects on both their physical and psychological health.

Dr. Janis Sanchez-Hucles, Professor of Psychology at Old Dominion University in Virginia, has studied the effect of living with racism on minority citizens. She argues that the consequences of chronic exposure to racism have been vastly underestimated and even unrecognized. Exposure to racism, Dr. Sanchez-Hucles says, "should be viewed as a form of emotional abusiveness and psychological trauma for ethnic minorities."[6] In fact, she says, chronic problems resulting from the severe stress of racism should be viewed as a type of post-traumatic stress disorder (PTSD)—a mental disorder recognized and treated by psychiatrists and psychologists in patients ranging from Vietnam war veterans to victims of natural catastrophes, such as floods or earthquakes. In the same way that psychiatry has begun to widen the definition and conception of PTSD to recognize the reaction to smaller-scale events like the abuse of spouses or children, Sanchez-Hucles argues that psychiatry needs to recognize the devastating impact of racism on the lives and health of African Americans, Latinos, and other minority citizens. For years, she says, blacks have been taught by their parents that in order to get along in the majority culture, they must swallow everyday slights and insults—ignore and internalize them.[7] "Micro aggressions" like racial profiling, concludes Sanchez-Hucles, give people of color "one more reason to be fearful and concerned about their safety and well being." Likewise, Vivian Martin, a newspaper columnist, says that the hypervigilance of blacks who face racism every day is necessary, "even as it creates the kind of chronic stress that leads to all sorts of chronic illnesses that afflict blacks more than whites." Racial profiling, she says, "is about a lot more than traffic stops. It's about a way of life."[8]

Linking this idea directly to racial profiling, Dr. Hugh F. Butts, a New York psychiatrist and psychoanalyst, calls racial profiling "one symptom of an intricate, widespread disease complex called racism" that many regard as "one of the most significant public health problems in America."[9] According to Butts, the failure of psychiatry to come to grips with the psychological and emotional problems of minority individuals created by racism stems from the fact that white psychiatrists assume that their knowledge of the psychodynamics and psychopathology of white patients fully equips them to deal with these issues in black patients. It is as if, Butts says, knowledge of black life and the black experience in America has no value in understanding black patients.[10]

Racial profiling has behavioral as well as emotional costs. It may cause many people of color to plan their driving and travel routes in certain ways, to take (or not take) particular jobs, even to wear clothing and behave in ways that minimize their potential to attract police attention. They may simply stay out of places and neighborhoods where they will "stand out"—typically white neighborhoods, suburbs, or towns—where police may feel they don't "belong." Or they may turn away and go in the opposite direction when they see a police officer.

When Wade Henderson, a well-known and highly respected civil rights lawyer in Washington, D.C., drives to Richmond, Virginia, to teach a class, he does not rent a flashy or fancy car. Instead, he sticks to bland, middle-of-the-road models.[11] *Chicago Tribune* columnist and academic Salim Muwakil prefers undistinguished rental vehicles for his trips through downstate Illinois.[12] "I drive a minivan because it doesn't grab attention," says Emmanuel Key, a sales executive for a large midwestern company. "If I was driving a BMW"—a car he could certainly afford—"different story."[13] Some even feel compelled to change the details of their personal behavior or appearance. They wear their suits, ties, and clerical collars as a kind of sartorial armor, or remove things they would normally wear. On any kind of extended drive outside the city he lives in, Muwakil remembers to remove his black beret—an item he likes and that he regards as something of a personal signature or statement, but that he thinks might attract more police attention than he wants.

The National Picture: The Police Public Contact Survey

The U.S. Department of Justice's Bureau of Justice Statistics (BJS) survey of contacts between police and approximately ninety thousand members of the public in the last six months of 1999 sought broader information on the impact of traffic stops and searches on African Americans, Hispanics, and other minorities.[14] The results served as a sharp reminder that, even with public discussion of racial profiling at full crescendo, as it was in 1999, being stopped and searched by the police remained a much more common experience for blacks and other people of color than for whites.

Fully 52 percent of all contacts between police and the public came during traffic stops. The next largest category—contacting police to report a crime—constituted only about 20 percent of all contacts. This difference underlines just how important traffic

stops are in forming public perceptions of police and their actions. Blacks were more likely than whites to be stopped at least
once—12.3 percent for blacks versus 10.4 percent for whites—
and blacks were almost 50 percent more likely than whites to
have experienced more than one stop. This proved true even
though whites have a higher rate of contact with the police generally (i.e., not just traffic stops) than blacks or Hispanics, and
even though a far higher percentage of whites (92 percent) than
blacks (74 percent) or Hispanics (86 percent) are licensed drivers. In sum, "survey results indicated that in 1999 blacks had
higher chances than whites of being stopped at least once and
higher chances than whites of being stopped more than once."[15]

Police searched a stopped driver or vehicle 6.6 percent of the
time, or approximately 1.3 million searches over the entire population. During the stop, police were more than twice as likely to
search an African American or Hispanic driver than a white
driver, and more than twice as likely to search the cars of African
American or Hispanic drivers.[16] Police were also more likely to
ticket blacks and Hispanics (60.4 and 65.6 percent, respectively)
than whites (51.8 percent). As reported in chapter 4, the searches
police did were fruitless in the overwhelming majority of cases.
Police officers recovered nothing—no evidence of crime whatsoever—almost 90 percent of the time that they conducted searches.
And hit rates for these searches differed by race. Officers found
contraband and evidence more often when they searched whites
and their cars (17 percent) than when they searched blacks (8 percent).[17] Given that police used stops and searches against African
Americans and Hispanics much more frequently than against
whites, it is not surprising that the survey indicated that significantly higher percentages of minority citizens expressed grave
doubts about the legitimacy of these searches. Though most of all
people surveyed doubted the legality of the searches, a noticeable
racial and ethnic gap remained.

One question often asked is whether racial profiling has anything to do with the race of the officer—that is, whether black officers use profiling and, if so, how their use of the tool might be

different than what white officers do. The survey gives us, for the first time, material with which to answer this set of questions. According to the data, racial disparities in stops, searches, and the like seem to have little or nothing to do with the officer's race. According to the report, "blacks generally had a worse outcome," that is, they experienced more stops, searches, and ticketing, "whether they were stopped by a white officer or a black officer." [18]

This is a very significant finding. Often, arguments over racial profiling become as charged as they do because the practice is assumed to be a manifestation of white racism against people of color. Some say that this means that rooting out profiling should center on finding the few racist "bad apples" in the department; others say that the "profiling-as-racism" theory means that a person making accusations of profiling is (at least implicitly) calling all white officers racists. Still others say that profiling as racism means African American police officers, or police departments headed by African Americans, couldn't have a profiling problem, since they would almost certainly not hold prejudices against blacks or other minorities.

The data showing that blacks experience higher rates of stops and searches at the hands of white *and* black officers alike mean that all of these conceptions and conclusions concerning profiling are far too simplistic. If both black and white officers seem to use traffic stops and searches disproportionately against blacks and other minorities, this implies that profiling is about more than the racism of a few racist whites with badges. Rather it is an institutional problem, and an institutional practice, that lies at the base of this thorny knot of difficulties. While we cannot tolerate racism among law enforcement officers, we must understand that the problem is not as simple as spotting those individuals and getting rid of them. Rather, profiling is about pervasive police and investigative strategies based on biases found throughout our society, to the great detriment of those who find themselves on the wrong end of police suspicion when they have done nothing wrong. And all of these experiences will have an unavoidable cost: a strong negative impact on the attitudes of these people toward police, toward courts, and toward the rule of law itself. These attitudes will damage the institutions that are important to all Americans, so we all pay part of this cost.

The Reinforcement of Residential Segregation

Racial profiling carries with it costs that go beyond psychological hardship and damage. Because profiling has such a strong impact on the mobility of those subjected to it—the diminished willingness of minorities to go where they feel they will get undesirable law enforcement attention—these tactics help to reinforce existing segregation in housing and employment. Thus the costs of profiling are quite real—having an impact on residential patterns and earning potential of minorities all over the country.

Several years ago, sales executive Emmanuel Key, his wife, and children lived in a suburban area outside Chicago.[19] Key's corporate job had brought them there. A corporate relocation firm had found the house, which happened to be one of the most expensive in the neighborhood. Key recalls vividly what happened to him when he went jogging after work. Although he wore neat sweat suits and new athletic shoes, the sight of a black man running in a white neighborhood often attracted the attention of police officers. During one run, a police officer drove by him. Key thought nothing of it at first, but when the same police officer came by a second time, he ordered Key to halt and asked Key what he was doing there. Key told the officer that he lived in the neighborhood. The officer reacted skeptically, but drove off, and Key resumed his run. But before he finished, the officer drove back around again and gave him another scowling once-over. Key got the unspoken message without having to hear it from the officer's mouth—it was "as though I'm not supposed to be in this neighborhood." Eventually, after a number of encounters like this, Key decided he'd had it. He was tired of getting stopped. He gave up jogging in his neighborhood, and eventually he and his family moved.

America remains a largely segregated nation. While the law no longer enforces this separation the way it used to, with legal rules like restrictive covenants on deeds, which prohibited selling property to people belonging to particular racial or ethnic groups,[20] the reality of residential segregation has not changed. Professor George Galster, who has studied the issue, says that racial segregation remains one of the signal characteristics of American cities; "virtually all of our major metropolitan centers where large numbers of minorities live are highly segregated."[21] Galster uses a "dissimilarity index" to demonstrate how evenly various racial and ethnic groups have spread across neighborhoods in cities. His data show high degrees of segregation in areas where African Americans and Latinos live. In these neighborhoods, members of those groups are virtually the only residents.[22] In his analysis of the interaction of race, class, and drugs, Professor William Stuntz sees many of the same patterns. In almost every American city with a multiracial, multiethnic population, he argues, poorer residential neighborhoods are both heavily segregated and mostly black.[23] None of this will surprise anyone who drives through an American city of any size on a regular basis, and the 2000 Census figures confirm it.[24]

Like Emmanuel Key, African American sales executive James Banks has felt the power of this segregated reality in America. And as in Key's experience, it came from an encounter with the police.[25] Banks has lost track of the number of times police have stopped him in white neighborhoods, even though he dresses neatly, drives a well-kept vehicle, and drives with extra caution in these areas. He recalls a recent visit to a friend whose family had just moved to a relatively new, virtually all-white subdivision. Banks had no sooner left his friend's house and backed out of the driveway when the police pulled him over. Banks felt puzzled; he hadn't reached the main street and had not even had enough time to get up to the posted speed. The officer walked up to the driver's window, but instead of telling Banks why he'd stopped him, the officer questioned him, asking where he was coming from and where he was going. Banks was upset—he felt he already knew what this was really about—but he answered the questions. The officer responded by telling Banks he'd been "weaving in the road," and took Banks's license and registration to the squad car to check it. When he returned, he threatened to give Banks a citation for failure to wear a seat belt, but ultimately let him go without one. Banks was glad to have escaped without a fine, but he felt violated—as if someone had put him through something just to teach him a lesson.

Others have experienced this same type of policing in neighborhoods in which they work. Suron Jacobs, a construction worker in his twenties who is African American, had a construction job as part of a crew on a project in a nearly all-white suburban area outside of Toledo, Ohio.[26] One day, Jacobs made arrangements to meet his brother on a corner near the construction site during his lunch break to exchange an apartment key. Unbeknownst to Jacobs, a resident who saw him waiting on the corner for his brother called 911 and reported him as a suspicious person. Responding to the call, a police officer drove by, stopped, and began to question Jacobs. What was he doing? Where was his brother, and how long had he been waiting? Why was he in this neighborhood? After a number of these questions, Jacobs became irritated. He refused to answer any more questions and began walking back to the construction site. Jacobs immediately learned the price of defying the police in a place where he "didn't belong"; the officer grabbed him, while another who had arrived on the scene handcuffed him. They arrested Jacobs and charged him with a variety of offenses, including resisting arrest, even though he'd done nothing wrong and under the law he had every right to refuse to answer questions and walk away. Though the charges were eventually dropped, the police response to the resident's 911 call told Jacobs everything he needed to know about his presence in this white area.

The experiences of Emmanuel Key, James Banks, and Suron Jacobs are unfortunately all too typical. We might call them "border stops"—stopping and questioning people as a method of policing the borders of communities against those who "don't belong." And all of these men understood the underlying, unspoken message of these encounters: stay out.

Segregation in housing patterns, reinforced by racial profiling, also has a direct impact on employment and the ability to get jobs. Over the past ten to twenty years, suburban areas have become the main location of job growth in America. As employment has increased in the service sector, in financial services, and in high-tech businesses, most of the businesses spawning these jobs have located away from city centers.[27] Because these jobs are in outlying areas, this creates problems for inner-city minority residents. Public transportation to these areas is often spotty, and commuting by car means running the risk of "border stops."

This can cause unexpectedly odd results. In Carmel, Indiana, an all-white upscale suburb outside Indianapolis, a communications company located there employed a high percentage of African Americans who did not live in the area.[28] Carmel's police had sometimes used traffic stops aggressively, and an African American state trooper sued the city and the police department in 1996, claiming that a Carmel officer had stopped him based on race. (The case was settled out of court for one hundred thousand dollars, under an agreement calling for the installation of video cameras in all squad cars and the collection of data on all traffic stops for several years.)[29] In order to help the communications company's black employees avoid these experiences, the police department created special tags for their cars that would be visible to any passing police officer. The tag would instantly identify the black driver as acceptable—as a black person who had a reason to be in Carmel and should not be stopped or otherwise bothered just because he or she was "out of place." According to the *Indianapolis Star,* an article in a company newsletter, accompanied by a photo of the police chief, the mayor, and the company president shaking hands and displaying one of the tags, said, "The tag's purpose is . . . to provide safe, easy passage to employees and to provide Carmel law enforcement authorities with instant identification of vehicles that may not bear [county] license plates." A stronger parallel to apartheid South Africa's pass system is hard to imagine.

The Overinclusiveness of Profiling   Profiling is, by nature, overinclusive. When being black (or Latino or Asian) is used as a proxy for criminality or dangerousness in a society in which a relative few are criminals, profiles based on or including race will always sweep too widely. A racial or ethnic profile is simply too blunt an instrument for its alleged statistical accuracy to give an officer any but the most general information about a class of likely suspects—a group that is so wide that the profile is of little practical use. The upshot is that even if police investigation using the profile yields some wrongdoers, it is almost certain to capture far more innocent people in its exceedingly wide net—all of whom will be stigmatized, angered, and perhaps traumatized by what happens.

A fascinating counterexample will illustrate the dangers that lurk in the use of any widely shared characteristics in a profile. In the wake of a string of school shootings in the late 1990s—at Columbine High School in Colorado and at other schools, in Paducah, Kentucky; Jonesboro, Arkansas; and other places across the country—parents, politicians, and school officials voiced their frustrations. Could nothing be done to avoid these senseless killings? How might we, as responsible adults, do something—anything—to stop this violence and the tragic loss of life? Eventually, the federal government tried to address the problem. In a report entitled "The School Shooter: A Threat Assessment Perspective," [30] the FBI provided an analysis of these crimes and presented "a systematic procedure for threat assessment and intervention," so that school officials would at least have a framework within which to exercise vigilance. The report points readers to a number of clues—everything from demonstrating a lack of empathy and a lack of respect for others[31] to the making of different kinds of threats[32]—to help understand the difference between a disgruntled teenager and one who presents a genuine danger. But what is so striking about the report is what it emphatically says it does *not* do.

This model is not a "profile" of the school shooter or a checklist of danger signs pointing to the next adolescent who will bring lethal violence to a school. Those things do not exist. . . . [I]n practice, trying to draw up a catalogue or "checklist" of warning signs . . . can be shortsighted, even dangerous. Such lists, publicized by the media, can end up unfairly labeling many nonviolent students as potentially dangerous or even lethal. In fact, a great many adolescents who will never commit violent acts will show some of the behaviors or personality traits included on the list.[33]

An inability to predict accurately who will commit crime in the future from the actions of others in the past—this is exactly the same problem of overinclusiveness and weak inferences from weak data that profiles always exhibit. The FBI is right to avoid a profile of school shooters, for exactly the reasons its report stated. Moreover, because school shootings are actually quite rare, far fewer than violent crimes in general, it seems prudent to be even more cautious about using any kind of a profile in these cases than in others. But the larger point still holds: profiles based on widely distributed characteristics are simply too sweeping and overinclusive to work, and they may also cause significant damage.

THE PRICE PAID BY THE NEXT GENERATION: "THE TALK"

In March 1998, the U.S. House of Representatives passed an amended version of Rep. John Conyers's anti-profiling bill, without a single dissenting vote. The legislation, introduced in 1997, was the first legislative proposal anywhere to attempt to address racial profiling. It would have required that police departments collect ten pieces of data on each traffic stop and that the attorney general conduct a study with the data. After the passage of the bill in the House, the media began to take interest, and state legislators around the country began to introduce their own proposals on profiling. In the fall of 1998, the U.S. Department of

Justice responded by calling a national summit on the problem of race and traffic stops.

The meeting, the first such gathering on the issue, took place in December 1998.[34] Long tables, arranged in a large rectangle, filled the room. A daunting array of the top-level law enforcement officials from around the nation filled most of the seats: members of the staff of Attorney General Janet Reno, chiefs and superintendents of state police forces and city police departments, United States attorneys from around the country, national officials of police unions and fraternal organizations, and officials of federal law enforcement agencies. There were also a few academics and representatives of several advocacy groups such as the National Urban League and the American Civil Liberties Union. An assortment of Justice Department and law enforcement personnel packed the periphery of the room. After short speeches from Justice Department officials, the moderator began the meeting by asking each of the people around the table to make a brief statement explaining his or her view of the problem. As the discussion started, a tone of defensiveness quickly emerged from the law enforcement people around the table. Their statements varied, but they had several common themes: There is no such thing as racial profiling. It doesn't exist. Collection of data on traffic stops that tracked race would be unnecessary, dangerous, an insult to every person who wore a badge. Merely raising the issue was a slap in the face to the brave officers who risked their lives on the street, day after day, in order to keep the peace.

Saul Green, the United States attorney from eastern Michigan and one of those invited to speak, listened to all of this.[35] Given where he happened to be sitting, he'd be one of the last to speak, and he felt uncomfortable with what he was hearing. He was the top federal law enforcement official in his jurisdiction, and he had tremendous respect for the agents and officers he worked with every day. He felt a strong bond to them, because he viewed himself as part of law enforcement. Yet he was also an African American man, and he knew firsthand that racial profiling and the use of skin color as a source of suspicion was reality, not a myth or a self-serving story. He'd been through it himself as a young man.

So when Green's turn came to speak, he attempted to address the problem differently. Green explained that he had a sixteen-year-old son. Tarik was a National Honor Society member and a competitive swimmer, but he was also something else: a young black man. Green explained that when Tarik turned sixteen and got his driver's license, he had had a special talk with his son about what to do if he was stopped by the police while driving. Green said he'd told his son two things. One was what any parent might tell his son—drive safely. Cars can kill if driven carelessly. Don't speed; obey the rules of the road. But the second thing Green told Tarik is what set their talk apart from a discussion that a white parent might have with a newly licensed sixteen year old. "African Americans are subject to profiling," Green said, and "it can occur in instances where the person stopped does not feel he's done anything wrong." Green warned his son that, even though Detroit had a large black population, he would likely find himself stopped by police as he moved across the city's borders into mostly white suburban areas. He wanted to make sure Tarik knew how to behave so as not to create any danger to himself. Green told the chiefs, superintendents, and agents around the table that this talk with his son was not an effort to cultivate hostility toward police. As a law enforcement official himself, Green said, he could hardly want that less. Instead, Green said, he viewed it as a simple, straightforward duty that any African American parent must fulfill to ensure his child's safety—something "unfortunate" but necessary. As Tarik's father, he had the obligation to "tell him that racism exists and that he might very well be subject to it." [36] Green says he felt somewhat uncomfortable talking about something so personal, but he felt he had an obligation to tell those in the room of his very personal discussion with his son. "Here I am a member of law enforcement, a person who is truly part of the system who believes in the system," Green said later, "and yet here I had to have this discussion with my son because as a father I felt it was important that he have all the warnings for his safety and his well being." [37]

The room was quiet after Green spoke. It was not just what he'd said that made an impact; it was who he was and the non-confrontational way he'd addressed the audience. Then the next person spoke. He introduced himself as Richard Deane, the United States attorney for Atlanta and much of Georgia. Like Saul Green, Deane was the top federal law enforcement official in his jurisdiction. Like Green, he is also an African American. And he, too, told of having "the Talk" with both of his teenage sons when they got their driver's licenses. He explained to the law enforcement officials arrayed around the table that, as far as any black parent was concerned, profiling was a reality that he had to prepare his children to confront. He said that he warned his sons about the dangers they would face—the likelihood that they might be stopped by the police because they were black. "You have to prepare your children to live with and live in the greater community in a fashion in which they'll be safe and treated with respect." [38]

The meeting continued. Much was said, but little of it had the impact of the statements of the two U.S. attorneys about counseling their children. Several of the chiefs and superintendents approached Green and Deane during the day and thanked them for sharing such a personal perspective on the problem. [39]

By the end of the meeting, the closing statements of the moderator and others revealed a subtle shift in tone. If U.S. attorneys had to deal with the issue in raising their children, perhaps there was something to it after all. Some months later, Attorney General Janet Reno recalled Green's and Deane's comments when she spoke at the National Press Club in Washington, D.C. "When even a U.S. attorney who is African-American feels he has to instruct his son to be cautious of the police when he drives," she said, "we have a problem." [40]

The stories told by Saul Green and Richard Deane that day revealed something of the effect of profiling on black life. Deborah Ramirez, a professor at Northeastern University Law School in

Boston and a mother, puts it sharply. As a Latina, she says, "it would be parental negligence not to prepare [our children] for what, inevitably, they're going to experience, so we do."[41] No matter who these parents may be in the larger community, and no matter how clean-cut and well behaved their children may be, these parents understand that there is no escaping the reality of police stops for people of color. Class doesn't matter, wealth doesn't matter, driving behavior doesn't matter, the type of car doesn't matter. *Race and ethnicity matter.* Parents know this, even if their children don't. They also know that if their kids do not handle these encounters with extreme care, they can quickly turn into confrontations that range from merely unpleasant to physically dangerous and even deadly. For them, talking about how to handle a police stop is just as important as discussing the dangers of driving itself—perhaps even more so.

What gets said in the Talk varies. Michael, the municipal executive who has had a number of confrontations with police, said his father told him years ago what to do. "My dad would tell me, 'if you get pulled over, you just keep your mouth shut and do exactly what they tell you to.'" Whether he'd done anything wrong or not, Michael's father said, "'doesn't make a difference.'" Other parents give much more specific, pointed instructions. John Solomon, a former police officer who now works as a child protective services officer in Minneapolis, told his son what to do in no uncertain terms.[42] "You will have your driver's license and registration and insurance verification in a convenient place where you don't have to do a lot of reaching," he said. "Pull those things out and put 'em on the dashboard so you're not going in your pockets. Talk politely, and if you're talked down to or whatever, just don't say anything. Because your main goal is to leave the situation and get home—safely." Solomon knows that his instructions sound dire, and as a former police officer he's aware that cops face danger in traffic stops. But he feels he has no choice. He knows the dangers for which he's prepared his son are real, and he does not feel he can ignore them just because they're unpleasant. Ramirez, the law professor, says that when the time comes, she'll tell her son, "Sit up straight. If you slouch to the right or the left, the police are gonna think you're carrying a gun. Put both hands on the wheel so the police can see you don't have a weapon in your hands," she says. No matter what the officer does, "don't resist arrest. Even if the officer hits you, don't hit back. Don't swear. Call us as soon as you are able to." Ova Tate, a veteran police officer with fifteen years on the force in Toledo, Ohio, understands this reality, too.[43] He also has a teenage son, and when the time came, Tate did not mince words. He explained to his son that, because he is black, he'd always attract extra police attention, like it or not. He told his son that it made no difference that his father was a police officer; he'd get no special treatment. "I said, 'you're black, you're out in the neighborhood, it's a fact of life you're going to be stopped.' " He stressed to his son that his behavior was all-important to how the stop would turn out, whether he was right or wrong. "How you deal with the police is how your life is going to be. They say you did something, you say 'Okay,' and let 'em get out of your life." Diana Jimenez, a welfare reform analyst in Monterey County, California, has done the same thing with her sons. Even though she finds it "hard to swallow," she tells her boys that "it's reality that because of the color of their skin and who they are, they are going to be subjected to this."[44] She calls it "a tough one," but she knows she has to do it.

And parents are not the only ones concerned with instructing young blacks, Latinos, and other minorities on how to act during an encounter with the police. Schools, community organizations, and even some police officers and organizations have taken on the task, too. A New York City group called 100 Blacks in Law Enforcement Who Care, a social service organization formed by African American police officers, has received more requests than it can handle for what *Time* magazine called its "survival workshops."[45] Thousands of young people have attended the sessions, which aim to teach kids how to deal with the police from the unique perspective of the officers themselves. The organization's written materials make emphatic what minority parents tell their kids: survive the encounter. Do nothing that might give an officer a reason to endanger your safety. If the police stop a citizen walking on the street, the group says, "REMAIN CALM. ... DO NOT reach into your pockets. ASK why you are being stopped." Whatever you do, the instructions say, "DO NOT BE-COME LOUD. ... Remember: Depending upon the circumstances, the officer may think he/she has probable cause to stop you or he/she will use any excuse to harass you." The officers give similar advice for traffic stops. "Pull over and sit tight. IF you are stopped at night—turn on your interior dome light. PLACE your hands on the steering wheel. PRODUCE your identification when asked. REMAIN CALM. NO SUDDEN MOVES!!!!" [46]

This instruction in the realities of police encounters for young blacks will have two consequences. The first is the one that parents and other concerned adults hope for: that young people will exercise greater caution when police stop them, never giving an officer reason to take any untoward actions that might escalate the situation and perhaps even threaten the child's well-being. The second impact of the Talk, while perhaps unintentional, is no less real: young African Americans, Latinos, and other minorities will inevitably have a devastatingly negative impression of police. They cannot help but surmise that, in their parent's eyes, the police mean danger for people of color. One could not realistically expect these young people to regard police officers as helpful, constructive forces in the community after such a lesson. In short, instructions on how to handle stops cannot help but pass the attitudes, resentments, and injuries created by profiling on to the next generation.

Of course, even in the absence of the Talk, many young people of color learn the lessons of racial profiling firsthand. Former police officer John Solomon and his thirteen-year-old son were returning from a basketball game when they pulled into a fast food place to pick up some hamburgers. As they pulled out of the parking lot to get back on the road, a police officer pulled them over. The officer told Solomon that he pulled them over because "we looked suspicious and he thought we might have had a weapon." Solomon is still irritated, as he thinks back to the incident. "Here we are with burgers in our hands, and I'm not exactly sure what [the officer] could have assumed that we were doing," he says. But his emotions become raw and his voice seems to break when he talks about how the incident affected his son. "I have an impressionable thirteen-year-old son [and] now . . . that's all he can think about," he says. Solomon fears even more strongly that the incident left his son with an impression of his own father as weak and powerless. His son knows him as a professional, a strong father figure who used to be a police officer. But "to see me in a helpless position," he fears, will degrade the father in the eyes of the son. Worse yet, his son will know that "when it's [his] turn, [he's] gonna be in a helpless position here, too."

Some children fare even worse, sustaining very direct damage to themselves. For Gregory, the son of Sergeant Rossano Gerald, the experience of being stopped in Oklahoma while traveling with his dad discussed in chapter 1 devastated him. The police officers told Gregory that his father was a drug dealer and that they'd be attacked by the fearsome police dogs at the scene if they tried to escape. Gregory was put in one of the squad cars with a police dog who barked horribly at him. As he watched the police search their bags, Gregory became convinced that officers had taken his airline tickets, and he would not be able to return home to Indiana at the end of his time with his father. Months later, the soft-spoken Gregory still cried when he talked about what had happened. He had nightmares about it for months, and he underwent therapy to help him deal with his fears.[47]

Few minority children emerge from their teen years without understanding that profiling can—and does—affect them. They know that racially biased policing can reach out its ugly hand to touch them, and so they have to be prepared to meet this challenge in order to get home safely. They know because their parents tell them so. And they hear it whether their parents are politicians or police officers, employers or employees, federal officials or family physicians.

These are the costs of using racial profiling and high-discretion police tactics to enforce the law. And as long as law enforcement continues to do business this way, the virus of division between police and communities of color will continue to infect our society.

THE DISTORTED REALITY OF RACIAL PROFILING: THE STORY OF PRE-PAID LEGAL AND LEGAL SHIELD

The story of Harland C. Stonecipher and his company, Pre-Paid Legal, Inc., supplies an unlikely example of how racial profiling has distorted society.[48] After an automobile accident in the early 1970s, Stonecipher found himself in a curious position. He had both auto and medical insurance, so he was protected against those types of expenses. What he hadn't expected was mounting legal costs that were not covered by insurance. Understanding that he was not alone in his experience, Stonecipher started Pre-Paid Legal, Inc. The company would provide low-cost legal insurance for millions of people who could not afford to purchase expensive legal services but who did not qualify for help from the public defender or legal aid services. Stonecipher's company resembles a health maintenance organization. A nationwide network of provider attorneys and law firms takes cases and legal matters for insured members. Pre-Paid Legal has grown tremendously. Numerous business publications have recognized it as an excellent small company,[49] and its stock is now traded on the New York Stock Exchange.[50]

In the late 1990s, with public awareness of racial profiling at an all-time high, Pre-Paid Legal launched a new product, Legal Shield, an additional benefit available to members for an extra one dollar per month. Legal Shield provides members with a card to give to a police officer if they find themselves arrested or detained, and it gives them access to a twenty-four-hour 800 number for legal help. (Pre-Paid Legal's regular plan provides members with legal services only during regular business hours.)

While a spokesperson for Pre-Paid Legal says that the company did not create Legal Shield specifically for African Americans and other minorities,[51] materials advertising the product ask what potential buyers would do if they were pulled over because of their age, gender, "or even your race?" According to the *Wall Street Journal,* Pre-Paid Legal founder Stonecipher sees middle-class minorities worried about racial profiling as a growing market his company can serve.[52] Some associates of the company who sell the product clearly aim to sell to the African American market. One member law firm begins an advertisement for Legal Shield with the phrase "remember the profiling of people and the Asian man in New York?"[53] Stonecipher credits Tony Brown, the black journalist and entrepreneur, with helping him understand the problem of police stops from the African American perspective. Brown, who spearheads Pre-Paid Legal's sales effort to the African American market in the New York metropolitan area, has talked about Legal Shield on his New York radio show, generating a tremendous response.[54] Brown points to the "New York Attorney General's Report on Stops and Frisks"—which showed blacks much more likely to be stopped and searched on the street than whites—as "solid evidence that a 'Shield' is needed."[55] Stonecipher sees the Legal Shield card and its benefits as a way to level the playing field. The idea is that, for those who fear that they may be "questioned, detained, or arrested" during off hours, Legal Shield should provide some peace of mind.

Pre-Paid Legal is careful to say there are limits on what the Legal Shield plan can do. It's no "get-out-of-jail-free" card. It simply gives the member twenty-four-hour-a-day access to a lawyer, and an easy way to inform the officer that the member has legal representation.[56] The company is also careful to note Legal Shield's benefits do not apply in many situations. The point is that under the free-market system, Legal Shield is a very logical development. Social forces have created a need; Pre-Paid Legal fills it with a perfectly legal products in the finest American entrepreneurial tradition.

But it is the fact that thousands of citizens feel a *need* to buy insurance as a hedge against police action, and that those citizens come disproportionately from minority racial and ethnic groups, that represents a truly disturbing situation. When the dynamic of police action in our society produce a mass market for insurance against abusive use of police authority, something has gone terribly wrong.

THE COSTS TO SOCIETY

The Legitimacy of the Rule of Law and the Legal System

Beyond the costs to individuals, racial profiling and other racially biased methods of law enforcement corrode the basic legitimacy of the entire American system of justice, from policing to the courts to the law itself. The legitimacy of courts and the willingness of both the public and the other branches of government to accept their decisions rest entirely on the judiciary's independence and trustworthiness. Profiling puts this very legitimacy—the legal and moral authority that courts have—at risk. If citizens feel that the legal system acts based on bias, that the courts allow and sanction racial and ethnic discrimination, and that judges bestow their legal blessings on police decisions based on race, the integrity of the system begins to dissipate. When people mistrust courts, they become that much less likely to accept their decisions as lawful and correct, and the whole system loses its legitimacy.

In a study focusing on residents of Cincinnati, Ohio,[57] Martha Henderson and her colleagues found a large gap between the perceptions of blacks and whites in their beliefs concerning racial injustice in the criminal justice system. Many more blacks than whites believed that police were more likely to stop blacks than whites. More blacks than whites also believed that when convicted of stealing, black defendants were more likely than white defendants to go to jail and that blacks would be more likely than whites to receive a sentence of death for murder. These racial gaps remained even when the researchers controlled for sociodemographic status, experience with the criminal justice system and crime, the level of neighborhood disorder where respondents lived, and ideology on political and criminal justice issues. Despite the gap, a substantial minority of whites—from 37.5 percent to 47.8 percent—agreed with blacks.[58] Henderson ties these results directly to the legal system's legitimacy and the consequences that might follow from damage to this legitimacy. If blacks and a substantial number of whites see the criminal justice system as racially unfair and generally inequitable, "they may be less likely to trust system officials and help to co-produce social order; they may be reluctant to assume certain occupational positions in the system . . . and as jurors in trials, they may be less willing to believe police testimony and to convict minority defendants."[59] A 1998 study of attitudes toward courts in Providence, Rhode Island, showed the same thing. Whereas 57 percent of whites called the performance of courts in Providence excellent or good, only 42 percent of nonwhites concurred—a statistically significant difference of 15 percent. The racial differences on the question of whether courts were fair were even more dramatic—a gap of 23 percent.[60]

Few people could explain the link between the perception of racial bias in the criminal justice system and the legitimacy of that system better than Saul Green.[61] Green, the former United States attorney for the Eastern District of Michigan, considers himself an integral part of the law enforcement and criminal justice structure, and he has great respect for the people with whom he works. "I know the vast majority of law enforcement officers that I have contact with on a daily basis do a really good job. I have a lot of trust in them," Green says. But his own experiences as a young man and the experiences of others that he hears about give him pause. "Unless there is confidence in the system and in the manner in which enforcement occurs, then there's an overall negative impact on the system," he says, "which has to function based on confidence. So much of what we do is based on nothing more than pieces of paper." Race-based mistreatment within the system has a profound impact. "It erodes your trust and confidence in the system," he says, "and everybody suffers."

Public belief that racial bias exists in policing is more wide-spread than many seem to think, and attitudes about profiling have played a key part in these perceptions. Consider the recent findings of the U.S. Department of Justice about public attitudes toward police. Americans in twelve cities around the country were asked, "In general, how satisfied are you with the police who serve your neighborhood?" In ten of these cities, levels of satisfaction ranged from 86 percent to as high as 97 percent; in the remaining two cities, about 80 percent said they felt satisfied.[62] Overall, African American citizens were almost two and a half times as likely to say they were dissatisfied as whites. In Chicago, the gap between blacks and whites was almost three times; in Knoxville, it was more than four times. Other statistics dovetail with these findings.[63] A survey taken in 2000 by the Harris polling organization asked the following question: "Do you think the police in your community treat all races fairly or do they tend to treat one or more of these groups unfairly?" Responses of blacks and whites were almost a mirror image of each other. For whites, 69 percent believed their police treated all races fairly and 20 percent thought that they treated one or more groups unfairly; 10 percent said they didn't know. For blacks, 36 percent responded that police treat all races fairly, but almost 60 percent said that police treat one or more groups unfairly.[64] A February 2000 Gallup Poll confirms this. Among blacks, 64 percent say that blacks are treated less fairly than whites by the police; 30 percent of whites agree—a gap of 34 percent.[65] All of this resonates with the split-screen televised images of blacks and whites reacting to the verdict in the O. J. Simpson criminal trial: African Americans jumping for joy and stunned, disbelieving whites silent and tearful. These differences simply cannot be healthy in a society that so deeply depends on the rule of law.

Polling data on racial profiling show us how African Americans' personal experiences contribute to this divide—and how their beliefs are spreading to whites. A Gallup Poll released in December 1999 asked respondents whether they believed police had stopped them because of their race or ethnic background. More than 40 percent of African Americans said they believed police had stopped them because of their race.[66] Among young black men, aged eighteen to thirty-four, 72 percent—almost three-quarters—said they had been stopped because of their race.[67] Of those who said they had been through these stops, 54 percent said they'd experienced it at least three times, and some of them as often as ten times. Fifteen percent said they'd experienced it eleven or more times. Seven percent of whites say they have been treated unfairly by their local police; nearly four times that number of blacks—27 percent—think local police have treated them unfairly. Four percent of whites think their state police officers have treated them unfairly; six times that number of blacks think state police have been unfair to them. Eight percent of whites think that state police from other states have treated them unfairly; more than twice that number of blacks—17 percent—believe this.[68] Blacks see their experiences with racial bias in police stops not as unusual or isolated events. Rather, they make up part of the everyday experience of African American life. Not surprisingly, blacks were two and a half times more likely than whites to say they feared being stopped and arrested by police when they are completely innocent. Latinos were one and a half times more likely than whites to say they fear false stops and arrests.[69] A study of potential jurors by the *National Law Journal* and DecisionQuest in 2000 showed deep racial divides concerning police. Whereas nearly 70 percent of whites agreed with the statement, "Police usually tell the truth when they testify at trial," only 36 percent of African Americans did. The study found that knowledge of racial profiling and other types of police misconduct had clearly taken a toll on police credibility. Thirty-five percent of all respondents, and 50 percent of African American respondents, said they were less likely to believe a police officer in court.[70]

In 1999, surveys of public attitudes began focusing on profiling in earnest, and the results seemed to show that profiling, particularly traffic stops, might be exhibit A on the list of experiences that persuaded people that racial discrimination pervaded the criminal justice system. The December 1999 Gallup

Poll asked whether Americans thought that racial profiling was widespread. Not surprisingly, more than three-quarters of all African Americans—77 percent—agreed that racial profiling was widespread. What was unexpected, perhaps, was that more than half of all whites—56 percent—agreed.[71] The same poll also asked respondents whether they approved of racial profiling. Eighty-one percent of *everyone, black or white,* disapproved.[72] A poll of drivers in Michigan commissioned by the Michigan Office of Highway Safety Planning on the state's new seat belt law found that 61 percent of African American drivers and almost half of all white drivers believed that the new law might "give rise to certain drivers being singled out" for stops. The data showed that "racial profiling may be at the root of selective enforcement."[73] What makes this important is that the awareness of racial bias in the criminal justice system has begun to cross demographic lines from those most directly affected into the consciousness of those who have seldom recognized this problem before.

The Damage Done to the Courts

When ordinary citizens serve as jurors, they bring attitudes about police credibility to court with them. And it is in courts that the damage to police credibility can have real, concrete consequences of the worst kind. In most criminal cases, police serve as witnesses. They have gathered the evidence, arrested the defendants, and interviewed the victims. They are usually central to the prosecution's case. They have information to convey to the jury that is legally required for conviction. And in a significant number of cases, the police aren't just central witnesses—they are *the only* witnesses. Think, for example, about the typical drug possession case. Although some of these cases involve informants or other police agents, it is usually police officers themselves who find the drugs, smell the burning marijuana, or observe the defendant making a street-corner sale. These types of legal cases are usually built entirely on the testimony of police officers. Therefore, if people who serve as jurors harbor skepticism about the truthfulness of police officers, it becomes increasingly difficult to convince jurors to convict guilty defendants.

James Carr, a federal judge and well-known authority on search-and-seizure issues, says that he has witnessed this phenomenon during his more than twenty years of selecting juries. One common question judges and lawyers everywhere ask prospective jurors during the jury-selection process, Carr says, is whether they would give the testimony of a police officer any more credence or weight than they would give the testimony of any other witnesses. "When I first started out, invariably, we'd have some people say, 'Yes, sure, of course I would, they're police officers, they're sworn to tell the truth,'" Carr says. But over the last five years, he says, things have changed. Now, he almost never hears potential jurors say that they would be more likely to believe a police officer than any other witness. Instead, a small but increasing number of potential jurors say exactly the opposite. "They say, 'What? God no, I'd be less likely to believe them, they're cops,'" Carr says, "and these are not urban minority jurors. They're mostly white jurors from small towns." People are simply "not giving police officers the credence they historically have," Carr says. While no one has gathered empirical evidence to support this change in attitude, Carr says that it has been "perceptible to me as a trial judge."[74] Lucas Miller, a detective with the New York Police Department, says police in New York have known about the damage to police credibility in minority communities for years. "It is common knowledge in law enforcement and legal circles that juries in the Bronx are unsympathetic to cops," Miller says. "It is harder to get a conviction in the Bronx when a cop testifies for the prosecution." Miller understands what this means in run-of-the-mill cases. "Many of these trials involve innocent people who must watch those who victimized them go free. Often, in the Bronx, justice is not done because residents mistrust the police."[75]

As skepticism toward police testimony increases, not just among minority citizens but among all potential jurors, an increasing number of cases will end either in undeserved acquittals or in hung juries. Gerard Lynch, a professor at Columbia Law School and the former top assistant to the United States attorney in Manhattan, believes this prediction to be quite sensible. "Police testimony is at the very heart of the criminal justice system," says Lynch, who became a federal trial judge in 2000. "If the public does not have confidence in the police, then acquittals or hung juries will become increasingly routine." [76] Though there have been no studies to test this hypothesis, there is some evidence that it may indeed be happening. Journalist and law professor Jeffrey Rosen has described this phenomenon in the courts in Washington, D.C., in which a single holdout juror—often an African American female—refuses to convict a black defendant, despite convincing, even overwhelming, evidence of guilt and the vociferous contrary opinions of fellow jurors, black and white. [77] Rosen speculated that the rising percentage of mistrials might have much to do with racial bias in the justice system against African Americans. Eric Holder, a former chief federal prosecutor and judge in Washington, D.C., who served as Attorney General Janet Reno's top deputy and is himself an African American, told Rosen that the perception that the system is racially biased may indeed play a role in warping jury decisions. "There are some folks who have been so seared by racism, so affected by what has happened to them because they are black, that, even if you're the most credible, upfront black man or woman in law enforcement, you're never going to be able to reach them." [78] And nullification by juries—cases in which jurors acquit defendants despite the law and convincing evidence of guilt—has begun to enjoy a rehabilitation of sorts into a respectable criminal justice device. In the twentieth century, jury nullification came to be associated with the odious legally enforced separatism of the Jim Crow South. Faced with serious charges against members of the Ku Klux Klan and other hate organizations in deaths of blacks and civil rights workers, all-white juries would acquit white defendants—nullify—despite overwhelming evidence of guilt. Now nullification has taken on a different complexion. Paul Butler, a respected law professor who is a former federal prosecutor and an African American, has urged blacks to nullify in drug cases against black defendants. Butler argues that African American jurors should use their power to vote not guilty as a form of political protest and an assertion of black control over the system. Even if the evidence clearly supports the defendant's guilt, Butler says, black jurors should not vote to convict nonviolent black drug defendants because doing so would serve only to apply and uphold an unjust, discriminatory law and legal structure.[79]

It is difficult to imagine anything more damaging to the rule of law than growing distrust and cynicism, failure to believe police witnesses, and even calls from respected authorities like Professor Butler to ignore evidence and law. All are symptoms of the damage racial profiling and its associated tactics have done to the very muscle and bone of the legal system.

Distortion of Criminal Records and Sentencing   Racial profiling and high-discretion police tactics, especially pretext traffic stops, can also distort the sentences that African Americans receive when courts convict them of crimes. Most people would agree that all criminals who commit the same crimes, and who have similar criminal histories, should receive the same sentences; the race, poverty, or class of the defendant should play no role. But profiling can distort this ideal badly.

A case decided in a federal court in Boston illustrates the point. In 1998, a defendant named Alexander Leviner came before the court for sentencing.[80] Leviner had pled guilty to the crime of being a felon in possession of a firearm. The prosecution and the defense essentially agreed on the facts of the case. The only real issue was what sentence Leviner should receive. As a defendant in the federal criminal justice system, Leviner's sentence would depend upon the federal Sentencing Guidelines. The Guidelines represent an attempt to deal with the problem of unjustified differences in sentencing: a way to make sure that similar defendants who do similar crimes get similar sentences. The Guidelines do this by having sentencing depend upon two numbers: an offense score and an offender score. The offense score is based on the seriousness of the offense and its factual context. The offender score is an attempt to assign a number to the defendant's prior criminal history. The more serious and consistent that criminal history, the higher the offender's score. Using a grid, the offense and offender scores give the sentencing judge a narrow range of punishment deemed appropriate for the particular offense and offender—for example, thirty-six to forty-two months. The judge may sentence the defendant to any length of imprisonment within that range. Any deviation from the prescribed range, whether upward or downward, requires a written opinion specifying reasons for the departure. The law accepts only certain reasons as adequate justification for sentencing outside the specified range.

Leviner's case presented a challenge to Nancy Gertner, the United States district judge assigned to the case. On the one hand, there were no real factual disputes about Leviner's case— he'd pled guilty. And the particulars of his criminal record were not seriously disputed, either. But as Judge Gertner's opinion in the case shows, something about Leviner's criminal record stood out. Examining Leviner's record, Judge Gertner noticed that it consisted "overwhelmingly" of "motor vehicle violations and minor drug possession offenses." [81] Since all of the available evidence indicated to Judge Gertner that African Americans like Leviner experienced a proportionally greater number of traffic stops than whites,[82] Judge Gertner reasoned that assessing Leviner's offender score as a straightforward, neutral indicator of his criminal behavior over time, without considering the ways that profiling and pretext traffic stops might have inflated his criminal record, represented nothing less than a continuation of the racial discrimination implicit in racial profiling into the sentencing process—and into her courtroom.[83] Judge Gertner refused to go along with this. Instead, she gave Leviner a "downward departure"—a cut in the usual sentence he would have gotten given his criminal record.[84]

It may be true that police, in general, discriminate against black motorists in their use of traffic stops, but this does not mean that the particular stops Leviner himself experienced in the past resulted from bias. An appellate court thus could find that Leviner or someone like him does not deserve the downward departure he received. But Judge Gertner's decision points out something important nevertheless, and it will no doubt serve as an example for judges in many other courts. Racial profiling can have grave consequences not just immediately, but in the longer term, as minor offenses build into serious criminal records that come back to haunt certain defendants down the road. And profiling makes this more likely to happen to blacks than to whites. Unnoticed, this will skew the sentences African Americans and other minorities receive under supposedly neutral sentencing criteria.

The upshot here, and throughout the legal system, is a set of rules, practices, and institutions distorted almost beyond recognition. As a society, we look for equal justice under the law; instead, we get a concentrated focus on minorities. We look for the Fourth Amendment to restrain police behavior; instead, we have a free-for-all, unrestrained by the Constitution in any practical sense. We look for punishment meted out on the basis of justice and fairness; instead, we get a prison system containing larger and larger numbers of minority citizens, while others get more lenient treatment.

The Damage to Community Policing   Only a handful of developments in policing and criminal justice in the last thirty years have had the impact of community policing and problem-oriented policing. Community and problem-oriented policing aims to restore the connections between police and their constituents—to bring police and residents together as partners to combat crime. This requires that the police and the community work together. Foot patrol, community meetings, and one-on-one contact with citizens must become the norm. Officers must trust the community to identify the real problems in the neighborhood—to determine what the priorities of law enforcement should be. In other words, the community, not the police, must decide what police would do. For their part, the members of the community have to trust the police enough to tell them what—and who—the real problems in the neighborhood are. To earn this trust, people have to know that officers would police not just with vigor, but with respect for constitutional rights and compassion for people. And residents must learn to take responsibility for solving their problems rather than simply leaving them in the hands of the police.

Many Americans are aware that New York City experienced a dramatic decrease in crime of all kinds in the 1990s. For Rudolph Giuliani, New York's mayor during these years, the central policy initiative responsible was simple: tougher law enforcement, organized around the idea of "zero tolerance" for even the most minor offenses.[85] And, in the media capital of the world, the politically ambitious Giuliani makes no secret of his feeling that he and his tough-guy policies should get the credit.

But whereas New York got all the media attention, cities elsewhere showed that there was more than one way to cut crime. Beginning in the late 1980s and early 1990s the San Diego Police Department fully committed itself to community and problem-oriented policing. Chief of Police Jerry Sanders made it clear that community and problem-oriented policing techniques would henceforth be the way that the department operated. Perhaps more to the point, it would also be the key to advancement, promotions, and plum assignments within the department, giving officers and their supervisors real incentives to adopt these new methods. The department put a premium on police-citizen cooperation and interaction; twelve hundred citizens joined a civilian police auxiliary that had real responsibility for coming up with ways to combat and prevent crime. The results were stunning. Under San Diego's community and problem-oriented policing approach, crime also dropped in the 1990s—as it did in many other cities—but it dropped *more* than in New York. This occurred across all categories of crime, including violent crimes such as homicide. And whereas New York will be dealing with the legacy of the Giuliani administration's zero-tolerance policies for many years to come—including a sharp antagonism between the police and racial minorities, who feel that they bore the brunt of the mayor's enforcement policies—San Diego's police department has been traveling in the other direction for a long time, building bridges, forging a common purpose, cultivating the trust of those they serve. And it has done this with less than half the number of police officers per citizen than New York has.

Obviously, each city must choose public safety and law enforcement policies that fit its situation. New York's methods may not have worked in San Diego, and vice versa. But as the experience in San Diego shows, there are alternatives to the zero-tolerance approach. Community and problem-oriented policing can make real inroads on crime. But this approach has a catch. Community and problem-oriented policing's centerpiece has always been trust. Racial profiling and other police methods that create the perception of racial and other biases in law enforcement carry with them yet another insidious problem: they will erode—even destroy—any possibility for the building of trust that community policing requires. If many Americans of every race feel that policing is not fair in an absolutely fundamental respect—that skin color may serve as evidence and that racial and ethnic bias may determine who gets treated like a criminal— the great potential of community policing will go unrealized. And given its notable successes so far amid a landscape cluttered with the failed law enforcement policies and initiatives of the past, this would represent the squandering of an irreplaceable opportunity.

Chapter Six

IT'S NOT JUST DRIVING WHILE BLACK: HOW PROFILING AFFECTS LATINOS, ASIANS, AND ARABS

When racial profiling first began to creep into the debate on race and policing, most of those who made their concerns public were African Americans. Black people connected these practices with their other experiences of discrimination both inside and outside the criminal justice system. In fact, long before the term *racial profiling* became common, African Americans had a different way of describing race-based traffic and pedestrian stops. They'd say that police had stopped them not for speeding or for a burned-out taillight or any of a thousand other possible offenses. Instead, they'd say that the officer stopped them for "driving while black"—a cynical twist on the offense of driving while intoxicated. "Driving while black," or DWB, is the form in which the problem first became known to the general public.[1]

Perhaps it is for this reason that racial profiling has sometimes become identified as a "black issue"—a concern for only African Americans. This perpetuates the idea that blacks alone suffer this treatment and thus isolates them from other groups with similar concerns and experiences. It also greatly oversimplifies the problem. Other minority groups also encounter this same set of problems—profiling combined with high-discretion police tactics—and also suffer stops and searches vastly disproportionate to their presence in the population, either on the road or on city streets. Context largely drives police focus; near reservations, Native Americans may be targets, whereas in certain West Coast cities police may suspect that young Asian Americans are potential gang members.[2] And Latinos have often complained that they receive the same treatment African Americans do from police. In fact, Latinos sometimes use the initials DWB themselves—to stand for "driving while brown."

At least three racial and ethnic groups other than African American have had regular experience with profiling. Their stories show that profiling is not just a black problem. Police can aim this weapon at any minority group.

PROFILING AT THE BORDER: LIVING UNDER THE DOUBLE SUSPICION OF BEING LATINO

Latinos live under the same cloud of statistically based criminal suspicion as African Americans. Like African Americans, Latinos are overrepresented among defendants arrested and incarcerated for many crimes. Therefore, just as with African Americans, a police officer playing the odds with a profile may think that stopping more Latinos "just makes common sense" if he or she wants to combat crime aggressively. As with blacks, Latinos—the vast majority of whom are law-abiding, not lawbreaking, citizens—will have to put up with this undesirable attention from police, regardless of their having done nothing to deserve it.

But Latinos actually bear another burden, one that is exclusively theirs. Unlike African Americans, Latinos face the suspicion that they may be illegal immigrants, subject to arrest, detention, and even deportation.

Recall the story of Judge Filemon Vela from chapter 1, the federal judge stopped twice in Texas and forced to answer questions about his citizenship by the Border Patrol. Judge Vela's experience demonstrates the vast power of government agents to conduct searches and seizures at the border or its functional equivalent (for example, an inland airport where international travelers reenter the country). At the border itself or anything that acts as a border, the rule is simple: government agents can stop and search people and their belongings. They need no warrant, no probable cause, no reasonable suspicion—in fact, no amount of evidence or suspicion at all. According to the Supreme Court, this power exists "pursuant to the long-standing right of the sovereign to protect itself" from persons or things considered dangerous or unwelcome.[3] True, the Fourth Amendment to the Constitution does require that all searches be reasonable. But according to the Court, border searches are "reasonable simply by virtue of the fact that they occur at the border."[4]

When the Border Patrol stops people in areas near the border, but not at the border, the rules change slightly. At fixed interior checkpoints—checkpoints some distance from the border itself but still close enough to get considerable border-related traffic— the Supreme Court has said that Mexican appearance is considered suspicious enough to justify the "minimal" intrusion of being stopped, detained, and questioned about immigration status.[5] The "minimal" nature of the intrusion justified giving the Border Patrol "wide discretion."[6] Mexican appearance, the Court said, "clearly is relevant" to finding illegal immigrants.[7]

Roving patrols—immigration policing in which agents in moving patrol cars stop individual vehicles of their choosing— raise more difficult issues, and the Supreme Court has applied somewhat stricter rules to them. Since, unlike agents at fixed checkpoints who stop everyone, agents in roving patrols decide whom to stop, and because these stops occur without notice, often on lightly traveled roads at night, increasing the possibility of frightening individual drivers,[8] even a brief stop of a vehicle during a roving patrol of the interior of the country requires that Border Patrol agents have "reasonable suspicion" of illegal entry into the country—a relatively small amount of evidence, but at least somewhat more than the "no suspicion" standard set for interior checkpoint stops.[9]

The Supreme Court has said that Mexican appearance, standing alone, does not justify a reasonable belief that the occupants might be illegal aliens, because so many native-born and naturalized Americans have these physical characteristics.[10] Even near the border, the Court said, a "relatively small proportion" of those who look like this are illegal immigrants.[11] But in the same breath, the justices said that because statistics that showed that as many as 85 percent of all illegal aliens in the United States come from Mexico,[12] "the likelihood that any given person of Mexican ancestry is an alien is high enough to make Mexican appearance a relevant factor" that could, along with others, constitute reasonable suspicion for a stop.[13] The upshot is that the Supreme Court has given law enforcement explicit permission to consider Hispanic or Mexican appearance in deciding whether someone is suspicious. In other words, skin color and physical features have become evidence in the world of immigration enforcement. "Driving (or walking or working or standing) while brown" is explicitly sanctioned by our highest court, as long as agents consider anything else—any other factor—along with it.

The Supreme Court's pronouncements in this area, combined with the universal stereotype of illegal immigrants as Latino, all but guarantee that police will use ethnicity in its crudest form, whether or not these agencies have immigration-related responsibilities. Because the law allows Mexican appearance to serve as one factor in deciding whom to stop, it can easily become the dominant factor. The use of the low reasonable suspicion standard does nothing to stop this; an officer can always find other factors to bring into the equation after the fact to justify what has already happened. As one author pointed out, "[O]fficers can easily strengthen their reasonable suspicion after [the stop]. . . . It is easy to come up with the necessary articulable facts after the fact, which is commonly referred to within the Border Patrol as 'canned p.c.' (probable cause)."[14] Because nearly limitless discretion invites abuse, combining this discretion with the right to use race and ethnicity virtually at will seems calculated to bring about the worst type of biased policing.

The great majority of Latinos in the United States are citizens, either native born or naturalized. Others are legal resident aliens, and others are in the United States with some form of legal permission (work and educational visas, for example). The Court's reasoning turns their legal status upside down—from something they have and enjoy to something they are assumed not to have and must assert and even prove, whenever challenged. The vast majority are judged guilty on sight until proven innocent, and they carry a heavy burden so that police may find a small minority who are actually guilty. This, of course, is the essence of racial and ethnic profiling.

Demographic shifts in our country ought to alert us to the reality that the profiling of Hispanics on immigration issues will spread. The U.S. Census Bureau tells us that the racial and ethnic mix of our population has recently undergone rapid change. From July 1, 1990, to July 1, 1999, the bureau estimates, the Hispanic population of the United States grew more than 38 percent.[15] And some of this growth happened in some surprising places. For example, the state with the biggest percentage increase in Hispanic population was neither Texas, nor California, nor New York—the three states with the largest Hispanic populations—but Arkansas, with an increase of more than 170 percent.[16] At the county level, some of the largest percentage increases in the Hispanic population came in two counties in suburban Atlanta.[17] These places have seldom faced immigration issues; clearly, that will change. Law enforcement targeting illegal immigration has already popped up in places with no border to Mexico and no new influx of immigrants. A surprising example comes from northwest Ohio—an area far from the Southwest, closer to Canada than Mexico, but an area that has an abundance of agricultural land that attracts migrant farm workers, many of them Hispanic.

In 1995, a group of Hispanic men reported that several police officers had stopped them on the Ohio Turnpike and confiscated their green cards.[18] The men spoke Spanish and the officers did not, so the men had no idea why their cards had been seized or what had happened to them. It took the threat of a lawsuit to get the cards back, and in the course of putting the legal papers together, lawyers for the men learned from an Ohio Highway Patrol officer that his agency regularly seized green cards this way to check immigration status. This shocked the lawyers, because federal law made it a crime for any alien not to have the card with him at all times.[19] These attorneys soon filed suit against the Ohio Highway Patrol, alleging that the practice of seizing green cards of Hispanics violated the law.[20]

The suit uncovered evidence that the highway patrol—not the Border Patrol or the U.S. Customs Service or some other agency involved in policing the country's borders, but a state police agency with absolutely no official role in immigration law enforcement—did, indeed, take green cards regularly. According to Mark Finnegan, an attorney who represented the Hispanic plaintiffs in the case, the highway patrol focused solely on Hispanics. They had no interest in immigration issues involving, for example, Asian or African drivers. Hispanics have also alleged that the highway patrol has used the same techniques against them to search for drugs.

Litigation of the northwest Ohio case demonstrates just how difficult it can be to limit law enforcement discretion over immigration matters. Initially, the judge hearing the case granted a preliminary injunction, preventing the Ohio Highway Patrol from questioning motorists about immigration status during traffic stops without some evidence of violation of immigration laws. The injunction also halted the practice of seizing green cards and other immigration documents without cause and stated that any lawful seizure of documents required that substitute documents be provided.[21] The court allowed the case to go forward as a class action,[22] but the judge later threw much of the case out of court because the named plaintiffs could not prove that they would experience a traffic stop with illegal immigration questioning and seizure of documents again.[23]

Other courts have been more receptive to the claims of Hispanics. In *U.S.* v. *Montero-Camargo*,[24] the U.S. Court of Appeals stated that while agents near the border could make brief temporary stops if they had reasonable suspicion, Latino appearance could not be considered as one of the factors that made officers suspicious. Given the huge explosion of the Latino population in the United States, especially in border areas, and the fact that the huge majority of these persons were not violating the immigration laws, "we conclude that, at this point in our nation's history, and given the continuing changes in our ethnic and racial composition, Hispanic appearance is, in general, of such little probative value that it may not be considered as a relevant factor where particularized or individualized suspicion is required. Moreover, we conclude, for the reasons we have indicated, that it is also not an appropriate factor." [25] But the *Montero-Camargo* case is unusual; it is the rare opinion that expresses any misgiving with the use of Latino appearance as a factor indicating suspicion—even though the United States saw unprecedented growth in the Latino population between 1990 and 2000.

PROFILING AND ASIAN GANGS: OF "MODEL MINORITIES" AND OTHER MYTHS

For many years, police in urban areas of America have targeted youth gangs as a source of crime. In the 1990s, a new wrinkle on this old problem emerged in areas of the country with substantial populations from China, Korea, Vietnam, and Japan: Asian gangs. California, the state with the largest Asian and Pacific Islander population in the nation, became the focus of police efforts to combat Asian gang activity. This may seem surprising. After all, most people think of Asians as the so-called model minority.[26] The term derives from the fact that Asians seem to have achieved success in business and higher education in outsized numbers. The stereotype tells us that Asians are smarter, work harder, and will not countenance failure because they would "lose face" with parents and family members if they did. Asians put a premium on family, education, and obedience, the thinking goes, and therefore succeed more often than others, whether in commerce, on campus, or in Silicon Valley. Thus the "model minority" stereotype makes it seem less likely that Asian young people would find gang membership attractive.

Clearly, Asian gangs exist, in California and elsewhere. And it only makes sense that the larger the Asian population of any given area, the larger and more numerous such gangs may be. But in some cities in California, the model minority view seems almost to have been entirely eclipsed by an outlook that sees many Asian young people not as overachievers and bookworms but as gang members. And especially in some areas of Southern California with large Asian populations, a new stereotype has emerged: the Asian "gang banger." Relying almost entirely on visual cues, police in a number of these small cities, especially in conservative Orange County, south of Los Angeles, began in the early 1990s to try to spot gang members by looking for a combination of Asian physical features with "gang clothing" and "gang cars." [27] These categories proved so wildly overbroad and overinclusive that enforcement efforts inevitably swept in many teens who had no gang affiliations at all. Using a profile, police picked out and stigmatized young people just because of what they looked like. And police did not just question Asian gang suspects about their actions or shoo them off corners. They also photographed these young people by the hundreds, most without their permission or the permission of their parents, and put the photos into "mug books" used to identify criminals, even though officers never arrested most of them and often had no firm proof of gang affiliation. Labeling these youths as gang members, the authorities put identifying information on many of the photos and logged them into a huge statewide antigang computer database. Thus the branding of young Asians as gang members, based on how they looked, became part of a permanent digital record.[28]

The report by a southern California police department on Asian gangs that discussed how officers could spot members of these gangs said the officers make special efforts to stop Hondas—"notorious" as the vehicle of choice for gang members.[29]

And students in Orange County report that they are stopped by the police especially frequently when they drive Japanese cars they have customized by tinting the windows, lowering the suspension, or adding acessories like fancy wheel covers.[30] But driving an accessorized Honda is not illegal, and it is not probable cause for suspicion, even if you are Asian American. The great majority of Asian American high school and college students who dress in what police describe as "gang clothes" or drive what they call "gang cars" have no involvement with gangs and have committed no crime. Nevertheless, they are routinely stopped by the police, questioned, and photographed. It makes no difference whether the police have seen the young people engaged in any criminal activity or that they are not arrested. Police then enter the names and personal information, as well as some of the photographs, into a statewide computer system called GREAT—Gang Reporting Evaluation and Tracking—designed to track "gang members" and "gang associates." With no systematic checks in place and no way to know what information police have put into it, GREAT was almost guaranteed to contain identifying information about thousands of innocent people. (GREAT was replaced in 1998 by a statewide system called Cal-Gang, which allows police anywhere in the state to use a person's name to find out if he or she is considered a gang member or associate.)[31]

Police in California insist that taking photographs and interviewing people they considered possible gang members only made sense. Ethnic gangs are notoriously difficult to penetrate, they say, and so this type of proxy-based profiling was the only realistic alternative. In short, justifications of these gang-suppression techniques mirror all of the arguments made in favor of profiling in all of the different contexts in which police have used it.

But there is evidence that the combination of widespread stops based on appearance and the taking of photographs combined with the power of a large-scale database is far too raw to be very productive, and so broad as to make an eventual disaster likely. From its earliest stages, some of those who were involved with the GREAT system viewed it as dangerously flawed. In 1991, even before Orange County police agencies joined the system, Jim Amound of the Orange County District Attorney's Office wrote in an internal memo that if a person is "just a want-to-be and the person he's hanging around with or the gang he's associating with has not been involved in criminal activity, I think we'd be hard-pressed to defend having that person in our gang-intelligence computer." [32] Minutes of official meetings on the GREAT system as far back as 1992 point to this same problem: "The attendees were in agreement that a problem exists with the definition of 'gang associate.' " [33] And in a 1994 memorandum, Margaret Venturi, supervising deputy attorney general of California, expressed doubt about the uses to which GREAT could be put. Any individual person's record in the system without a "criminal predicate" could be challenged by a defendant in court. Yet by 1997, the GREAT database contained more than twenty thousand people—an astonishing 1 percent of Orange County's population.

With such a weak set of assumptions driving policing policy, it was only a matter of time before something went awry. For some years, the San Jose police were among those law enforcement agencies in California that compiled photographs of suspected Asian gang members. (The practice has since been discontinued there.) Danny Nguyen was arrested after a crime victim identified him from a mug book. Nguyen's photo got into the book after police stopped him on suspicion of gang membership and took his picture. Nguyen was not arrested or charged for any crime at the time the police stopped him, but months later the victim picked out his picture in the book. Nguyen and his family protested, but he was held in jail for three months before the authorities realized he was innocent and released him. Nguyen's ordeal began with the same experience as the two honor students, Minhtran Tran and Quyen Pham in chapter 1. Police identified him as an Asian gang member and took his picture on the basis of ethnic criteria and an extremely broad set of visual indicators. Fortunately, the girls' story had a happier ending than Nguyen's. Their lawsuit ended in a settlement that required the police department that took their pictures and personal information to purge all of this material and to put safeguards in place that would prevent an incident like theirs from happening again. The settlement also included a procedure to allow others to ask that their photographs and personal information be removed from any police records and computer systems, as well as a monetary settlement and an apology from the police chief.[34]

Unfortunately, even though years have passed since the police stopped Minhtran Tran and Quyen Pham, not everyone seems to have learned the lesson their case teaches. More than six years after the girls' encounter with police, Chief Charles Brobeck of the Irvine, California, Police Department and one of his top aides met with students from the University of California at Irvine to discuss police stops.[35] The university sits in the same general area of southern California, in which the two girls had their encounter with police. Many of the Asian students at the Irvine meeting complained to Chief Brobeck that police had singled them out, stopped them, and questioned them about possible gang affiliation—often many times. Chief Brobeck's reaction to these complaints spoke volumes. First, he laughed with his aide. Then he suggested that the problem lay not with the police action but with the students themselves. "I'd look at my car and ask, 'How can I change it so I don't get stopped again?' "

ANTI-TERRORISM PROFILING: ARAB AMERICANS AND MUSLIMS IN AIRPORTS

For some years, American air travelers have been occasional targets of terrorism involving air travel. This has ranged from hijacking and hostage taking to bombings of airliners that have killed all on board the aircraft, such as the bombing of Pan Am Flight 103 over Lockerbie, Scotland. Some of these crimes have involved Middle Eastern or Muslim perpetrators. Because of these and other types of terrorism directed at American and other Western interests, a broad perception exists that Muslims or Arab people represent a potential terrorist threat that the government and the airlines must address. Constant use in the media of such terms as *Muslim extremists* and *Arab terrorists* has perpetuated this belief among the general populace.

Government actions in response to these perceptions have ranged from thoughtless to outrageous. The problems began when airline ground personnel—people who manned ticket counters and gate podiums in airports—seemed to have been granted the lead operational role in selecting people who might be terrorists. When these personnel spotted someone they thought was suspicious, airline employees flagged these passengers in some way, marking their tickets or boarding passes, for example, or tagging their luggage. Once in the gate and boarding areas, Arabs and Muslims often reported that they were taken out of the normal passenger lines and waiting areas and directed to special areas for questioning, searches of bags and other personal items, and sometimes even intrusive types of personal searches such as frisks. Airport personnel often marked suspects' suitcases with bright strips of colorful tape, with words like "SECURITY" printed in bold, black letters clearly visible to other passengers. Many Arab passengers couldn't fail to notice that the only people selected for this treatment were other Arabs, especially if they were dark skinned, spoke only Arabic, or spoke English with an Arabic accent.

Just as aggravating and angering, the airlines and the federal government responded to complaints about these procedures from Arab Americans and Muslims in a classically bureaucratic fashion. Airlines typically said that their ground personnel acted on the explicit instructions of the Federal Aviation Administration (FAA), the government body charged with insuring the safety of air travel. Sometimes the airlines said that they had been given a specific, written profile by the FAA, as a way to help ferret out potential security risks among their passengers. When passengers complained to the FAA, the agency vigorously denied this; they had given the airlines no directives or instructions of any kind, and certainly no "profiles" designed to focus on Arab Americans as potential terrorists and security threats.

By the middle 1990s, airport "stops" of Arab Americans and Muslims had become a regular occurrence. And nearly every time a terrorist incident made headlines, the authorities automatically responded by attempting to apprehend people of Middle Eastern origin. For example, in the wake of the bombing of the federal building in Oklahoma City, law enforcement immediately posted bulletins looking for Arabs. One man, an Arab on his way to Jordan, was in fact detained. This was just one example of a constant series of incidents and irritations directed at one group of people, often conducted by airline and other nonpolice officials without even minimal training in how to handle such situations. These actions created and perpetuated a stigma attached to being Arab in American society—a thousand small indications, visible both to Arabs and everyone else, that Arabs were untrustworthy types who might even be terrorists.

Most Arab Americans trace the worst of their treatment at the hands of airport personnel to July 1996 and the crash of TWA Flight 800 off the coast of Long Island. In the immediate aftermath of the disaster, which was ultimately determined to have been caused by an explosion in the plane's center fuel tank,[36] many thought that it had been an act of terrorism originating in the Middle East. Much of the media reporting on TWA Flight 800 highlighted the unsubstantiated possibility that the crash was a terrorist act.[37] Large numbers of Arab Americans, Muslims, and other airline passengers of Middle Eastern origin began to experience harsh questioning, demeaning treatment, and public searches of their possessions. Many reported that airline employees told them that they were singled out for this treatment because they "fit a profile."[38] And they noticed that Arabs were almost always the only ones treated this way—sometimes through methods as blunt and publicly embarrassing as flight attendants ordering all Arabic-speaking people to come to the front of the plane.

In response to the TWA Flight 800 crash, President Clinton

quickly appointed a commission, headed by Vice President Gore, to investigate and propose new measures to insure aviation safety and security. Among the commission's many recommendations were a number meant to address terrorist threats. These included the nationwide implementation of a computerized profiling system to spot those passengers thought to pose a higher risk of being terrorist suspects than others. The computerized system, known as CAPS (Computer Assisted Passenger Screening), would replace investigation by airline personnel.[39] According to James Padgett of the Office of Civil Aviation Security and Intelligence of the FAA, the old system consisted of an FAA "mental checklist" for airline employees to use when considering whether passengers presented a threat. If a passenger presented a certain (unspecified) number of those factors, they were sent for additional scrutiny that could include questioning, hand searches of bags, and the like.[40] (Although these "manual procedures" are no longer used, Padgett would not disclose what the factors in the checklist were, because he said doing so would still pose a security risk.)[41] Neither the FAA nor the Gore Commission would release the elements of the computerized profile that CAPS would use,[42] but James Padgett did say that CAPS selects people based on their current reservation and not on travel history.[43] He points out that a U.S. Department of Justice report declares that CAPS uses neither race, ethnicity, national origin, or any other factors, like surname, that would correlate with race or ethnicity.

Along with other recommendations by the Gore Commission, CAPS was adopted and put into operation at the beginning of 1998. At the very least, it was hoped, this would end selection based on skin color, accent, and clothing. Since neither the FAA nor the airlines nor any other agency would reveal what factors constituted the CAPS profile, some feared that CAPS could end up having the same effect that the old profiles had, picking out a disparate number of Arab Americans and others with connections to the Middle East. As a consequence, few expected the situation to change much, and many braced themselves for what was to come.

But the airlines and the FAA implemented other changes along with CAPS. First, the worst abuses of the prior system—public searches of possessions, stigmatizing announcements, and visible signs of suspicion such as "SECURITY" tape on luggage—were virtually eliminated through regulation and by requiring special training of airline agents. According to James Padgett, some of the procedures in the past had indeed been abusive—harsh tone and language used in questioning, the use of very public areas for security procedures, and what Padgett called "wholesale, intrusive, highly resented dump searches," in which all clothing and personal possessions were unceremoniously dumped on the floor and searched, with hapless passengers told to repack without any assistance. (Padgett says that some in the FAA speculated that this was "malicious compliance" by airline employees with FAA rules—implementing FAA procedure in a way guaranteed to generate complaints, which would then force the FAA to give up on having airlines bear these burdens.)[44] Second, and perhaps more important, the FAA limited the actions that airline personnel could take when a passenger was selected by CAPS. Rather than intrusive questioning, searches, and other procedures, the FAA declared that one of only two possible actions could occur: the selected passenger's luggage could be put through an electronic explosive detection system or the luggage could be "bag matched." Bag matching means that the selected passenger's checked luggage cannot be on the plane unless it is confirmed that the passenger matched to those bags is on; if the passenger does not board, for any reason, the passenger's bags must be removed. (After the bombing of Pan Am Flight 103 over Lockerbie, Scotland, investigators learned that the killers had gotten the bomb onto the plane by checking luggage [actually, a large radio] containing explosives but not boarding the plane.) Third, CAPS selects a certain number of passengers for bag matching or explosive detection at random. (The FAA will not disclose the percentage of selections made randomly.) These passengers could be anyone, even the airline's premium frequent travelers paying full first-class fares. This has helped to reeducate the airline workforce. In James Padgett's words, "They see enough little old ladies selected every day" that they know not everyone selected is bad. The message is clear: draw no conclusion from who is selected. These folks could be anyone—even our best, highest-paying customers—so treat them with care.[45]

The results of these changes have been striking: according to both Arab American groups and the FAA, complaints about these types of encounters in American airports have fallen drastically since CAPS was put into place.

Chapter Seven

MEETING THE CHALLENGE OF RACIAL PROFILING

Racial profiling doesn't work as a crime-fighting tactic. Focusing on minorities does not, as many believe, give police better odds of apprehending criminals in possession of drugs or guns. And taken together, the individual and societal costs of profiling based on race or ethnic appearance threaten to destroy the legitimacy of policing and the law.

Fortunately, there are alternatives—successful ways of fighting crime—that do not rely on racial and ethnic bias. These alternatives demand a different view of policing, and a different view of crime prevention and the role of police officers, but the results can be substantial: effective policing, improved race relations, and restored faith in the fairness and integrity of the criminal justice system.

ACCOUNTABILITY-BASED POLICING

In a twenty-five-year career in law enforcement, Charles Moose has served as chief in two very different police departments. He began his career as a patrol officer in Portland, Oregon, a fast-growing western city that combines blue-collar industry with a burgeoning high-tech sector. Moose rose through the ranks while earning a Ph.D. He became chief in Portland in 1993 and spent six years in the job, earning praise and national recognition as a tough, innovative, and forward-thinking public servant. In 1999, Moose left Portland to become chief of police in Montgomery County, Maryland. Montgomery County lies just north of Washington, D.C., and combines urban areas with suburban development and a diminishing number of rural tracts. His officers have the main patrol responsibilities in the entire county, covering everything from wealthy bedroom communities like Potomac, where many of Washington's elite make their homes, to substantial pockets of chronic poverty, crime, and social disorder. As different as Montgomery County is from Portland, Moose says that all of modern policing must confront a central issue as it moves into the twenty-first century. That challenge, he says, is not just to confront racial profiling. Rather, it is to remove race from police decision making altogether. What Moose calls "race-based policing," which includes racial profiling, must go. He says that police departments and their leaders need to make up their minds that they will root race out of policing. To the extent that using race has been "thought of as a viable method to catch the bad guys," Moose says, this thinking must change. Instead, he says, police "need to just focus on behavior." [1]

Moose is right. If policing is to improve and progress—to do a better job of crime fighting while treating all citizens with respect and dignity—police departments must confront racial profiling. One way to remove race from routine police decision making is to adopt what we might call accountability-based policing—a new set of principles and strategies to guide police departments away from profiling and toward a model that requires and assures greater public accountability for police behavior and for the actions of police departments. Accountability-based policing would require accountability not just of line patrol officers, but of all supervisory and command personnel for the conduct of their subordinates, in order to insure that *all* levels of the police structure are part of the adoption of these principles and strategies. The specific reforms involved are not new, and many are being used in the field right now with good results. Accountability-based policing pulls these methods together, with an eye toward rooting out the poison of race and racial profiling, producing sharper, more efficient and effective policing, and treating all citizens with respect and compassion. To accomplish these goals, accountability-based policing employs five basic precepts.

One: Recognize and Count All Costs

Racial profiling and high-discretion police tactics impose substantial costs on innocent citizens of color, who as a result must bear the burden of public humiliation and personal degradation at a level unimaginable to whites. Racial profiling burdens the legal system and also distorts the social world around us—for example, reinforcing segregation and alienating police from the communities they serve. Perhaps most telling of all, African American and Latino parents are forced to counsel their children on how to act when stopped by the police, and end up unintentionally passing distrust of police to the next generation.

Alone and collectively, these injuries constitute a cost to this method of doing police work. Yet these costs are routinely ignored. Police departments do not pay these costs directly, and most act as if they simply do not exist. Many of the costs of enforcing the law with profiles and high-discretion police tactics are hidden, and most are *external* to the police; they are borne by those whose neighborhoods get patrolled in this way or who experience multiple vehicle stops on the roadways. These costs do not translate well into dollars and cents, and they are difficult to compare to more tangible things, such as the number of arrests made or the quantity of contraband seized.

But even if the police do not pay in the short term, the longer-term costs may still end up on their bill—for example, in the form of accumulating cynicism about police and courts. That is why these costs cannot be ignored. All of the costs of our law enforcement tactics and efforts—not just those paid directly by the police—must be counted as a real part of the expense of the tactics and strategies we employ.

Two: Understand That Public Perception Matters

Police culture faces inward. Officers can become quite insular in their thinking and attitudes. Officers find themselves regularly exposed to deviant behavior of many kinds, and their job is to suppress it. The result is a world in which the day-to-day experience is so different from that of almost any other citizen that officers feel both naturally isolated from ordinary people and drawn to each other as kindred souls. The only ones who can understand the reality police officers face, they often think, are other police officers. Most citizens, they may think, simply have no idea of the difficulties officers face day to day. And because of this, they may also come to believe that what the public thinks concerning how they do their jobs does not matter.

While this attitude may be understandable, it can only impede efforts to make progress on racial profiling and a host of other issues concerning policing. Public perception of what police do—whether they act fairly or are biased, whether they perform their duties in a respectful way or instead seem concerned only with bending citizens to their will—can have a substantial impact on law enforcement.

Effective policing requires the public's understanding and goodwill. Otherwise, police testimony will be discounted, juries will nullify, and citizens will decline to cooperate with police in other ways large and small. Citizen opinion can affect the resources police have—everything from the condition and sophistication of their equipment to departmental manpower—in the political arena. Didi Nelson, a Georgia sheriff's deputy who now does police training, tells officers that everything they do, every encounter they have with citizens, has the potential to have an impact on police department budgets and resources. "People vote," she says, speaking of those who have been stopped, intimidated, or mistreated. "People who have been treated badly by the police won't vote for a pro-law-enforcement candidate."[2]

Public perception is very real—a vital part of the environment in which police officers work and in which police policy, strategy, and tactics prove either effective or weak. For all of these reasons, the law enforcement community ignores public perception at its peril.

Three: Focus on Behavior

Much of what we think of as racial profiling comes from attitudes and beliefs people hold about certain racial or ethnic groups. Sometimes we think of these attitudes as stereotypes; others might describe them as beliefs stemming from life's experiences or as prejudice. To the extent that stereotypical beliefs about black and brown criminality develop early in life, efforts to change them will require us to reach far down into family life, relationships, and education. If these beliefs come from the constant bombardment of media images all Americans encounter, changing them will require us to deal with profound questions about mass culture. And, perhaps most discouraging of all, to the extent that these attitudes are deeply ingrained in the population as a whole, changing them will take time.

Yet while changing *attitudes* is surely both appropriate and important, it is not, strictly speaking, absolutely necessary—providing that we decide in no uncertain terms to change *behavior*. It is the police officer's *behavior* that makes an impact on the citizen's experience with law enforcement—for good or for ill. It is the police's officer's *behavior* that we deal with when we ask whether minorities are stopped and frisked more than whites and whether blacks and Latinos are treated rudely more often than whites. Officer *behavior* influences not only public perception, but the success of police efforts to cut crime. And unlike attitudes, which may change only very slowly, behavior is easier to change and can be changed relatively quickly. Changing police behavior takes several steps, beginning with the determination at the leadership level that behavior *will* be changed in particular ways. The desired changes—the new behaviors that superiors want and expect to replace old ones—must then be clearly explained to line officers and field supervisors themselves, those whose behavior leaders want to change. There must then be a corresponding change in incentive structures. If the organization wants different behavior it must set up a structure to reward this behavior when it appears. At the same time, leaders must remove incentives that existed in the past for other behaviors that are now no longer desired, and they must add sanctions for behavior they want to discourage. When these steps are followed, police officers—perhaps not all, but most—will do the rational thing: they will change their behavior to respond to the incentives and disincentives in their environment. And once behavior changes, problems will begin to recede. Changes in attitudes may even follow. But changes in behavior, even without changes in attitudes, can nevertheless produce concrete results.

Four: Do What Works

The more police officers, chiefs, and administrators one meets, the more one realizes that police are largely practical and pragmatic people. Ideas are great, as long as they work. Theories can help, as long as they translate into something that gets the job done.

That is why implementing accountability-based policing requires drawing on strategies that have already been proved. Every one of the tools discussed here is something that can be done, and has been done, by police departments. This not only makes the analysis and proposals here more solid and sound but should also give anyone interested in taking on the issue of racial profiling real confidence that progress can be made. If some departments are already using these tools successfully, others can adopt them, adapt them to their own contexts, and succeed with them.

Five: Set Realistic Goals

There are many who will throw up their hands at the prospect of any reform designed to confront racial profiling. There is just no real, practical way, they will say, to eliminate race from police decision making. But the task is not the *absolute elimination* of racial profiling and the use of race in police decision making—these cannot be eliminated any more than we can entirely eliminate all misuse of deadly force or all police corruption. Rather, a realistic goal is to curtail these practices—first to bring them under control, then to make them uncommon, and eventually to have them become rare exceptions to the general rule. Our aim should be to have the officer who uses race as the basis for decisions about whom to stop, frisk, and search be perceived by his or her fellow officers as an aberration.

STRATEGIES

The following are specific strategies designed to implement accountability-based policing. They reflect the five precepts described above—they take all costs into account, consider public perception, focus on behavior, have been proved effective, and have realistic goals. They are drawn from police departments across the country. No one department employed all of them, though some have made use of several in pursuit of other goals. A common theme among them is bringing police and communities together instead of continuing the largely racial and ethnic divisions we see so often. Best of all, there is nothing radical about the changes it would take to put these strategies in place. Most of these ideas have become accepted within policing, even if they have been praised more often than they have been implemented. But by bringing them together, and applying them specifically to curtailing racial profiling and implementing accountability-based policing, we can advance law enforcement in a profound way, confronting racial issues even as we create the conditions for more effective crime fighting.

Enacting Departmental Policies About the Appropriate Use of Race in Law Enforcement

Although we cannot and would not want to order police officers to entirely ignore color or other racial or ethnic characteristics, we can require that these characteristics be considered as factors only in strictly limited ways. It does make sense to use racial or ethnic characteristics in enforcement, but only in one context: *cases in which race or ethnic characteristics describe actual suspects.* When we have a description of one or a group of suspected perpetrators, race or ethnic group is clearly relevant— just as relevant as height or weight. Skin color can be just as important an identifier of particular individuals as eye color, and considerably more useful, since it can be observed so much more easily. In this situation, a description of the suspect's skin color serves not as a predictor of criminality, but as an identifying physical attribute that can be used, in conjunction with others, to determine whether a person observed might be someone wanted by the police as a suspect in an actual crime. Take, for example, what police sometimes refer to as a "BOLO" stop—a stop of a pedestrian or driver because he or she resembled someone described in a "be on the lookout" police broadcast that included a physical description. There is absolutely no reason to prohibit this; race serves only to identify a particular person, along with the person's other physical characteristics. And there is every reason to want to encourage accuracy and detail in these descriptions. The more specific they are, the more likely they are to help officers find and identify the right suspects and help them avoid accosting the wrong ones.

What must *not* be allowed is using race or ethnic appearance, alone or in combination with other factors, to stop a particular person based on a *prediction* that he or she is more likely to be involved in crime. This would not interfere with any legitimate and effective law enforcement activity; since using race as a predictor doesn't help fight crime, law enforcement could use its available resources to greater effect instead of spending them on useless racial profiling. There would be more police time and energy to go around for more effective enforcement and crime prevention after the elimination of wasteful and harmful profile stops.

Using race appropriately in law enforcement decision making

should affect not only whom police stop but also what happens *after* the stop. Which drivers do police question about things having nothing to do with the vehicle infraction alleged? Do they ask *all* drivers, "Where are you going? Where did you come from? Do you have any drugs or guns in your car?" Or do they ask these questions *only* of minority drivers? Is everyone asked for consent to search their cars and possessions or just blacks and Hispanics? Do officers frisk the pedestrians they stop on reasonable suspicion under *Terry* v. *Ohio* at roughly the same rates in similar minority and nonminority neighborhoods, or do they use this tool more often against people of color, as we have seen in the New York attorney general's study of the NYPD's stop-and-frisk practices?

Language from the New Jersey State Police consent decree with the United States Department of Justice offers a good model of a policy designed to limit the use of race or ethnicity in police decision making:

> Except in the "suspect-specific" ("be on the lookout," or "BOLO") situation . . . , state troopers shall continue to be prohibited from considering in any fashion and to any degree the race or national or ethnic origin of civilian drivers or passengers in deciding which vehicles to subject to any motor vehicle stop and in deciding upon the scope or substance of any enforcement action or procedure in connection with or during the course of a motor vehicle stop. Where state troopers are seeking to detain, apprehend, or otherwise be on the lookout for one or more specific suspects who have been identified or described in part by race or national or ethnic origin, state troopers may rely in part on race or national or ethnic origin in determining whether reasonable suspicion exists that a given individual is the person being sought.[3]

New Jersey State Police policy now reflects this part of the consent decree.[4]

The Police Executives Research Forum (PERF), a nonprofit

group that helps police chiefs and administrators keep up with important research in the criminal justice arena and formulate goals and policies in their departments, has drafted a model policy for its members. According to Research Director Lorie Fridell, PERF's model policy on "racially biased policing" requires officers to enforce the law based only on strict Fourth Amendment standards and not on race. Officers, the policy says, "shall not consider race/ethnicity in establishing either reasonable suspicion or probable cause, or in making requests for consent to search. The policy then goes on to describe a limited exception:

> Officers may take into account the reported race or ethnicity of a specific suspect or suspects based on trustworthy, locally relevant information that links a person or persons of a specific race/ethnicity to a particular unlawful incident(s). Race/ethnicity can never be used as the sole basis for probable cause as reasonable suspicion. Except as provided [here], race/ethnicity shall not be motivating factors in making law enforcement decisions.[5]

These policies state, clearly and precisely, that police officers can use race or ethnicity only as part of the *physical* description of particular suspects and for no other purpose. With this type of policy in place, every member of the department would understand that police conduct that uses race as a proxy for criminal offending does not comply with departmental standards. Note also that the policies are not limited to stops; race also cannot be the basis for anything that comes after the stop, such as deciding who is detained, questioned, and asked for consent to search. And because violation of departmental standards can be the basis for discipline and sanctions, and at the very least might prevent a person from advancing or succeeding on a long-term basis in the department, officers will know that this conduct is unacceptable.

Enact Departmental Policies Limiting Police Discretion

Research on policing during the last forty years has largely centered on police discretion and the effectiveness of various efforts to limit it. During that same period, regulation of the criminal justice system has come mostly from the courts. This began with the Warren Court and its focus in the late 1950s and early 1960s on remedying long-standing racial injustices in law enforcement, just as it sought to do with racial inequities in such other areas as voting, housing, and education. In these early years, the courts were virtually the only way to redress racial discrimination in the justice system, and the Warren Court proved hospitable to these arguments in a way that neither legislatures nor any other governmental bodies had. Thus the Supreme Court became the leading (if not the only) institution changing criminal law in ways concerned with racial justice. As the composition of the Supreme Court changed—slowly in the 1970s, and then more rapidly and drastically in the 1980s—the Court still retained the central decision-making role in questions on police procedure, but it no longer seemed much concerned with racial inequity in law enforcement. Instead, the Justices began an enlargement of police discretion to an almost unimaginably wide degree. Even in cases in which the Court retained limits on police methods set by the Warren Court, these new cases seemed to have devices built right into them to allow police to make constitutional end runs around these limits. For example, the Court decided in 1996 in the *Whren* case that the police did indeed need probable cause to stop drivers, but that any traffic offense would serve for that purpose. Since no driver could go even a short distance without violating *some* aspect of the traffic law, the upshot was a rule that, effectively, imposed no limits at all.

But just because police departments *can* legally use a particular tactic—that is, because the Supreme Court allows officers to use a particular method—does not mean that police departments *should* use it. Put another way, just because the Supreme Court blesses a particular tactic does not make it effective, smart, or morally right. Instead of simply using all the discretion the Court gives police, we need to determine when it makes sense to use police discretion.

There are several good models that suggest a solution to this problem. On the subject of consent searches, which the Supreme Court allows police to do without any evidence at all of a crime, the consent decree between the New Jersey State Police and the U.S. Department of Justice is again a good place to start. The consent decree reads, in pertinent part,

> In order to help ensure that state troopers use their authority to conduct consensual motor vehicle searches in a nondiscriminatory manner, the State Police shall continue to require: that state troopers may request consent to search a motor vehicle only where troopers can articulate a reasonable suspicion that a search would reveal evidence of a crime; that every consent search of a vehicle be based on written consent of the driver or other person authorized to give consent which precedes the search; that the scope of a consent search be limited to the scope of the consent that is given by the driver or other person authorized to give consent; that the driver or other person authorized to give consent has the right to be present during a consent search at a location consistent with the safety of both the state trooper and the motor vehicle occupants, which right can only be waived after the driver or other person authorized to give consent is advised of such right; that the driver or other person authorized to give consent who has granted written consent may orally withdraw that consent at any time during the search without giving a reason; and that state troopers immediately must stop a consent search of a vehicle if and when consent is withdrawn (except that a search may continue if permitted on some non-consensual basis).[6]

The Supreme Court tells us that police can ask for consent to search under any circumstances—whether or not they have some reason to be suspicious; officers have unlimited discretion to use this tool. But the New Jersey consent decree changes this by explicitly limiting and channeling how officers may use this discretion. They may still ask for consent to search, but only when they have a reasonable, articulable basis for suspicion of the occupants of the vehicle. The consent must be in writing, and the driver or owner of the vehicle may watch the search, as long as this does not endanger anyone's safety.

Other police departments have also adopted policies that limit their officers to doing less than what the Supreme Court would permit. For example, the Michigan State Police have also formulated a policy on consent searches that requires officers to have some articulable reason before they can ask drivers for consent to search. That policy, set out in an August 2, 1999, memorandum from the deputy director of the force's Uniform Services Bureau, reads as follows:

> While the courts have recognized [the consent search] exception to the search warrant requirement for many years, this department is committed to a higher standard which precludes the use of this exception without an articulable reason. . . . [O]fficers shall not use consent searches indiscriminately without regard to the totality of the circumstances. . . . [O]fficers are reminded that it is not appropriate to request a consent to search during every traffic stop or other public contact. The officer must weigh the reasons for the search against the intrusiveness upon the citizen. Officers may request a consent to search from an individual only where there is an articulable reason for this course of action to be pursued, developed through the officer's observations and questioning.[7]

The state police explained this policy in a recent departmental report on traffic enforcement practices. "Overly aggressive" policing during traffic stops, the report says, does not necessarily make for good law enforcement and may engender bitterness toward police officers. Therefore, based on departmental policy, a consent search may only be requested from an individual when there is an articulable reason for this course of action to be pursued and developed through the officer's observations and questioning. The officer is also required to consider the totality of the circumstances including such factors as the reason for the search balanced with the intrusiveness on the citizen. It is against departmental policy to consider a consent search during every traffic stop.[8]

The Michigan State Police is only one of many of the law enforcement agencies in the state. But in one of the most interesting demonstrations of the influence police policy can have, the state police consent search policy has been adopted not just by other police agencies but by actors in another part of the criminal justice system: prosecutors. Prosecutors have control over which cases they will pursue in court—which ones they will charge, bring to the grand jury, or throw out. If prosecutors have a policy that requires police to have reasonable suspicion before they can ask for consent to a vehicle search, this means in effect that they will not prosecute cases in which police officers have violated the policy. In other words, though both the U.S. Supreme Court and their own police departments may permit consent searches without an articulable suspicion, prosecutors will still drop these cases. This would discourage police from asking for consent without articulable suspicion, even if this is otherwise allowed, since their enforcement efforts will be effectively wasted if they do not comply with the prosecutor's policy.

Brian Mackie, the elected prosecutor of Washtenaw County, Michigan, a jurisdiction west of Detroit, has adopted just such a policy.[9] Washtenaw County brings Mackie and his prosecutors a mix of cases, everything from homicides to the full range of misdemeanors one sees everywhere. Mackie and the prosecutors who work for him have had to take stands in a number of cases to enforce the policy by refusing to pursue cases in which consent searches would have been allowed by U.S. Supreme Court law.

He says that although the policy sometimes angers police officers, the number of problem searches he has had to deal with has dropped off as word that the policy must be followed has gotten out. "What percentage of minorities are asked to consent to a search as opposed to majority white drivers?" Mackie asks. "I think it's a tremendous cause of friction with some minority communities that are constantly asked, 'May I look in your vehicle? Do you have anything in your vehicle you shouldn't have?' " It is, of course, possible that refusing to pursue cases in which police officers have done what the Supreme Court allows them to do may carry a political price. If that happens, Mackie says, he's ready to take the heat. As an accountable elected official, he says, he "can live with that kind of criticism," which has included opposition to his reelection from police unions and from opposing candidates who charge that, unlike Mackie, they will back up the police a hundred percent of the time. But Mackie recognizes that high-discretion law enforcement has begun to generate increasingly negative attitudes toward police, and using these tactics has begun to hurt the integrity and credibility not just of the police but of all institutions in the criminal justice system, including his own office. In essence, Mackie is exercising his own discretion—prosecutorial discretion—to limit the discretion exercised by police officers.[10] At the beginning of 2000, the Prosecuting Attorneys Association of Michigan, a statewide professional organization that represents prosecutors all over the state on a variety of legislative, administrative, and policy issues before the state government, decided to take the same position as Brian Mackie, and they unanimously voted to adopt a policy on consent searches that required articulable suspicion.[11]

Consent searches are just one part of the picture of high-discretion police tactics that go along with profiling. As with the use of race, we should look for ways to limit and channel discretion not just in the stop itself but in all aspects of the encounter between police and citizens that follow the stop. A single policy might be designed to cover all parts of routine law enforcement encounters by requiring that any action that follows a traffic stop—questioning, removing drivers or other occupants from vehicles, asking for consent to search, or anything else—must be based on reasonable suspicion of involvement in crime. Such a policy might be worded as follows:

> Traffic stops are an integral part of the duty of police officers to insure the safety of the public. Increased, active traffic enforcement will bring down the number of motor vehicle accidents, and with it the number of deaths and injuries on the road. Nevertheless, any attempt to use traffic enforcement as a pretext for other law enforcement purposes must be strictly limited because of the danger that pretext stops pose to effective law enforcement, the public's perception of the integrity of the criminal justice system, and the possibility that pretext-based law enforcement may be misused in a biased fashion. Accordingly, officers conducting a traffic stop are limited to performing functions related to traffic enforcement, such as requesting driver's license, registration, and other documents, discussing the alleged violation, and the like. Any other police conduct—detention for any period beyond what is necessary to resolve and document the traffic charge, inquiries concerning destination or place of origin, questions concerning what the driver has in the car, or requests for consent to search—must be based upon a reasonable articulable suspicion of involvement in criminal activity. Absent such a fact-based suspicion based on the behavior of the particular individual involved, nothing other than traffic-enforcement activity may take place.

Any policy like this must also include an obligation to make an official report or record of the encounter articulating the basis for actions beyond the stop and traffic enforcement itself. Requiring a written report that articulates the basis for the officer's actions also serves to limit and channel discretion. When he became commissioner of the Philadelphia Police Department, John Timoney, a former assistant chief in New York under William

Bratton, spent some time reviewing the reports his officers filed after encounters with citizens.[12] Timoney found that these reports, known in the department as "Form 48," usually told him very little, and often told him nothing. They were completely open-ended; officers could write as much or as little as they wanted, and there was no requirement that these reports show justification for what the officer had done. Timoney promptly changed this. He ordered a complete redesign of Form 48 to include enough detail to show whether the facts legally justified what the officer did. "We could have made it pages and pages, but we didn't. No one would have filled it out," Timoney explained. The idea, he said, was to come up with a form just long enough so that officers would fill it out with sufficient detail. Timoney had two goals in doing this. First, he wanted the important information the form could give him and his command staff about patterns of enforcement action. But second, and just as important, Timoney knew that the requirement that the form be filled out would make police officers think twice before making a stop—that is, it would force them to *self-limit* their use of their discretion. If they knew they were going to be held accountable for what they did, officers would be less likely to go ahead with a stop, a search, or questioning in marginal cases in which there was little concrete evidence.

Change the Interaction Between Officers and Citizens

Racial profiling has two distinct parts. First, there is the issue of the stop itself—why a particular person or group gets stopped and whether this represents treatment that differs from that received by people from different racial or ethnic groups. The stop may anger people; they may feel anything from perplexed to afraid to fed up when the blue lights of a police car signal them to pull over. But this is not the only event of significance when a traffic stop takes place. At least as important as the stop itself is what happens *after* the stop, how police treat people whom they stop. Speaking to African Americans and Latinos makes clear that it is often these aspects of the interaction that they feel most deeply aggrieved about, not the stop itself. The way events unfold after the stop has everything to do with the perception they carry away from these encounters. While it is true that encounters between police and citizens often begin with some tension and can lead to unpleasant outcomes like traffic citations, these events need not always degenerate into a downward spiral of conflict, confrontation, and mutual contempt. Surely, most police departments have a general policy that officers must treat citizens respectfully, but something more specific to the traffic and pedestrian encounters that so often engender bad feelings seems necessary. It is important that officers control situations in which they deal with citizens; they must carry out their enforcement duties, the results of which can sometimes be unpleasant for the citizens involved and make them angry. But officers can accomplish this with a minimum of conflict. Citizens have begun to demand fair and respectful treatment. Police department policy should require no less of their officers. When even a minority of officers regularly treat the public with contempt, this injures every officer in the department and eats away at all of the efforts we might make to connect police and community in crime-fighting efforts.

In order to change the interaction between police officers and citizens, departmental policy should identify the fair and respectful treatment of citizens as a value of paramount importance—not just generally, but specifically in face-to-face encounters between police officers and drivers and between officers and pedestrians. These are the most common interactions between officers and regular folks, and any feelings of resentment they cause in citizens will linger long and penetrate deep. A model policy to prevent this might read as follows:

> During any encounter between police officers and citizens, including traffic and pedestrian stops, citizens must be treated courteously. This includes addressing citizens as "sir" or "ma'am," using the word "please" with any request, and thanking the citizen when appropriate. Officers must always

identify themselves by name and badge number, and immediately inform the driver or pedestrian why the officer stopped them with enough detail and in language sufficiently clear for a layperson to understand. The officer should be prepared to answer any reasonable question, including the reason for any procedures the officer is engaged in, even if the officer does not think it important. Any detention past the minimum necessary to handle the issue that caused the stop should be minimal, fully explained, and legally justified. Any disturbance of the citizen's vehicle or other property should be minimized, and officers must do whatever is necessary to help citizens put their vehicles and property back as they were before the police encounter, including helping reassemble items and vehicle parts as the citizen may request. Detentions and searches that conclude without the recovery of contraband should be ended with thanks to the citizen an intelligible explanation and an apology for any inconvenience that was caused.

The Police Executive Research Forum's model policy can also supply some guidance.

In an effort to prevent inappropriate perceptions of biased law enforcement, officers shall do the following when conducting pedestrian and vehicle stops:

- Be courteous and professional.
- Introduce him- or herself to the citizen (providing name and agency affiliation), and state the reason for the stop as soon as practical, unless providing this information will compromise officer or public safety. In vehicle stops, the officer shall provide this information before asking the driver for his or her license and registration.
- Ensure that the detention is no longer than necessary to take appropriate action for the known or suspected offense and that the citizen understands the purpose of reasonable delays.

- Answer any questions the citizen may have, including explaining options for traffic citation disposition, if relevant.
- Provide hir or her name and badge number when requested, in writing or on a business card.
- Apologize and/or explain if he or she determines that the reasonable suspicion was unfounded (e.g., after an investigatory stop).[13]

The Prince Georges County, Maryland, police department operates under a policy encompassing many of these ideas. John Farrell became chief of the Prince Georges County Police in 1995.[14] For many years prior to his arrival, the Prince Georges Police Department had had a reputation for brutality, especially with young blacks. Farrell was determined to change this, and he knew that one of the key points of tension involved traffic and other stops of citizens by his officers. At the same time, he wanted to make use of traffic stops as a key ingredient to focus on gun violence in selected target areas. "[M]uch of this had to do with communications issues, police officers on traffic stops dealing with individuals that were confused, became angry, and some of the officers apparently lacked the skills to de-escalate the situation," Farrell said. As a consequence, he put a policy mandating courteous and professional treatment of citizens in place shortly after taking the job, and he mandated extra training. Farrell's solution involved changing the way the interaction between officer and citizen unfolded in each and every stop. When an officer stops someone, he or she must immediately identify him- or herself and tell the driver the reason for the stop. Officers must treat drivers with courtesy and answer their questions politely. When the encounter is over, officers give the driver their business card and a sheet that tells them how they can file a complaint if they want. Farrell is not thinking that citizens will complain. He simply wants them to know they can if they wish. So far, the policy is working well. While the number of stops is up— a direct consequence of the fact that the department is using traffic stops to combat gun violence in hot spots where crime has long festered—the number of complaints from traffic stops has fallen dramatically. With "well over 100,000 traffic stops," Farrell says, "I've not had a handful of complaints" from that program.[15]

A policy mandating respectful treatment of citizens stopped and searched by police may seem like a small, even insignificant, item. It has the ring of a "politeness plan" that a mother might impose on her misbehaving children or of a kind of political correctness soaked in manners. Nothing could be further from the truth. Respectful treatment will go a long way toward helping citizens accept what law enforcement officers must sometimes do in the course of their very difficult jobs. Understanding treatment will create understanding. Talking to people as if they mean something and deserve to get the answers to the questions they ask will build bridges between the police and the people they serve. At the very least, it will keep the wounds sometimes caused by profiling from getting larger, more ugly, and more likely to cause further problems. It takes only one incident to spark a confrontation, community outrage, or a crisis; many of the major race riots of the 1960s began with a traffic stop that escalated into violence.[16] Building connections comes slowly, one police-citizen encounter at a time. But if we fail to insist on fair, even-handed, and respectful treatment for all of our citizens, we risk further alienating everyone who encounters a police officer.

Change the Incentive Structures Within Police Departments

In any institution that employs people, there are incentive structures: the employer rewards certain behaviors that benefit the institution and may also create disincentives for behavior the employer wants to discourage. Like other employers, police departments also have incentive systems. Pay raises, commendations, promotions, and favored assignments depend on doing what the department's incentive structure encourages. In the past, the incentive structures within many police departments often focused on traditional tasks built around calls for service. This was, after all, the model most departments were built on.

More officers in cars on the street, with lower response times, was supposed to mean better law enforcement. Officers reaped rewards in the same proportion that they gave tickets, made stops, and arrested people. The more arrests an officer made, the better that officer was considered to be.

There is nothing inherently wrong with an incentive structure like this, but its value depends on what kind of policing we want. The incentive structure not only reflects the type of law enforcement a police department does; it also reinforces it and shapes it, by advancing within the ranks those who behave in the ways that are rewarded. The result should not surprise anyone. In a police department that gives credit to officers based on the number of traffic stops made, officers will make a lot of traffic stops. If the department rewards proactive, gung-ho policing that relies on aggressiveness and brawn to catch criminals, rather than relying on brains to prevent crime from occurring, that is the type of department that will emerge.

The debate over racial profiling has given us an object lesson in how this works. When we tell officers to use a group of characteristics—a profile—to spot potential drug couriers, and then give them intelligence reports that say that the dealers and couriers come from particular racial and ethnic minority groups, we need only stand aside and wait until racial profiling begins to happen. When we tell officers this "works" as a way to find the big drug shipments, they will act accordingly. When we tell them that our top priority is the war on drugs and then we make those officers who find large shipments of narcotics on the highway Officers of the Year, others in the department will follow. When we make those same officers the head of drug-interdiction units, canine team leaders, and anticrime squad members, the message is clear.

To change police behavior, we must change the incentive structures to which officers respond. If we want a police department that relies on smarts to head off crime, we have to reward examples of that type of behavior. If we want officers who work with the community, building confidence and solving problems in conjunction with community members so crime does not happen, we must reward that behavior. If we want drug interdiction to concentrate on large narcotics shipments learned about through intelligence gathering instead of random stopping of certain racial and ethnic groups, that behavior must be rewarded. And, along with these rewards, the behaviors we want to discourage must be punished, through denial of the very things officers want and through sanctions and discipline.

In San Diego, which has used community policing and problem-oriented policing intensively for more than ten years, the entire incentive structure has undergone a drastic change. Under former chief Jerry Sanders, the department moved from a classic response-to-calls-for-service system to one in which officers are rewarded based on the community policing work they do and its effectiveness in reducing crime. "The old system was two tickets and two FI's [field interrogations] and an arrest per shift," says Steve Creighton, a twenty-eight-year veteran of the force in San Diego and now an assistant chief. Creighton says that any ambitious young officer knew what he or she should do: check off those boxes every time and handle radio calls.

Things have changed markedly in San Diego in the last decade, with its emphasis on neighborhood policing and problem solving. The department encourages officers to think of themselves as problem-solving entrepreneurs—people looking for long-term solutions instead of such short-term fixes as arrests and clearing troublesome people off corners. And it rewards them for it by advancing them when they show themselves to be effective problem solvers, whether this means getting abandoned cars towed out of a neighborhood, having a crack house demolished, or refurbishing a city park so kids have a place to go. Creighton says the incentives work, but change is slow. Real change, he says, will come only after "a generation" of police officers have been trained and "raised" under the new structure, to the point that "problem solving becomes the standard" and rewards aren't as necessary.[17] In Stamford, Connecticut, Chief Dean Esserman, who is deeply committed to community policing, has also changed his department's incentive structure.[18] The department's highest praise and accolades go not only to those who lock up dangerous criminals but also to those officers who figure out ways to solve problems in cooperation with community residents. And even more important, Esserman says, is structuring officers' tasks so that the real reward comes from the contact officers have with the community itself. His goal, he says, is "creating an environment where there is a sense of momentum and a sense of change and where everyone's starting to feel, 'Wow, I'm part of it, I'm part of the change.' " This, he says, motivates officers to come to him with creative ideas oriented toward crime fighting. The results of Esserman's efforts have surprised even his most ardent backers: in 1999, his department tripled the decline in crime seen in New York—without, Esserman says, alienating the communities in his city.

Not all examples of changes in incentive structure involve community policing. When John Timoney became the commissioner of Philadelphia's police department, he learned that officers got credit for the number of traffic stops they made, whatever the outcome—citation or warning, release or arrest. Timoney thought the practice was nothing short of silly and guaranteed to produce a surplus of often-irritating and mostly meaningless traffic stops. He changed the department's policy to say that it was arrests and citations that counted, not just raw numbers of stops. Timoney remembers going to a roll call to talk to officers about this change. "[An officer] says, 'You mean we're not getting credit for when we stop people anymore?' Timoney explained that he wanted different behavior from the officer and her colleagues, and the new policy was meant to see that he got it.

If we no longer want policing with profiles and high-discretion tactics, we must remove the incentives to engage in this behavior and replace them with incentives for the type of enforcement we prefer. It may not be as easy as it sounds, because the incentive structure in any police department is tied very deeply to the department's history and ethic—the type of force it is and has been and the type of people in it. But unless we undertake this change, we can make no other progress.

Training

The room is full of police officers—more than a hundred of them of all ranks.[19] They're listening and watching as a man and a woman talk to them about one of the most taboo subjects in America—race. And the man and the woman leave no doubt that they think racial profiling is the point where race and policing intersect. The officers sit quietly, but tension, not boredom, fills the air. Body language communicates that some officers just do not want to be here.

The man speaking could be a typical police officer himself: white, middle aged, well but not fancily dressed in a conservative suit, neatly trimmed mustache. A bit of gray streaks both the mustache and the sandy blond hair. He'd fit right in in any police station in any city in the country, though his southern accent gives his origins away. "Tell me," he says to the class, "what comes to your mind when I ask you to envision the face of crime? What do you think is the typical image of a criminal?"

The class says nothing. A shifting around in the chairs in the middle rows betrays some discomfort as the silence stretches on. Two men about a third of the way back look at each other discreetly, mouthing three short words to each other behind their hands. Finally, a voice from the back of the room says those same three words, barely loud enough to be heard in the front of the room: "Young black male." The man nods his head, acknowledging what most in the room were apparently thinking. The woman, also white and southern, with brown hair past her shoulders and the bearing of a person comfortable around police officers, has been watching the class and listening carefully the whole time. "Sure," she says, "isn't that what we see all the time on TV? Isn't that what we're all used to thinking?"

Then the man asks a different question. "Suppose you're out on patrol and you spot a sixteen-year-old white kid driving along in a fancy, brand-new BMW. What's your first thought?" This time the class seems more willing to answer the question. "Spoiled brat," says one voice. "Rich parents," says another. A third voice says, "A present from his daddy." The man asks another question. "Now let me ask you. Same fancy car, but the kid is black. What's your immediate reaction?" Again there is silence, but this time it doesn't last long. "Stolen car," one officer says. "Whose car is it?" asks another. "Drug dealer," several officers sing out, almost simultaneously.

The man and the woman stop talking and look at each other, then at the class. "This is the kind of thing we're talking about," the man says. "You may not even realize it or think that you're doing it, but race is there. And you need to start being aware that it is."

The man and the woman, Tom Hayes and Didi Nelson, both come from Georgia and have spent their careers firmly on the law enforcement side of the spectrum. For Nelson, a sworn sheriff's deputy in Georgia for fourteen years, law enforcement runs in her family. Her father recently retired after a long career as a deputy, and her brother has been on the force for more than twenty years. She has a ready smile and a friendly way with people that would never clue a stranger in to the fact that she spent a significant number of years tracking down fugitives. Hayes, an attorney, is a career prosecutor who has put in years convicting criminals in Atlanta. He comes across as quiet, unassuming, and serious about his business without taking himself too seriously. For the past two years, Nelson and Hayes have spent considerable time traveling the country training law enforcement personnel about racial profiling as part of an ongoing effort by Richard Deane, the U.S. attorney in Atlanta, to bring police the training they need on the subject. In some ways, it is hard to imagine two people less likely to do law enforcement training about race issues than these two white southerners. Yet they have both become convinced that law enforcement must confront the issue of racial profiling head-on and in the most direct way possible, without burying its head in the sand. Indeed, Nelson and Hayes say, there is simply no other way to handle the issue of race and criminal justice.

Most law enforcement agencies have administered training in racial and cultural issues for some years. Variously referred to as diversity training or cultural awareness or sensitivity training, in some departments this training is minimal and quite general, but in other departments it is emphasized. In such cases, the aim is to bring trainees to a level of "cultural competence"—that is, a level of awareness that will enable officers to deal with the many different racial and ethnic groups that they might encounter in the course of their jobs. Commander Jerry Clayton, a veteran of the Washtenaw County, Michigan, Sheriff's Department, has done much of this training.[20] He explains cultural competence for police officers as part of the vital set of skills he wants his officers to have when they deal with the public on a daily basis. Clayton says that he and his superiors knew that there were some cultural considerations that had to be taken into account as part of their comprehensive effort to address profiling and related issues of race.

Cultural competence and diversity training surely serve as an important piece of the puzzle in helping officers deal with citizens of different backgrounds as part of their daily routine. It may also help them understand how race can creep into police decision making in ways such as racial profiling. But this type of general training in cultural awareness alone is not enough to address profiling because officers see this practice as an enforcement issue rather than a racial one. For this reason, profiling must be confronted directly—not just as part of racial and cultural awareness, but as an issue of whether it is morally right and/or the best way to fight crime. This approach is what makes the training that Nelson and Hayes do unique. It not only addresses race but also attempts to show police officers how race may play a subtle and insidious role in their actions, and how in moving away from profiling they can become better as crime fighters. Only this kind of direct discussion will enable law enforcement to see what they have at stake in coming to terms with profiling.

Nelson and Hayes deliberately focus their training away from the legalities of profiling. "Our experience is that officers really want to do the right thing, that they're in law enforcement to do good," Nelson says. She knows that most police officers, like her, got into policing to help people. Most law enforcement training, she says, concentrates on "what is legally allowable," but she feels that, at least on this issue, that particular approach obsures the underlying flaw: "You can do something that's legal but it's not necessarily right." So Nelson and Hayes focus explicitly on the "moral and ethical problem" of racial profiling. Others who do training for police officers on racial profiling address other aspects of the issue. Rose Ochi, who headed the U.S. Justice Department's Community Relations Service under the Clinton administration, says that her agency's trainers emphasize officer safety.[21] Failing to come to grips with racial profiling, Ochi says, causes community antagonism and makes every encounter officers have with members of the public more difficult, and potentially more dangerous. Other agencies, including the Ohio Highway Patrol and the Columbus, Ohio, Police Department, have designed their own materials and training regarding racial profiling.

Nelson and Hayes admit that they do not know how effective their training is. No one will see any difference except over the long term, and they won't be able to know what causes any changes in police behavior that do happen. They candidly admit that they do not always get a friendly reception, though negative experiences have been the exception. Most officers in their classes give them a hearing, and many become engaged in the debate in class. But however police officers receive their efforts, what they are doing is groundbreaking and should be both strengthened and made widespread. African American, Latino, and other minority officers might be well positioned to help their brother and sister officers understand the impact of racial profiling. Think back to the story of U.S. Attorney Saul Green's statement at the first U.S. Department of Justice meeting on profiling, discussed in chapter 5. The story he told that day of explaining to his son how to conduct himself when police inevitably stopped him had a huge impact on the police officials assembled. No doubt this was because Green was not only an African American but a high-ranking member of the law enforcement establishment. Police officials could not dismiss his statement as the complaint of a disgruntled citizen who felt wronged by police. He was one of them. Green's courage teaches the valuable lesson that those in law enforcement will listen more readily to someone they perceive as one of their own. If possible, any training on racial profiling and on the use of race in law enforcement decision making should include personal stories and testimonies from fellow officers—officers the class members will automatically respect and accept. The impact of profiling as explained by a fellow officer will be harder to explain away and more likely to generate empathy and serious thought. Some minority officers would surely be willing to speak to this issue, even if others would hesitate, seeing a risk to their careers. Clearly, they should not be required to shoulder the responsibility.

But perhaps this difficulty could be overcome by involving organizations of minority police officers instead of just individuals. The New York organization 100 Blacks in Law Enforcement already does outreach and training for teens on how to respond to police stops. They would be well positioned to do parallel teaching for their police colleagues. Cecil Thomas, a retired veteran of the police force in Cincinnati and the former leader of Cincinnati's Black Sentinels police organization, says that the members of the Sentinels would value the chance to teach officers in the Cincinnati Police Department or in other agencies what profiling is like from firsthand experience.[22] Thomas, now director of Cincinnati's Human Relations Commission, says that black and Latino officers understand the stakes in the discussion of profiling and in getting police officers to come to grips with the problem. Ida Gillis, president of the National Organization of Black Law Enforcement Executives (NOBLE), vigorously seconds Thomas.[23] NOBLE has been running training and presenting programs on racial profiling for police and other types of audiences since the issue first emerged. NOBLE's former executive director, Bob Stewart, became one of the most respected authorities on the issue and Captain Ron Davis of the Oakland, California, Police Deparment has written excellent training materials for NOBLE on what he calls bias-based policing. The organization has taken a leadership role in these efforts, whether in the form of presenting the training itself, supplying individuals to talk about their personal experiences, or training for trainers. Organizations for Latino and Asian police officers have become part of the effort, too.

As we look to the future, we may be able to offer police officers even more advanced methods of training on race and racial profiling. Bob Wasserman, a former police officer and chief and a high-ranking administrator at police departments in a number of major cities, offers a vision for how this might work.[24] Wasserman, who now heads a consulting company in Rockville, Maryland, called PSComm, says the key may be to use self-training methods that can give officers solid, immediate feedback on whether or not biases play a role in whom they decide to stop and how they treat people, even when those biases are hidden or are very subtle. Wasserman envisions doing this with interactive CD-ROM products, in which an officer at a computer terminal would be confronted with a very realistic scenario on a screen. The trainee would make choices about whom to stop and what happens after that point. Depending on the choices made by the trainee, the scenario would change; an hour or more of interactive material covering a number of realistic scenarios would allow race to recede into the background and operate at an almost subconscious level, in order to measure very subtle distinctions officers might make.

At the end of the training, a scoring system would give the trainee officer direct feedback concerning whether or not racial or ethnic biases seemed to be playing a role in the officer's choices. This kind of interactive computer-based training has been very effective in other professions. For example, a similar CD-ROM–based product called "Interactive Courtroom" presents lawyers and law students with realistic scenarios in order to teach them trial skills, the law of evidence and objections, and even client-interviewing techniques.[25] The police-bias version of such a product might be expensive and complicated to develop, but it would undoubtedly prove worthwhile—a way to train more officers in more departments with the advantage of individual feedback. Since officers would essentially use the training alone, it would not have the limitations of speaking up in a classroom setting in which a trainee might be afraid to be seen as politically incorrect. And it could be the perfect complement to classroom training such as that done by Didi Nelson and Tom Hayes of Georgia.

Data Collection

Any plan to address racial profiling must include data collection—the systematic collection of basic information on each and every encounter between police and citizens. There are many questions about police activity that most police forces could not answer concerning their enforcement efforts. For example, we saw in chapter 5 that no one in the state attorney general's office knew how many law-abiding citizens state police in Ohio had stopped for each stop that resulted in a seizure of evidence and criminal charges. Even though this information would seem absolutely basic to understanding the effectiveness of law enforcement as well as the costs involved, few agencies had done any such data gathering on a consistent basis until recently. With the public debate on racial profiling over the last several years, things have begun to change. The mere existence of the debate has led to a search for real information to answer the public's concerns, not the least of which is whether profiling is actually occurring in any given place. Up to this point, citizens who had made allegations of racially biased law enforcement were often dismissed. At best, they were told that if true, their stories were anomalies—exceptions to the general rule, and as such nothing to worry about in any larger sense. At worst, the victims were portrayed as crackpots, malcontents, criminals, or race baiters. Now, with allegations becoming more frequent and with some well-known cases, such as those in New Jersey, Maryland, and New York, in which data have proved that citizens had indeed experienced real patterns of discrimination, police departments cannot easily dismiss these concerns as "mere anecdotes" or exceptions. Often, they find the shoe on the other foot—without numbers to refute the charges, their denials of responsibility or of the existence of a problem fail to quell public dissatisfaction.

The importance of collecting data, including information on race and ethnicity, on traffic, pedestrian, and other police encounters, cannot be underestimated. It is crucial from a public policy point of view, and it is critical from a police management and public service point of view. A police chief or other administrator who does not have data on the specifics of what officers under her command are doing and how they are doing it is at an extreme disadvantage. She will find it hard to know what decisions to make, what personnel she needs, or how to deploy existing assets without information that will tell her how effective her current efforts are. Accurate and timely information is a prerequisite for managing any organization, including law enforcement agencies. Robert McNeilly, chief of police in Pittsburgh and the architect of what is probably the state-of-the-art personnel management and early warning system in policing today, makes a striking analogy on this point.[26] "I look at police chiefs and assistant chiefs and commanders as being CEOs and executive officers of businesses," he says. The police department in Pittsburgh has a budget of more than a hundred million dollars a year—roughly a third of all municipal expenditures. "How can anyone run a hundred-million-dollar business without knowing what's going on in their business?" It takes information, McNeilly says, not just crime statistics but information on how officers perform in their jobs. Deborah Ramirez, a law professor at Northeastern University School of Law who often does police training, has a phrase she uses to explain the necessity of data collection: "You can't manage what you don't measure."[27] There are ways to confront the problem through management-driven solutions and training. But all approaches like this start with, and depend upon, the measurement of the problem.

Suppose, for example, a chief thought that one or more of his officers, or even the whole department, had a problem with profiling in one form or another. Assume the chief felt inclined to do something about the problem—at the very least to find out whether allegations of profiling coming from the public were true. How could the chief do this, without data that illuminated stop-and-search patterns? A related example will help illustrate the dilemma an uninformed chief would face. Ron Jornd, chief of police in Ottawa Hills, Ohio, a small municipality outside Toledo, says that a few years back he received information that one of his male officers was using traffic stops as opportunities to "hit" on female drivers—traffic stops as dating service, one might say.[28] This kind of behavior represented a highly inappropriate use of police powers as well as intentional discrimination and perhaps even sexual harassment, all of which might conceivably form the basis for multiple lawsuits not only against the officer but also against the police department, its command staff, and the town. Jornd's police force had been tracking demographic information on stops since the early to mid-1990s, including gender. Thus it was relatively easy for him to pull up records that helped him find any patterns in the officer's activities. Without that information—without data tracking the activities of his officers—he would have been in the difficult position of trying to manage a problem that had not been measured. With the information he needed, he was able to pinpoint the problem and take appropriate action.

Nevertheless, many departments all over the country work without crucial information on police stops and searches. Even now, after several years of public controversy over profiling, many police administrators simply insist that the public should trust them when they say there is no problem, even as they refuse to collect the data necessary to back up their assertions. Some even contend that since profiling can't be "proved" through existing data resources, that means we aren't doing it, therefore we refuse to collect any data. Thus the question is never fully addressed and resolved.[29]

Fortunately, many in police leadership understand that they cannot simply ignore racial profiling. John Timoney, the commissioner of police in Philadelphia, put it well when he testified before a committee of the Pennsylvania state legislature. Looking out over the American political and social landscape, Timoney said, any police administrator would "have to be brain dead" in order to ignore the fact that law enforcement would be forced to grapple with issues of race and policing in the years ahead.[30] The smartest, most forward-thinking police departments will take the problem on and address it on their own terms. And they'll do so not just because their customers—the public—want them to do this. They'll collect data because it is in their interest to have accurate, comprehensive information to help them understand officer and departmental behavior and to address complaints before they undermine the effectiveness of efforts police make at reaching out to members of the community.

William Bratton, who has served as head of police departments in Boston and New York, says that accurate data collection and analysis of criminal activity had much to do with his success in bringing crime down dramatically in both of those cities.[31] When he came to New York, Bratton says, he was amazed to find that he could not get information on current crime patterns that was less than forty-five days old. Bratton knew that the department had to be able to respond to crime patterns much more quickly than that, so he and his top assistants set up a computerized information-gathering and analysis system so that they had information on all crimes within twenty-four hours. The information was mapped so that commanders could see exactly where crime was happening and could make concrete adjustments in deployment of officers. This system, which became known as Compstat, became a very effective tool for the management of the crime problem in New York; variations on it are now in use in a number of cities around the country. And it is all based on data collection and analysis to insure accountability—the same approach resisted by many departments as a way to track racial profiling.

What exactly does data collection on police stops and searches entail? Different jurisdictions have answered the question differently, but the basic idea is simple. For every traffic stop or pedestrian stop, the officer would record several pieces of data. Police would do this whether the stop resulted in a citation or a warning, a pat down or an arrest. Most jurisdictions have recorded about ten pieces of data; some have required more, and at least one as few as four. A good example is the data that would be required under legislation introduced in the 105th and 106th Congresses by Representative John Conyers. The Conyers bills, which have become the model for many state laws and proposals around the country and the data-collection efforts of many police departments,[32] required the collection of the following data for every traffic stop:

A. The traffic infraction alleged to have been committed that led to the stop.
B. Identifying characteristics of the driver stopped, including the race, gender, ethnicity, and approximate age of the driver.
C. Whether immigration status was questioned, immigration documents were requested, or an inquiry was made to the Immigration and Naturalization Service with regard to any person in the vehicle.
D. The number of individuals in the stopped vehicle.
E. Whether a search was instituted as a result of the stop and whether consent was requested for the search.
F. Any alleged criminal behavior by the driver that justified the search.
G. Any items seized, including contraband or money.
H. Whether any warning or citation was issued as a result of the stop.
I. Whether an arrest was made as a result of either the stop or the search and the justification for the arrest.
J. The duration of the stop.[33]

Connecticut's legislation, one of the first laws enacted on the issue in the country, requires a similar list of data to be kept by police in that state.

1. The number of persons stopped for traffic violations;
2. characteristics of race, color, ethnicity, gender and age of such persons, provided the identification of such characteristics shall be based on the observation and perception of the police officer responsible for reporting the stop and the information shall not be required to be provided by the person stopped;
3. the nature of the alleged traffic violation that resulted in the stop;
4. whether a warning or citation was issued, an arrest made or a search conducted as a result of the stop; and
5. any additional information that such municipal police department or the Department of Public Safety, as the case may be, deems appropriate.[34]

Missouri's legislation, enacted in 2000, requires ten pieces of data.

1. The age, gender and race or minority group of the individual stopped;
2. The traffic violation or violation alleged to have been committed that led to the stop;
3. Whether a search was conducted as a result of the stop;
4. If a search was conducted, whether the individual consented to the search, the probable cause for the search, whether the person was searched, whether the person's property was searched, and the duration of the search;
5. Whether any type of contraband was discovered in the course of the search and the type of any contraband discovered;
6. Whether any warning or citation was issued as a result of the stop;
7. If a warning or citation was issued, the violation charged or warning provided;
8. Whether an arrest was made as a result of either the stop or the search;

9. If an arrest was made, the crime charged; and
10. The location of the stop.[35]

Other examples of what data should be collected can be found in a recent U.S. Department of Justice monograph, *A Resource Guide on Racial Profiling Data Collection Systems: Promising Practices and Lessons Learned,* by Deborah Ramirez, Jack McDevitt, and Amy Farrell of Northeastern University.[36]

These data-collection systems can make use of virtually any medium to collect and transmit the information to some central repository for analysis. Some are paper based, using or augmenting existing forms for traffic citations and warnings to make a record. One such form, used by Chief Ron Jornd's department in Ottawa Hills, Ohio, simply adds a "check the boxes" area on ticket and warning forms so that officers can record demographic information and facts about any search that occurs. During the early morning hours, when police radio traffic in Jornd's jurisdiction is slowest, the dispatcher types the data from these forms into the department's computer system. The San Diego Police Department also uses a paper form, with somewhat more detail. Other forms of data collection use technology. These range from San Jose's radio-code-based system (the dispatcher receiving the radio call types the letter codes into the department's computers) to the use of pull-down menus on mobile data terminals in patrol cars to handheld personal digital assistants, like those in use in Montgomery County, Maryland.

Police usually raise three objections to data collection. The first has to do with the mechanics of the process itself. Collecting any data on race or ethnicity, opponents say, has the potential to inflame an already tense situation, because having a police officer ask a driver what race or ethnic group he or she belongs to might make the citizen angry or even provoke a hostile reaction.

The answer is that it is not necessary—in fact, it is not even desirable—to have police officers ask drivers to identify their racial or ethnic group. When we collect data on the racial or ethnic group of the driver or pedestrian, the important thing is not what race or ethnic group drivers *actually* belong to, but what race or ethnic group the officers *think* they belong to. That means that it is entirely sufficient for purposes of tracking traffic or pedestrian stops to record officers' impressions of the driver's or pedestrian's race.

The second and third objections to data collection both relate to resources—specifically, officer time and departmental funds. Many object that data collection will take too much of officers' time—time that could go into "real" crime-fighting activities instead of mere paperwork or record keeping. Both of these concerns have turned out to be much less important than almost anyone thought they would be. In most departments, officers have spent only a minimal amount of time to collect the information for each stop—usually less than two minutes, and sometimes much less that that. Indeed, the relative ease and low cost of the efforts mounted thus far have come as a pleasant surprise to almost everyone involved. In San Jose, the radio-code system adds less than thirty seconds to most stops. And costs have been lower than anyone anticipated, with most departments able to put these efforts together without making supplemental budget requests. According to Marc Thompson, city manager for Ottawa Hills, the municipality's experience with data gathering on traffic stops has been entirely positive. Without the statistics officers keep, Thompson says, the police department could neither deny allegations of profiling nor credibly investigate them. "We have found our statistics gathering to be extremely helpful and not particularly cumbersome," Thompson adds.[37] The relative simplicity of the idea has enabled many municipal-data-collection efforts to go forward more easily and rapidly than would have seemed possible when the idea of data collection first surfaced.

There are several key issues to consider before undertaking any data collection effort.

Location and other context-specific information. One of police officers' most frequent objections to data collection concerns context. They feel that their assignments—perhaps to neighborhoods in which an overwhelming majority of citizens are African American or Latino—will inevitably skew the numbers of their stops of drivers and pedestrians. Given their duty assignments, these officers simply do not patrol in areas or situations in which they would be likely to stop members of more than one race. This, they fear, will make them look like racists when the data emerge. This same concern can emerge when officers have special tasks or assignments, such as looking for drunk drivers outside bars frequented by particular ethnic groups. These officers have a point. According to John Lamberth, the expert statistician in the New Jersey and Maryland cases, "When 90 percent of the traffic they're patrolling is black and they stop 90 percent black (drivers), that's perfectly appropriate for them to do so." [38] This makes it critical to collect information on the location, time, and date for each stop. Location should include the most specific information possible—approximate address, intersection, precinct, neighborhood, or the like. Time and date, as well as information concerning any special assignment, would allow the analysis to take into account special circumstances such as those of the state police officer detailed to watching particular bars. Context is all important; collecting data without it means that interpretations of the numbers can easily go wrong.

Research and analysis partners. In order to have the greatest chance of success, law enforcement agencies should ally themselves with partners—university researchers, think tanks, or expert consultants—to help them design their studies and to perform the analysis of data. There are at least two good reasons to do this. First, there is no point in undertaking the effort of collecting data to study traffic- or pedestrian-stops activity unless this is done in a way that will actually produce answers. Whereas some of the largest police departments might have staff capable of designing a successful data-collection effort and performing a sophisticated statistical analysis, many would not. Partners with statistical training can help make sure that the numbers gathered can, in the end, be meaningfully analyzed. The other reason for involving partners for research and analysis involves independence. Unfortunately, communities in which people believe officers use racial profiling often harbor considerable distrust of police. They will likely regard any data collection, research, or analysis performed by the police agencies themselves as suspect—an instance of the fox guarding the henhouse. Against that kind of background, few citizens will likely accept whatever the results of the study were, good or bad, if they come directly from the police themselves. The independence of an academic or research partner can give the public confidence in the result that they simply would not have if both the design of the study and the analysis came from the police themselves.

Community task force. A crucial step in any data-collection effort begins with the community. A law enforcement agency that decides to collect data should first convene a community task force. The task force should include members of law enforcement (including representatives of rank-and-file patrol officers and/or police unions), members of the local community, and representatives of concerned citizens groups like the NAACP, the ACLU, and the National Urban League, for example. The task force should have input on the whole effort to address profiling, from conceiving what the problem is to the specifics and problems the jurisdiction's data-collection effort will face. Police officers, for example, will have considerable knowledge concerning questions of context that could affect data analysis. Community members will have a strong feel for where complaints come from, as well as particular practices that grate on residents. Citizens groups will bring credibility and standing, as well as a degree of expertise and institutional memory concerning the history of police and community relations.

The diversity of viewpoints guarantees that the effort to collect data will occur against the backdrop of the fullest, most accurate picture of the whole problem. The result will be more complex, more nuanced, and ultimately more useful. Perhaps even more important, when all of these constituencies become a real part of the process from the beginning, the result is likely to be not only a better outcome but an outcome in which all of the participants have a stake. The best examples of this combined effort come from San Jose and San Diego, California. In both instances, the police departments brought citizens and representatives of advocacy groups into the data-collection process early on in a community task force. When both of these police departments released their first reports and analyses, certain numbers "stuck out"—numbers that, looked at in one light, might indicate the presence of racial bias. But in both cities, when the chiefs of police released the data, reaction was muted. Instead, prominent citizens and community groups gave their support to the police departments, with representatives of such groups as the ACLU—the organization that has clearly done the most to promote action against profiling across the country—standing with the police chief and lending support to his efforts.[39]

Ongoing management perspective. Some data-collection efforts have been proposed or undertaken for limited periods of time—a year, six months, even three months. The idea is to do a relatively rapid study of a single discrete question: Is racial profiling occurring? This approach has at least two important flaws. First, limiting the data-collection period has the potential to skew the results, and very short time frames like three or six months will almost always change the results. Werner Heisenberg's uncertainty principle derives from physics, but it has an application in the social sciences, too: observation affects the observed. In this case, if police officers feel they will be under close observation for possible racial bias in traffic stops for several months, some will almost certainly modify behavior for that short period, then return to unrestrained behavior once the observation period is over.

Perhaps more important, data collection should be viewed not as a one-time test period but as an ongoing effort to assist in the management of the department by providing solid information. In other words, data collection on police behavior should not be a test or a study of police behavior during some particular time period but a tool to help supervising officers and administrators to *manage* police officers, force deployment, and effectiveness of enforcement efforts *over the long term*.

Chief Bill Lansdowne of San Jose, California, the first big-city chief to release traffic stop data to the public and one of the pioneers within law enforcement on the issue, has seen the management benefits of data collection firsthand. When his first sets of data showed little law enforcement benefit from stops—only 1 percent of stops resulted in an arrest—and some members of the public still complained about how they were treated, Lansdowne modified department training to emphasize better interaction with the public and the inefficiency of judging people as suspects by appearance. The results were striking—public complaints dropped 45 percent in 2000 over the level of 1999.

Use of appropriate benchmarks. This may be the single most important issue in the design of any data-collection effort—and probably also the one most often ignored. To get an answer to the question of whether a given police department stops a disproportionate number of minorities, the data-collection effort must result in the calculation of two different numbers. First, we ask how many drivers of each racial or ethnic group (or pedestrians, if we are conducting a study of stop-and-frisk activity) police stopped during some particular period of time. Note that it is important that we look at *all* stops, not just those that result in citations or arrests; otherwise, we will have an incomplete picture. Second, we need to compare the first number to something in order to know whether the number of stops of each group is out of line with what we should expect. This second number is the *benchmark*—the number of stops of this group that we would expect if there was no bias present. Recall from chapter 3 that there are no racial or ethnic differences in driving; all drivers violate the traffic laws at the same very high rate. And while the cars of poor people would almost certainly have more vehicle-equipment violations than the cars of those more well off, and more of the poor are minorities, virtually any car, from the oldest rusted-out clunker to any showroom-fresh vehicle, can be stopped for *something*—if not for defective equipment, then for the details of driving behavior. Therefore a proper comparison focuses on the actual population of drivers. That is, the correct benchmark is the population of drivers on the road in the place we are interested in, broken down by race and ethnic group. We then compare the number of stops actually made for each racial or ethnic group to the benchmark number of drivers in each racial or ethnic group. This is what John Lamberth did in his studies in New Jersey and Maryland, and he is now using a variation on this method to calculate driving populations in non-highway urban and suburban settings involving traffic on typical surface roads. This means that, time and resources permitting, Lamberth can now calculate accurate, usable benchmarks for virtually any environment.[40] Matthew Zingraff of North Carolina State University and his colleagues are sharpening Lamberth's method further by devising a way to calculate the number of "drivers driving" on North Carolina highways.[41]

Unfortunately, some police agencies or others looking at statistics have used unadjusted residential population or census figures as a benchmark. This is a mistake, because the racial mix of the population that lives in an area is frequently different from the population of people who drive through it. Take, for example, Ottawa Hills, Ohio, outside Toledo. Ottawa Hills has a negligible minority population—well under 1 percent. But the driving population on the five thoroughfares that run through it ranges from 22 to 25 percent. Using the residential population as a benchmark would have produced a picture of biased police activity, since virtually any enforcement against African Americans would look disproportionate to the (nonexistent) black population. But compared to the rate of African American drivers who pass through the town, the latest figures show that there is nothing remarkable about police activity involving African Americans in Ottawa Hills.[42]

Assuring data integrity. Without some assurance of the accuracy of the data collected, no analysis can produce anything credible. If the data that go into the analysis do not represent what actually happens out on the street, no analysis can come to an accurate, useful conclusion. And unfortunately many citizens feel considerable suspicion that police officers—who must, after all, collect the data when they make the stops—will collect it in a biased way. And there have even been some concrete examples of police doing exactly that. In New Jersey, two troopers were indicted for filing false reports on stops—reporting that the black drivers they stopped were white, in order to change the racial balance in the figures they collected.[43]

In order that any data-collection effort and resulting analysis has the integrity necessary to stand up to criticism, the effort must include the use of integrity-assurance mechanisms. There are numerous ways to do this, and they need not be complicated. Most involve some type of cross-checking of the officers' data on particular stops with other processes that generate records. An integrity system could make use of the department's CAD, or computer assisted dispatch, system. Most police departments use a CAD system, which generates a computer record of each and every radio contact between officers in the field and the department's dispatch center. Most departments also require that officers performing a traffic stop call the stop in to the dispatcher, often with some kind of identifying and location information. All of this would generate a record that could then be cross-checked against any particular officer's own data. If randomly selected stops do not match CAD data this would raise questions concerning the data's integrity. Another integrity process would work well for any department that has in-car video cameras installed in its vehicles. The videos are themselves records of stops. As long as they are preserved for some length of time, officer data could be compared to the videotape records of randomly selected stops. Beyond helping to insure the integrity of the data-collection system, this would also insure that officers did not attempt to tamper with the video system; that is, it would serve as a check on the use of those systems as well. A third possibility would involve the use of post-encounter-feedback systems, such as "customer satisfaction surveys" like the ones used by private industry (see p. 205). The department would choose randomly selected records of stops and contact the driver to get information on how the police officer conducted the stop. This information could also include data to cross-check with the data in the officer's own records.

Another, more technically sophisticated idea for assuring data integrity comes from the consulting firm PSComm.[44] It has designed a software product to collect traffic-stop data in conjunction with any computing system used by a police force. Any department that equips its officers with in-car mobile data terminals, laptops, or handheld computers could use the system, called StopTracker. The software would come packaged with police computers, mobile data terminals, or handheld PDAs, such as the Palm Pilot. Any time an officer makes a request to check a license plate or driver's license, as would be the case in almost any traffic stop, the StopTracker software would take several actions automatically. First, it would communicate with the department's computer assisted dispatch (CAD) system, and create a CAD record and a unique record number. When information comes back to the officer on the plate or driver's license, that information would "autopopulate" the data fields in the software—that is, the information "pops" right into the blanks on the screens that will record data for the traffic stop, without the officer having to spend any time filling in this routine information by hand. Once the officer completes the record of the stop, the entire record goes to the CAD system by wireless data transmission. According to PSComm, StopTracker addresses two important issues. First, it greatly minimizes the requirement for the officer to record information. The system uses no paper record-keeping at all, and most of the information will pop right onto the screen without the officer having to lift a finger. The rest will be recorded on a series of easily used pull-down menus. Second, and most important from a data-integrity standpoint, the system will make sure that every stop an officer makes will leave an "audit trail." Because the system automatically generates a record and a CAD number every time the officer does a license-plate check, which precedes almost every stop, all stops will be recorded. Officers will not be able to subvert the data-collection system by making stops that they do not record. And every stop will be easily traceable with the CAD record. Since state driver's license authorities almost never include the race of the driver on their licenses, the record will usually not record any race information; the police officer will have to add it. This should be relatively easy to do, using a "check the boxes" or pull-down menu format on the computer screen.

Identification of individual officers. This is surely one of the most difficult issues any department will face as it mounts a data-collection effort. On the one hand, it makes sense when collecting data on stops to include with it the name or badge number of the officer making the stop. If the data indicate that a problem exists in the pattern of stops by the officer, the department can hold that officer accountable and see that he receives retraining, counseling, or discipline, as appropriate. On the other hand, the identification of particular officers in data-collection systems and early-warning systems (see p. 196, "Response and Tracking Mechanisms") has proved a contentious issue between police departments and the unions representing officers—so contentious as to be a "deal breaker" in terms of the rank and file and the police unions signing on to be part of and support any data-collection effort. For example, in San Jose, using a system that does not identify the officer involved in a particular stop assuaged officers' concerns that the data might be misused to portray individual officers unfairly. Jim Tomaino, a twenty-nine-year veteran of the department and head of the Police Officers Association in San Jose since 1994, says that officers became much more comfortable with the idea of data collection once they understood that the data would create a statistical picture of the department and not of any individual officers.[45] In Montgomery County, Maryland, Walter Bader, head of the local Fraternal Order of Police, says much the same thing. The agreement between the U.S. Department of Justice and Montgomery County includes data collection, but Bader says that his union signed on only with a promise that the data-collection system would not identify individual officers making stops. Instead, it tracks data for clusters of eight officers. Bader says the union would have strongly opposed the entire agreement without this concession.[46]

Ultimately, this issue almost certainly comes down to difficult calculations of employer-union relations and local politics. Chiefs of police and mayors and other officials will have to make the best arrangements they can to get these systems into place with the support of both individual officers and unions, and they may decide in any particular circumstance that while having individual officers identified would surely be beneficial, they do not want to sacrifice the entire system over this one item. Data-collection systems that do not identify the officer will not have the utility or the potential for good that systems including this information do. Perhaps union concerns could be addressed by requiring that the information on individual officers not be used for disciplinary purposes, or at least not for disciplinary purposes in the first instance. The issue looms large for any police department putting a data-collection system in place. Being able to identify a problem officer in the context of the data collected makes sense. It is an efficient use of the data-collection effort, and it serves the public interest by allowing the police department to address a problem employee in the most direct manner, instead of limiting the department to "group-" or department-wide solutions. It will be a tough call, but one that will have to be made.

In the end, data collection will become a reality—not because it raises no contentious issues (it surely does) or because it will be easy (it won't be). But it will happen because it is very much in the interest of law enforcement itself to have solid information with which to manage its people and address the concerns of the community. In San Diego, former chief Jerry Sanders became the first big-city police chief to begin data collection in his department because, he said, the department needed the trust of the community for its successful community-policing efforts. His successor, Chief David Berajano, and Assistant Chief Rulette

Armstead, have continued the effort. As a police agency, Armstead says, if there is even the slightest perception of police bias among members of the public, "we owe it to the community to actually look into it." [47] In San Jose, Chief Bill Lansdowne and Captain Rob Davis[48] designed a relatively simple system that cost little to implement and operate, generates no paper, and is quick and easy for the officers to use. Ottawa Hills, Ohio, a small suburban community, uses a paper-based system of simple records; officers in Montgomery County, Maryland, put their information into handheld computers. The important thing is not how data collection is done, but that it *is* done.

Technology's Role: Making It Easier, and Increasing Confidence and Capability

Most police departments make some use of computers to store, sort, and process information; it seems obvious to make use of computing power in the effort to address racial profiling. Once the data are collected, entered, and ready to work with, basic programs can detect patterns, using different types of analyses to illustrate how enforcement activities affect various groups. But technology can also help ease and speed the actual collection of data and the input of the information. There need be nothing especially "high tech" about this. Recall the way that the San Jose Police Department has implemented its data-collection effort. San Jose uses a technology that has been around for decades—police radio communications—in conjunction with its CAD system to collect and input traffic-stop data. The system is easy to use and understand, with no additional paperwork for officers. Officers already used letter codes over the radio for a variety of purposes; additional training costs for the operation of the system were minimal, and the only additional equipment required was a laminated plastic card listing the new letter codes for race and other new categories. It entailed no new paperwork for officers, and even additional data-input costs were minimal.

Where somewhat more sophisticated technology is available, the process can be even easier and more useful. For example, an increasing number of police departments have equipped police cars with mobile data terminals (MDTs) or laptop computers. These machines make it possible to have each officer in the field wired in to the departmental computer network either continuously or as needed. Data from each traffic stop can be recorded right on the computer screen using the ubiquitous pull-down menus and lists so common in computers using Microsoft Windows software or equivalents. This is exactly what PSComm's StopTracker is designed to do. The Montgomery County, Maryland, Police Department has done something similar, at an even lower cost than it would take to give each officer a laptop. Each of the department's approximately twelve hundred officers has received a personal digital assistant (PDA)—a palm-sized handheld computer that fits in a pocket. The PDAs issued to Montgomery County police also allow officers to track and record twenty-two categories of traffic-enforcement data by touching a few simple screens with a stylus, in a check-the-box format using pull-down menus. According to David Linn, the department's chief technology officer, the reaction of the average officer has been uncomplicated: "The officers love 'em," he says,[49] and Walter Bader, the head of the county's FOP local, agrees.

In-car video and audio recording. The technology needed to make audio and video recordings of traffic stops has existed for some time—at least since the early 1990s. Equipping each patrol car costs anywhere from four to six thousand dollars; some departments have found the cost prohibitive, while others have encountered resistance from officers who fear that supervisors will use the technology to "spy" on them. There have also been concerns by some citizens that officers might tamper or interfere with the recording equipment. But even with these possible problems, police departments should strongly consider making the widest use of in-car video and audio recording that departmental finances will allow. Despite the initial skepticism of individual officers, experience shows that these devices not only help get the profiling problem under control—after all, who isn't more careful and better behaved when they know they are being watched?—but also help protect officers. In New Jersey, where virtually all state police cars now have in-car recording systems, they have been used to defend officers more often than anyone anticipated. When allegations have been made of improper stops or biased treatment, supervising officers need only examine the tape to see whether there is anything to the allegations. In forty cases in New Jersey, allegations by the public of improper conduct by officers, including accusations that the stops were based on race or profiles, were dismissed after review of videotapes of stops.[50] In one case, in which a civilian had alleged that an officer had used racial epithets, even putting these allegations into the form of an official complaint, the tape proved that the officer had done nothing of the kind. (The citizen was subsequently charged with the crime of making a false report.)[51] This may be the greatest utility of these systems: they protect both the officer involved and the public by recording whether proper procedures were followed, and whether behavior following the stop was courteous, respectful, and lawful. They can also serve as part of an auditing system to check on data-collection integrity. Randomly selected records of traffic stops from paper or computer-based data-collection systems could be compared to video records of these same stops, to see if the data collected are accurate. Was the driver of the racial or ethnic group recorded? Did he or she in fact consent to a search? And tapes can, of course, serve as the best possible adjunct to training and individual performance review imaginable. A police department with cars equipped with recording equipment could set policy obligating supervisors to review randomly selected pieces of tape every month for each officer under his or her command. This would give the supervisor the chance to see what would normally only be visible had he or she happened upon the scene by chance and to pick up any bad habits or patterns that require correction, advice, or even retraining. If a pattern is seen in the conduct of a number of officers in the department, perhaps departmentwide training or other changes is warranted.

Chief Ron Jornd of the Ottawa Hills Police Department has

been through the whole cycle of reactions to in-car cameras with the officers in his department.[52] Resistance by his officers killed the first proposal to install cameras in the early 1990s. Some years later, all cars in the department were equipped with video- and audio-recording systems, despite the skepticism. The turning point in officers' attitudes came when an officer was accused of using a racial epithet in speaking to an African American. The tape showed that the officer had not done this, and had in fact gone out of his way to help the man. The tape, Jornd says, effectively saved the officer's job, and this convinced his other person- nel of the value of the cameras. Jornd says his officers now say two things about the devices. First, they regard them as elec- tronic notebooks—"files" they can go back to for information that they might forget (or be too busy) to write down. Second, most officers will not take a patrol car out for a shift unless the camera and recording equipment are in working condition. Jornd himself had made use of the tapes as an administrator. Be- sides using them to review individual officer performance, he now sees to it that each and every tape is preserved. He has made the videotapes into an open library. "Anybody who wants to come in, it's public information, and we'll sit there and go through whatever videotape they point out," he says. "And if they find anything in question, we'll pull the [paperwork] on it" and go through all of the officer's records for the stop—citations, arrest records, anything. The idea, Jornd says, is that the tapes are not only highly nuanced records of interactions between citi- zens and police, but they also serve to build both public confi- dence in police, and officers' confidence that their reactions will be judged fairly and objectively.

Response-and-Tracking Mechanisms

A fourth tool needed to combat racial profiling consists of what we might broadly call response-and-tracking mechanisms. These are systems that are designed to generate, collect, and/or track a variety of information on police officers in a comprehen- sive format that will allow supervisory personnel to monitor, track, and take appropriate actions when conduct does not meet policies and standards. Much of this information is routinely collected but only available in isolated pieces that are difficult to obtain and bring together; some of it is not routinely collected at all. These mechanisms form crucial parts of any bona fide commitment to the accountability of police forces to the public they serve. When that commitment to police accountability is in place, response-and-tracking mechanisms follow as a matter of course—as a measure obvious to anyone interested in doing what it takes to earn public trust and confidence and to run an open department strongly committed to the service of all citizens.

Departments should use two types of response-and-tracking mechanisms. The first is the early-warning system: a system in which information—most of which already exists internally in the police department in varying places—is brought together and tracked to give supervisory personnel a wealth of information about each officer's performance. If these performance data suggest some problem, counseling, retraining, or treatment would follow. The second device consists of feedback systems from external sources—including follow-up investigations and police-contact surveys that focus on public knowledge, perception, and reporting of experiences with police in order to gain insight into the delivery of police services from the public's side.

Early-warning systems. Until recently, no police department anywhere made any kind of systematic, comprehensive effort to gather and analyze data on crimes in ways that would allow supervisors to see patterns in criminal activity and to assign officers and deploy other resources according to where they were needed. This began to change in the early 1990s, with the advent of a system for tracking crimes called Compstat. Known largely as the brainchild of William Bratton, the outspoken leader of police forces in Boston and New York, Compstat was a revelation in modern law enforcement: crime was systematically tracked and "mapped," and supervisory and command personnel were held responsible for coming up with ways to address the hot spots of crime in their districts. These supervisors were required to appear before command staff to demonstrate knowledge of the problem and to explain what they'd done in response and what they planned to do. Compstat brought together in one system accountability for crime-fighting results with the intelligent use of data and analysis on crime trends and activity.

Early-warning systems utilize a similar idea: they bring together and analyze all of the relevant data on current officer behavior in order to prevent problems before they occur. They are set up to track this data—citizen complaints, use of force, disciplinary proceedings, and the like—for each officer so that supervisory personnel can have all of it at their fingertips. Thresholds built into these systems alert supervisors to possible problems when the thresholds are crossed. Most of these data already exist, but at different places in the police department, making it difficult or even impossible to view the picture as a whole.[53]

According to Samuel Walker and Geoffrey Alpert, professors of criminal justice and the leading authorities on early-warning systems, the basic idea of early-warning systems is to bring together data on officer performance "to identify those officers who appear to be having recurring problems interacting with citizens."[54] They work by identifying critical criteria for measuring officer performance: citizen complaints filed, use of force, civil litigation filed, reprimands, damage to property, resisting arrest charges, and other indicators. For each criterion, exceeding a particular threshold would mean that the officer should be reviewed for possible problems. Once the system identifies these officers, they could receive training, counseling, or other help necessary to correct the problems. The idea of "warning," Walker and Alpert explain, is that these systems are intended not as disciplinary tools but as devices to point out performance shortcomings that can still be corrected.[55] There is no real method, they point out, to predict which police recruits will have problems before the department hires them. But "it is definitely possible to spot (problem officers) on the basis of the performance histories once they begin to manifest problems."

The oft-quoted remark of former Baltimore police chief

Thomas Frazier—that " '10 percent of your officers create 90 percent of your problems' "[56]—may be a bit of an exaggeration, but not by much. For example, the Christopher Commission, which investigated the Los Angeles Police Department in the wake of the police beating of Rodney King, found that just forty-four "readily identifiable" officers within the department had extremely high rates of citizen complaints, yet none received any significant discipline.[57] In 1991, the *New York Times* found that 50 percent of the citizen complaints involved just 2 percent of all of the officers in Kansas City;[58] in Boston, almost two-thirds of the complaints involved 11 percent of the force.[59] An early-warning system is, by far, the most promising tool one could imagine to identify and respond to these problems.

Early-warning systems obviously can do much to improve policing. This is no doubt why important organizations on all sides of the criminal justice spectrum, from the United States Civil Rights Commission to the International Association of Chiefs of Police, have endorsed the concept for years. But what has not been considered until recently is how these systems can help to address the question of racial profiling: whether particular officers stop larger numbers of minority drivers than one would expect and whether their after-the-stop conduct—who gets searched, who gets treated disrespectfully, and the like—is different for different racial and ethnic groups. This can be accomplished by including in early-warning systems not only the traditional criteria of police problems discussed above but also racial-profiling data. By incorporating racial and ethnic data on stops and searches, early-warning systems allow us to see how officers in the same police departments with the same assignments—same neighborhood patrolled, same shift, same special assignment—compare to one other. Early-warning systems expert Samuel Walker argues that integrating racial profiling data into early-warning systems is in fact the best way to attempt to come to grips with profiling and is considerably easier than attempting to create realistic benchmarks for comparison with traffic stop data. "A national evaluation found that officers selected by [early-warning] systems do in fact have more serious disciplinary histories than their peers," Walker reports. If we integrate data on traffic or pedestrian stops and searches into early-warning systems, analysis of the data "can successfully identify those officers with a disproportionate number of traffic stops of racial and ethnic minority drivers *relative to their peer officers.*" Supervising officers can then use this information to correct the behavior. This can be accomplished by measuring the performance of each officer against "the activity levels of other officers working comparable assignments"—an automatic factoring in of each officer's work environment.[60]

Pittsburgh's state-of-the-art early-warning system, called Performance Assessment Review System (PARS), is a fully computerized database that contains twenty-two different pieces of information on each officer's performance, including data on stops and searches of drivers and pedestrians and their race or ethnic group, as well as complaints against officers, commendations, sick days taken, vehicle accidents, civil judgments, and a host of other categories.[61] Computer screens using graphs and pie charts allow Chief Robert McNeilly or any other supervisor to track any of these data. As in other early-warning systems, thresholds are set that trigger intervention by a supervisor. This intervention consists of counseling, retraining, or help for the officer and a supervisor's report on each and every officer under their command who has tripped one of the PARS thresholds in any category. The supervisors are asked to discuss the officer's situation—what, in particular, may have given rise to the problem—and what actions the supervisor has planned or undertaken to address it. Supervisors also report periodically on officers who have been identified by PARS in the recent past. This required follow-up keeps troubled officers from falling through the cracks and emphasizes to supervisors their responsibility for addressing the problems.

McNeilly makes no bones about his goal: to handle personnel issues, to see trends in police behavior, and to spot and correct potential problem officers just as efficiently as Compstat allows police departments to track and address crime. He says that he has also discovered an unforeseen benefit: the system has allowed him to find and make the best use of his star officers. For example, McNeilly says that in certain areas of Pittsburgh, robberies were up recently despite an overall drop in virtually every other category of crime. McNeilly decided to form a special detail to combat robberies, and he turned to PARS for help. The system helped him identify star performers on robbery cases within the department's ranks—officers who were good cops and whose records showed special talent for solving robberies.

To be sure, PARS has detractors. Chuck Bossetti, a Pittsburgh police officer and former Fraternal Order of Police official, says PARS has significant problems.[62] Bossetti says the thresholds the department has set for determining when an officer receives supervisory attention are arbitrary and have little relation to the realities of police work. He also says that, at least initially, the system focused only on line officers and had no mechanisms for assuring the accountability of supervisory personnel. Still, he concedes that a system like PARS is a solid idea, one that could improve policing, if constructed correctly and run with integrity.

Professors Walker and Alpert have been careful to point out that early-warning systems are neither panaceas nor easily executed automatic systems. They caution that planning and administration play key roles in the success of these systems; they cannot be regarded as computer-based "alarm clocks" that ring automatically whenever danger arises. They require careful consideration of such issues as the data to be included, the proper thresholds to be used, the accountability of supervisors to the system, and how the data will be entered, accessed, and maintained. But despite these requirements, making racial profiling part of an active early-warning system adds a crucially important tool to the comparison of data on traffic and pedestrian stops and proper benchmarks. Combining the two approaches gives us the best hope for painting a complete, accurate, and fully contextual picture of the problem on both an individual and departmentwide basis.

With early-warning systems used to track and analyze internal data that can help us combat racial profiling as well as a host of other problems, we must also incorporate external feedback systems. These systems are designed to collect, correlate, and analyze information from outside the police department on police-citizen encounters. In other words, instead of counting and analyzing data generated by police officers themselves for the police department on traffic and pedestrian stops, external feedback systems gather data from the public—the citizens that officers have stopped, questioned, and searched. This will give the department data on stops from the citizens' perspective: what happened after the stop, whether the officer acted properly, and whether the citizen feels that he or she was treated with respect. This data would be collected using several tools: police-contact surveys of the jurisdiction's general population, follow-up surveys of citizens who have themselves been stopped by police, and customer-contact cards handed out after every police encounter.

Bob Wasserman, law enforcement veteran and head of PSComm, especially likes the idea of gathering feedback on every encounter between a police officer and a citizen.[63] Wasserman suggests that every police contact with a citizen should end with the officer giving the citizen the equivalent of a "customer comment card" that one sees in so many for-profit businesses. The idea is to attempt to gather information from the citizen's perspective on as many police-citizen encounters as possible and not just a selected sample. It would also give each and every citizen who has dealings with the police an easy, quick way to "have their say" about the incident, be it a complaint or a compliment, a suggestion or a denunciation. All of these methods are designed to gather useful information, and the comment card would do this in the most thorough and easy way possible.

"Pattern-and-Practice" Authority

The work of the U.S. Department of Justice's Special Litigation Section represents one of the best hopes in the fight against racial profiling and other systematic problems in modern policing. In its first few years of existence, the Special Litigation Section used authority granted to the Justice Department under a new law to transform several troubled police departments into agencies using state-of-the-art management to assure that fighting crime goes hand in hand with respect for citizens and their civil liberties. The Special Litigation Section gets its authority to investigate state and local police departments from a trio of federal laws. The first, newest, and most important of these is the police misconduct provision of the Violent Crime Control and Law Enforcement Act of 1994, better known as the pattern-and-practice law. The phrase *pattern and practice* comes directly from the law itself, which reads in part as follows:

> It shall be unlawful for any governmental authority, or any agent thereof, or any person acting on behalf of a governmental authority, to engage in a pattern or practice of conduct by law enforcement officers . . . that deprives persons of rights, privileges, or immunities secured or protected by the Constitution or laws of the United States.[64]

In other words, law enforcement agencies or their officers cannot deprive citizens of their constitutional rights in any systematic way. The law gives the Department of Justice the authority to get *injunctive relief*—not monetary damages for any individuals, but a remedy in the form of a federal court order—to reform police departments engaging in civil rights violations as a regular practice. These types of remedies target the police department itself and its overall management. They are not aimed at obaining redress for a particular person. According to the Special Litigation Section's own description of what it does, "Sporadic bad incidents or the actions of an occasional bad police officer do not constitute a pattern and practice of misconduct."[65] Examples of a pattern and practice of misconduct might include repeated use of excessive force, false arrests, unreasonable searches and seizures, or racial and ethnic discrimination.[66] Drawing an analogy to similar standards in the area of employment-discrimination law, the

Special Litigation Section explains that "a pattern or practice violation exists when police misconduct is the agency's 'standard operating procedure—the regular, rather than the unusual, practice.' " [67] A private citizen cannot sue under the pattern-and-practice law; only the Department of Justice can. Still, the pattern-and-practice statute represents a real and powerful tool. It gives the federal government, with its virtually unlimited resources and considerable power and prestige, the ability to ask judges to impose reforms on police departments if it proves a pattern and practice of civil rights deprivations, whether they result from negligence, intentional wrongdoing, or simple sloppiness. And the department need not prove discrimination; rather, the pattern and practice itself constitutes the harm the law seeks to address, regardless of whether it involves some kind of discriminatory treatment. The pattern-and-practice law gives the Special Litigation Section the authority needed to exercise leverage over a police department in which officers violate citizens' rights not occasionally, or in the context of some especially egregious incident, but as part of the usual course of events. As of June 2000, the Special Litigation Section had fourteen active investigations, including large-scale investigations in Los Angeles (settled later that year), New York City (actually two investigations), New Orleans, and Washington, D.C. Steven Rosenbaum, the head of the Special Litigation Section, described the investigations and the Section's authority to conduct them as a focused remedy to be used only sparingly, for a situation when no other possibility for reform seems to exist. "The exercise of our pattern or practice authority must be based on competent, concrete evidence of systemic problems of great magnitude," he said. "Our focus is management, not just the alleged bad conduct by problem officers." [68] If an investigation shows a pattern and practice of civil rights violations, the Special Litigation Section can sue the offending police department in federal court.

In practice, most pattern-and-practice cases have resulted in negotiated settlement agreements, called consent decrees, spelling out a comprehensive package of agreed-upon reforms.

As of January 2001, the Special Litigation Section had entered into consent decrees with four police departments: the Los Angeles Police Department,[69] the New Jersey State Police,[70] the Pittsburgh Bureau of Police,[71] and the police department in Steubenville, Ohio.[72] The Section also entered into a "Memorandum of Agreement" with the police department, the police union local, and the county government in Montgomery County, Maryland—a voluntary arrangement in which all the parties obligate themselves to the same types of reforms one sees in consent decrees, motivated not by allegations of misconduct but by the desire of all parties involved to "provide for a cooperative effort ... to institute management practices ... that will promote nondiscriminatory law enforcement and community support" for the police department.[73] A proposed consent decree between the Section and the city of Columbus, Ohio, and its police department was scuttled by opposition from the Columbus police union, which objected to some of the terms of the agreement that would have changed certain provisions of its contract.[74] The Columbus case is now in litigation, and promises to be the first court to test the pattern-and-practice law. The consent decrees have all reflected a desire to address and correct management deficiencies in the areas of policy, procedure, oversight, and data collection in an effort to move these departments away from such tactics as racial profiling and instead toward the best practices in law enforcement.

The threat of federal intervention has served as a catalyst, moving police departments to become better, more sophisticated, more respectful of those they serve. The leverage provided by the statute can make a real difference—for leaders of those police departments who want to bring about change from the inside but find themselves stymied by the failure of political leadership in their jurisdictions to stand with them and to provide resources, or by recalcitrant unions or rank and file who do not wish to see change come. In short, the pattern-and-practice law provides a way to force the worst police departments toward the best practices in policing or to help those that wish to move in that direction to do so.

Thus it is absolutely essential that pattern-and-practice authority be preserved and enhanced. It has provided a crucial incentive to departments all over the country to do what they can to improve their practices and internal management—on their own, before the Special Litigation Section gets interested in investigating them. As one would surely guess, there is no appetite among chiefs to take on the Department of Justice on this issue. Rather, chiefs want to know how they can *avoid* having a pattern-and-practice case brought against them. In fact, the "frequently asked questions" on the Special Litigation Section's web site include exactly this query. The list of questions and answers, the Section says, includes "the question frequently asked by police executives of what they can do in their agencies to ensure that they are in compliance with the law and thereby avoid a pattern or practice investigation and lawsuit." [75] Joseph Brann, a consultant with PSComm and former head of the Department of Justice's Office of Community Oriented Policing Services, says that most chiefs not only want to avoid pattern-and-practice litigation; they really do want to meet the pattern-and-practice standards. The question, he says, is how we can assist these chiefs in "managing their way into compliance." [76]

If the pattern-and-practice law is designed to create better police management and to compel police departments to adopt the best management practices (with the objective of heading off conflict between citizens and police officers before it starts), we should look for a way to help law enforcement executives manage their departments toward these very goals. At the same time, we should couple any such efforts with continuing pressure toward those goals, embodied in the enforcement of the pattern-and-practice laws. This is nothing more than the classic carrot-and-stick approach—incentives and rewards for desired behavior, punishment or some form of unpleasantness for behavior we wish to discourage. As things currently stand, there is a stick: the possibility of pattern-and-practice investigations, lawsuits, and court-imposed remedies. But there is no corresponding carrot targeted at this specific set of goals. Proposed federal legislation the End Racial Profiling Act of 2001, S. 989 H.R. 2074, sponsored by Senator Russell Feingold, Congressman John Con-yers, and many other members of Congress, could be used to move in the right direction on both dimensions at once.[77] The proposed law defines racial profiling and gives both the federal government and private parties the authority to bring legal ac-tion to stop the practice and to ask for structural reform of of-fending police departments that would address racial-profiling practices. The bill would also tie federal criminal justice funding of state and local police agencies to required efforts to address racial profiling. And it would also authorize the Department of Justice to give agencies federal grant money to enhance their ef-forts toward better management—data collection on traffic stops, early-warning systems, the use of technology like in-car video cameras, and better management practices, among other examples.

Some say that the federal government should have no role in telling state or local police departments how to run their opera-tions. For example, Heather MacDonald of the Manhattan Insti-tute accuses the Department of Justice, and especially the Special Litigation Section, of "persecuting the police."[78] Of course, this perspective ignores the pervasive federal role in creating the problem in the first place, through the DEA's Operation Pipeline program. It ignores as well the historic role that the federal gov-ernment has played throughout the second half of the twentieth century in securing federal civil rights for citizens when state and local government refused to do so. Nevertheless, this criticism does highlight another possibility: creating pattern-and-practice authority in the states themselves. In 2001, California did just that. Under a new law, California's attorney general now has the same kind of authority that the U.S. Department of Justice does to investigate patterns or practices of deprivations of civil rights by law enforcement agencies in the state.[79] The California law al-lows the attorney general to bring civil actions to get injunctive relief to end this conduct, and it gives officials the appropriate authority to conduct investigations, including the power to issue subpoenas to compel testimony under oath and to produce documents. The creation of this state-level pattern-and-practice authority has already borne fruit, allowing the state to enter into a consent decree of its own with Riverside, California.[80] The decree was negotiated by state and local officials; it will be administered that way, too, thus obviating the need for federal intervention.

With these strategies in focus, we can see that there are ways out of the profiling thicket that point toward eliminating the inappropriate use of race from police decision making and toward fostering better policing. Where there's a will, there's a way, and these strategies show that there is, indeed, a way; what's missing now—in political leadership and in police leadership—is the will. Fortunately, the leaders of the police departments mentioned in this chapter (and many others throughout the nation) have shown that it is possible to move forward and to take action. It is now up to all Americans who care about the integrity of policing and the entire criminal justice system to insist that more be done.

Chapter Eight

A CASE STUDY: HOW ONE POLICE AGENCY CHANGED FOR THE BETTER

In the late 1990s, allegations surfaced that the U.S. Customs Service—the agency charged with keeping drugs and other contraband from coming into the country at international borders, including international airports—had made a practice of stopping black women for investigation at highly disproportionate rates. These women were then subjected to what Customs called "intrusive searches," but what happened to them is far more harrowing and degrading than this clinical term would suggest. Yet the story of racial profiling and the Customs Service stands out for another reason. Once these allegations became public, new leadership at Customs confronted the agency's problems openly and forthrightly. The Customs Service was completely turned around, and it now stands as an example of what can be achieved when police leadership determines to remove race and ethnic appearance from its arsenal.

Yvette Bradley and her sister Lori flew into the United States through Newark International Airport around 10:00 P.M. on April 5, 1999.[1] The two women, African Americans, were returning from a vacation to Jamaica, and as passengers on an international flight, both sisters had to clear Customs. They stood in separate lines, and they were sent to a separate area to have their bags hand searched by U.S. Customs officers. The women noticed that the officers singled out a large percentage of black female passengers for these searches, but almost no white passengers. Yvette Bradley remarked on this to the Customs officer assigned to search her bags, but he ignored her and looked through every single item in her suitcase, backpack, and purse. He questioned Bradley, and she told him that she'd been vacationing in Jamaica, that she lived in a penthouse on Fifth Avenue in New York City, and that she was a veteran advertising professional. Exasperated, Bradley had to repack all of her things, but at least, she figured, she'd be going home after the agent finished checking her passport. But her ordeal was just beginning.

The officer directed Bradley toward the closed door of a room off to the side. She asked for an explanation, but got none; he just pointed toward the door and yelled at Bradley to go over to the two female Customs officers standing there. She remembers feeling upset and angry, but also afraid. She didn't know what was going to happen to her, and no one—neither the inspector nor the two female agents—would tell her anything. When she complained, one of the female officers said to the other, "Oh no, not another one, I want to go home." They directed Bradley into a small windowless room, containing only two tables. Once they had the door closed, one officer told Bradley to place her hands against the wall. This was the beginning, Bradley says, of "one of the most humiliating moments of my life. She proceeded to run her hands and fingers over and against every area of my body," Bradley says. "She wasn't patting me down. She was rubbing and running her hands over me, [including] my breasts and the inner and outer labia of my vagina." Calling what happened to her "a sexual assault," Bradley says the officer's fingers penetrated her. Nothing was found, and the officers eventually told Bradley she could go, still refusing to give her any reason that they had selected her for this treatment. She filed a complaint; in response, officials told her she'd been stopped and searched because of her unusual hat. Bradley had, in fact, been wearing a striking piece of headgear by the designer Anna Sui. But Bradley says the hat wasn't even an issue. "None of the officers involved ever asked to examine the hat or even asked me to remove it," she says. Unsatisfied with the flimsy justification, Bradley has filed a lawsuit in federal court.

Unfortunately, Yvette Bradley was not the only black woman to have such an experience. In fact, it eventually became clear that a broad pattern of intrusive searches of black women had been occurring at the hands of Customs agents for some time. Denise Pullian, a Chicago businesswoman, was stopped and searched at O'Hare International Airport.[2] Like Yvette Bradley, the female Customs agent searched her thoroughly—arms, legs, breasts, waist, and crotch. The agent found nothing but asked Pullian something completely unexpected. "She said, 'Is your period on?' And I said, 'Yes.' And she said, 'Well, I just need to verify that your period's on.' " Pullian describes an overwhelming humiliation at the hands of a complete stranger. "So I pulled my clothing down and I took the Kotex out, put that on the counter and took the tampon out and put that on top of the Kotex and asked her, 'Are you satisfied?' " She pauses. "And I said, 'You know, I was married eight years, and my husband never saw what you people saw here.' "

Jenneral Denson's experience was just as terrifying, but longer and more intrusive than many others.[3] Like Bradley and Pullian, Customs officers pulled Denson, an African American female, out of line as she returned to the United States after a trip from Jamaica. Agents detained Denson, who was almost seven months pregnant, and eventually decided that she was smuggling drugs inside her body. They took Denson to a hospital, where they handcuffed her to a bed rail. She asked many times to call her mother or a lawyer; the agents refused. A doctor examined her and, Denson remembers, told the agents that "I didn't have anything inside of me" except the baby, but the agents didn't believe it. They suspected she had swallowed small bundles of illegal drugs wrapped in condoms, and they were determined to catch her. The agents told her she'd have to drink a powerful laxative so that they could check her stool for narcotics. Denson says she didn't want to do it, but she felt she had no choice but to drink the four cups of the stuff they gave her. The next day, with no evidence of drugs, the agents took her back to the airport. Just eight days later, amid bouts of diarrhea and bleeding, Denson underwent an emergency Caesarean section. She later told a congressional committee that she didn't know what effect her ordeal may have had on her son's premature birth, but she wonders all the time.

Outside of the women themselves, few seemed to know anything about these Customs searches. But almost as soon as she arrived home after her ordeal, Denise Pullian did something to change that. Pullian called Renee Ferguson, an award-winning investigative journalist with the NBC television station in Chicago.[4] Ferguson, herself an African American woman, has the kind of credibility with the public that most journalists can only dream about, and she has frequently covered stories in which members of the public have suffered some kind of abuse at the hands of the powerful. Ferguson could feel Pullian's anger as she described her ordeal over the phone. A professional skeptic, Ferguson at first doubted what Pullian had told her, but Pullian told a convincing story—logical, full of details and specifics. Ferguson asked Pullian if she had a criminal record. When Pullian angrily declared she was no criminal and agreed to appear on camera, Ferguson interviewed her. Pullian also agreed to take a polygraph test, than signed a release so that Customs officials could discuss her case.

When Ferguson's story aired, the station received calls from many others—all black women—who said that Customs had put them through the same type of ordeal. Ferguson interviewed many of them, too. "What was most striking," Ferguson said later, was that "these were not ordinary women. They were strong professionals, interesting, educated, articulate with dynamic lives outside of what had happened to them inside a locked room at the airport."[5] Research by Ferguson's producer turned up a lawsuit filed against Customs in San Francisco. A black woman named Amanda Buritica was held for twenty-six hours upon her return from India.[6] Like Jenneral Denson, she had been strip searched, taken to a hospital, and given laxatives because Customs agents suspected her of smuggling drugs internally. The Buritica case gave Ferguson access to a trove of internal Customs documents, such as training manuals that explained the reasons agents searched people. She also found a memorandum outlining a financial incentive program for agents who found drugs on people. Ferguson's report aired on the NBC Nightly News and Dateline NBC, as well as her own station; other stations around the country aired similar stories. (Ferguson later won a DuPont award for her work.)

At the time Ferguson's reports aired, Edward Fox was one of the few other people who seemed to know about strip searches of black women by Customs, but he had no idea of the scope of the problem.[7] Fox, a civil rights lawyer, represented Sharon Anderson, a middle-aged African American schoolteacher who claimed that Customs agents unlawfully searched her on her return from a vacation to Jamaica. Fox filed Anderson's complaint in October 1997, and in March 1998, Anderson told Fox that she had seen Renee Ferguson's report about Denise Pullian. Fox began to get many telephone calls from other African American women with nearly identical stories. As more and more of these women came forward, Fox began to notice the same patterns Renee Ferguson had. First, almost all of the women were African American. Second, most reported that inspectors asked questions that showed that they did not believe that the particular woman had the financial means to travel. Whatever answers the women gave, inspectors directed them to a secondary area for more questioning and a thorough hand search of their baggage and all of their belongings. Third, although these searches rarely recovered anything that could be regarded as suspicious—for example, lubricants used in carrying narcotics in the body, drugs used to suppress bowel movements, or large amounts of cash—the women said that female agents then took them to a small windowless room with a bench or chair and a toilet that did not flush. The women reported that they then were subjected to invasive "pat-down" searches like the one experienced by Yvette Bradley. Fox describes these frisks as "very abusive"—less a pat down of outer clothing and much more of a "groping." Although Fox never heard of any of the pat-down searches turning up any evidence, almost all of the women were then strip-searched. The agents put their hands up under the women's clothes, and many were asked to take off all their clothes and underwear. Some of the women had to stand naked in these inspection rooms for a long time. Many of the women were then subjected to "cavity searches," in which agents instructed them to bend over while they inspected their vaginas and anuses— sometimes visually and sometimes with their fingers. Fox heard over and over that, as far as the women could tell, these intimate searches were conducted on the say-so of a single low-ranking agent, without even the approval of a supervisor. And all of this happened while the women were held incommunicado, their requests to call loved ones or lawyers summarily refused.

Fox now represents about ninety African American women who allege that they were illegally and intrusively searched by Customs agents at O'Hare airport in Chicago. He estimates that a class-action lawsuit will eventually include about thirteen hundred women. In none of these cases were drugs or anything else found; every one of them was a search of an innocent person.

POLICING THE BORDERS

Policing the borders of a country as large as the United States is a huge task. The sheer number of people entering the United States on international flights makes clear the extraordinary size of Customs' job: approximately 140 million airline passengers during fiscal years 1997 and 1998 alone. Each passenger constitutes a discrete screening—a separate person to look over, to question, and to observe in order to decide whether to conduct a more intensive investigation. The Customs Service is, of course, concerned with general merchandise and goods brought in to the country untaxed and unseen. But its highest priority today is not uncovering untaxed bottles of liquor or perfume but stopping illegal drugs. Drug smugglers import some of these substances through international airline flights.[8] The individuals hired to do this are known as "mules." Some carry the drugs strapped to their bodies; some swallow balloons or condoms filled with these substances before their journeys. It is these passengers that Customs agents try to spot in the stream of the tens of millions of international passengers coming into the United States every year. Since there are simply too many passengers to scrutinize each one carefully, Customs relied for years on a list of forty-three factors to use in deciding which passengers deserved the extra scrutiny of a further search—a complex and multilayered profile if ever there was one.

Air passengers entering the country first encounter an agent of the Immigration and Naturalization Service at the control point, for "primary" inspection. This is the place where passengers line up and, when it is their turn, approach the agents at a gate or portal. Passengers present their passports and other travel documents, and often undergo some basic questioning concerning their travel. Then the Immigration agent chooses whether to allow the traveler to pass through the inspection and into the country without further delay or to refer them to Customs for further examination, the so-called secondary inspection. At the secondary inspection, passengers encounter a Customs agent who usually questions them further and may search their luggage or their personal belongings. It is at this point that the agent brings to bear the profile or factors that supposedly indicate that particular persons present a higher than normal risk of involvement in drug smuggling. If the agent suspects that the passenger may be carrying contraband of any kind, the agent may search the passenger's clothing and ultimately subject the passenger to what the Customs Service calls a personal search. These searches are always performed by agents of the same sex as the passenger, but they still go beyond anything that any domestic police department could do without a court order. Personal searches can include frisks, or hand searches like the one performed on Yvette

Bradley. If the pat down does not satisfy the agent, the passenger can be subjected to a continuum of ever-more-intrusive search techniques, such as strip searches, close visual inspections of passengers' bodies, body cavity searches, X rays that allow medical personnel to tell if passengers have contraband inside their bodies, and monitored bowel movements (MBMs). Passengers undergoing MBMs, like Jenneral Denson, are sometimes given strong laxatives to hasten the process.

Given the intrusive nature of these searches, what does the law have to say about them? The Fourth Amendment to the Constitution requires that all searches be reasonable, but searches at the border present a special case. Whether those entering the country are American citizens or foreigners, the Supreme Court has given the Customs Service and other agencies with jurisdiction over the national border complete discretion to pick its methods, its suspects, and its tactics in the effort to insure that objects of objectionable character make their way into the country. It is, quite literally, the most sweeping set of police powers that exists under our laws. Those charged with policing the border operate outside the usual requirements for probable cause or reasonable suspicion that regulate law enforcement in almost every other situation. The Customs Service has free rein to seize whom they want, to search whom they want, and to search how they want, without having to demonstrate any need, cause, or reason to suspect the commission of a crime. In short, if police in other situations use high-discretion tactics to put profiles to work, police at the border can use discretion unbounded by any rules at all.

THE FACTS: THE GENERAL ACCOUNTING OFFICE REPORT ON SEARCHES BY THE CUSTOMS SERVICE

The intense media coverage that began with Renee Ferguson's report about Denise Pullian generated a good deal of public criticism of Customs. Congressional hearings took place in May 1999. Amanda Buritica and Jenneral Denson testified about what had happened to them, and attorney Edward Fox discussed the patterns of conduct by Customs in these cases.[9] Ray Kelly, the former head of the New York Police Department who had become U.S. Commissioner of Customs only a short time before, promised the congressional committee that racial bias in intrusive searches "is certainly not the Customs Service policy, and it will not be tolerated as a Customs Service practice anywhere."[10] Kelly said that these tactics might have flourished because "there may be a mindset, and we have to ferret it out, and then we have to deal with it through discipline."[11] Senator Richard Durbin of Illinois ordered an investigation by the General Accounting Office (GAO), and Kelly appointed his own group, the Personal Search Review Committee, to study the problem. He also made some substantive changes in agency operation before either the GAO or Personal Search Review Committee delivered their reports.

When it was released in March 2000, the GAO report[12] confirmed that the stories heard at the congressional hearing were not aberrations or accidents. They were part of an ongoing pattern: African American women were, in fact, subjected to intrusive personal searches at higher rates than their presence in the traveling population would predict. First, data from all of the 102,000 personal searches in fiscal years 1997 and 1998 revealed that fully 43 percent of all of those subjected to some kind of personal search were minorities—a figure far greater than their proportion of the traveling population.[13] Among U.S. citizens searched in 1998, black women were *nine times* more likely to be x-rayed on suspicion of internal drug smuggling than white women.[14] Data from 1997 showed that Customs agents strip-searched black women more often than any other group of passengers.[15] Whereas white men and women were equally likely to be strip searched, black, Hispanic, and Asian women were all almost three times as likely to be strip searched than black, Hispanic, and Asian men[16]—demonstrating that these searches were not just based on racial and ethnic discrimination but on gender bias as well. Some of the same patterns seen in searches of black women emerged in searches of Hispanics, who were four times as likely to be x-rayed as either white women or white men.[17] In other words, the pattern was real; black women (and, to a lesser extent, all minority women) were having their bodies searched, inspected, probed, and x-rayed out of proportion to what their presence among air travelers would suggest.

Perhaps even more startling was the evidence on the rates at which Customs agents found drugs and other contraband. Black women, who were the most likely of all racial and gender groups to be strip searched, were only half as likely as black men to actually be found with drugs or other contraband as a result of these searches. Black women were much more likely than either Hispanic men or women to be strip searched, but again much less likely to be found carrying drugs.[18] Black women were also almost twice as likely to be strip searched as white women, but they were not twice as likely to be carrying drugs or other contraband.[19] The data on X-ray searches were even more skewed. Black women were the *most* likely among all groups to be x-rayed but were actually the *least* likely to be found carrying drugs in their bodies. They were nine times as likely as white women to be x-rayed but only about half as likely to actually be found with drugs. Similarly, Hispanic women were four times as likely as white women to be x-rayed, but only about two-thirds as likely to have contraband found during an X-ray. White and black men were equally likely to be found with drugs by an X-ray; all other minorities were less likely to be found carrying drugs or other contraband by an X-ray.[20] Overall, Customs' "hit rates" for the 51,000 searches it conducted in 1998 were wildly out of balance with who inspectors searched (see chapter 4).

The Customs Service did not seem to be aware of the ineffectiveness of its efforts. It directed its resources into targeting particular groups of people for searches—even though its own numbers showed that this was in fact the least effective way to find the drugs they were after. The GAO report confirmed the numbers showed that black women and other minorities were being searched "at rates that were not consistent with the rates of finding contraband." It recommended "that Customs compare the characteristics of those passengers subjected to personal searches with the results of those searches to better target passengers carrying contraband."

Commissioner Kelly's Personal Search Review Committee issued its report just a few months after the GAO report.[21] It received harsh criticism for focusing too little attention on the evidence of racial profiling; indeed, the report pointedly refused to draw any conclusions at all on that issue.[22] But, like the GAO report, it contained some interesting information of the percentage of "hits"—that is, the percentage of personal searches that actually turned up drugs or other contraband. Again, for anyone holding the "commonsense" belief that drug dealers are predominantly minority citizens, these numbers would come as something of a surprise.

Period	Racial or Ethnic Group	% of All "Hits"
Sept. '96–Sept. '97	Whites	28
	Blacks	22
	Hispanics	20
Sept. '97–Sept. '98	Whites	45
	Blacks	24
	Hispanics	14
Sept. '98–Sept. '99	Whites	42
	Blacks	27
	Hispanics	17[23]

In other words, the Customs Service searched blacks and Hispanics more often, sometimes by a substantial margin. But these searches were misdirected. Searches of whites turned up evidence more often. The right hand did not seem to know what the left hand was doing.

Customs' Response: Changes and Preliminary Results

Commissioner Kelly began to act on the accusations of disproportionate use of intrusive seizures against black women before the GAO report was issued in March 2000. Two interim reviews helped move some of these efforts forward. In June

1999, the U.S. Treasury Department's Office of Professional Responsibility issued a report on Customs search practices. Noting that "Customs did not conduct routine reviews to ensure that the criteria and targeting policy . . . are accurate and do not become discriminatory," the report recommended periodic reviews of the factors Customs used to target passengers to assure that these factors "continue to be reasonable predictors of illegal behavior."[24] Just a month later, Customs' own Passenger Targeting Committee reported that Customs' methods for selecting passengers required regular review and updating because "use of a standard list of targeting criteria has little value in a constantly changing environment."[25] Specifically, the Committee recommended that Customs eliminate the use of its list of forty-three articulable factors; that the agency emphasize to its agents that some factors thought to indicate suspiciousness may no longer do so; and that the agency adopt better technology for data collection on searches, which would allow it to make routine assessments of its effort to target drug-smuggling passengers.[26]

Amid all of this public controversy and media attention, Kelly began responding. He dramatically increased the involvement of supervisors in the process. In the past, any Customs agent could decide, on his or her own, to search a passenger. Kelly changed this. Starting in May 1999, personal searches, including pat downs,[27] required a supervisor's approval. For more intrusive searches, like strip searches, body-cavity searches, X rays, and MBMs, agents would need the approval of the port director if the passenger consented to the procedure. Without consent, agents would have to get a court order.[28] In other words, before conducting any personal searches, Customs agents would have to get the permission of their supervisors or higher officials. At the very least, this would cause agents to think twice before recommending a search.

Agents were also required to meet particular standards of evidence in order to conduct these searches. No search could take place unless the agent had reasonable articulable suspicion of wrongdoing by the person to be searched. The list of forty-three

factors indicating suspicion that Customs had long used was
eliminated, as the Passenger Targeting Committee had recommended, and in its place, Customs adopted the following six
"categories" of information to guide agents deciding whether to
conduct personal searches:

- Behavioral analysis—recognition of physical signs of ner-
  vousness, such as sweating and avoidance of eye contact.
- Observational techniques—the recognition of physical
  oddities in appearance, such as an unnatural gait or an unexpected bulge.
- Inconsistencies—interviews or documents that yield information that doesn't mesh.
- Intelligence—sources of information from outside the encounter.
- K-9—"alert" from a drug-sniffing dog that drugs are present.
- Searches incident to arrest or seizure—when a seizure or
  arrest results in the discovery of evidence, other searches
  may be considered.[29]

Customs agents would also have to get a court order from a
federal magistrate any time they detained a passenger for more
than four hours. And when a passenger was detained for more
than eight hours but probable cause had still not become apparent, agents would alert the United States attorney for their district. The requirement for a court order and the involvement of
the U.S. attorney would, at the very least, cause Customs agents
and supervisors to think through the legalities of the situation
with care. It would also bring legal expertise to the Customs
agents in a very direct way. Customs also moved to address a
common complaint. Much of the time that Customs agents had
conducted personal searches, it held passengers incommunicado,
and agents routinely refused requests to call family members and
friends—even when people were waiting to pick up the passengers. Now agents would be required to notify a friend, family

member, or an attorney for a passenger when asked to do so. Finally, Customs introduced electronic body-scanning equipment at several major airports. These machines would allow agents to search for contraband under the clothing of passengers unintrusively—in effect, to do an electronic pat down and strip search of the individual without ever touching them. Passengers could choose to have the scanner used on them instead of other, more invasive, procedures.[30]

These changes, along with extensive new training programs Kelly put in place, seemed calculated to respond to the complaints about Customs' heavy-handedness and to create a better balance between the agency's drug interdiction mission and its relationships with the millions of people that passed through its jurisdiction. And, looking back over more than two years, the changes Kelly made have begun to make a difference. The number of personal searches has fallen since Kelly's reforms took place. Data on the first six months of fiscal year 2000 show that Customs searches dropped 75 percent from the levels seen in the first six months of fiscal 1999.[31] This followed a large drop the previous year. Customs conducted 47 percent fewer searches on arriving passengers in fiscal year 1999 than it had in 1998. Some saw their worst nightmare in these numbers. Softer drug-interdiction policy making agents gun-shy and hesitant to do their jobs. Several officials blamed Kelly's directives requiring supervisory approval and "reasonable suspicion"; one official said that "there's a concern out there, that we're letting our guard down on the first line of defense in the war on drugs, our borders."[32] But the real surprise came when the numbers showing these declines were compared to the percentages of searches in which agents found drugs or other contraband. Even as the numbers of searches fell, hit rates were going up. Customs agents were finding what they were after *in much higher percentages of searches than ever.* In FY 1998, Customs' hit rate had been 3.5 percent. In FY 1999, as the number of searches fell, the hit rate increased to 5.8 percent—a jump of 60 percent.[33] In the first six months of FY 2000, as searches fell 75 percent, the hit rate increased again—to more than 13 percent. As the number of searches dropped, the "efficiency" of those searches—the rate at which they produced evidence—increased dramatically.[34] Kelly himself received daily reports on search activity by Customs agents around the country so that he could keep on top of problems and communicate with supervisors in the field about any trends or difficulties he noticed. What happened is that Customs agents narrowed their focus to a better set of candidates for searches. Reined in by closer supervision and regulation, they became better, more precise, and efficient police officers. And in the bargain, the number of innocent travelers subjected to invasive, humiliating personal searches has decreased drastically—surely a tangible benefit. Kelly summed it up simply—his agents were "doing it smarter." [35] And the latest numbers on searches by Customs back him up. Searches fell dramatically between 1998 and 2000, overall hit rates *increased,* racial disparities in searches nearly disappeared, and hit rates for all racial and ethnic groups have become nearly even—just as all the rest of the hit-rate data (see chapter 4) predict it would be.

The Customs Service's experience with racial profiling is instructive—both as a cautionary tale and a story of what can happen with strong leadership determined to root out these types of abuses. Under Ray Kelly, the Customs Service stopped its misguided and abusive profiling practices and strove to do better. The result was not only the fair and respectful treatment that passengers deserve but also better, sharper, more efficient policing.

The lesson is clear. Police agencies are difficult to change, and change takes imagination, effort, and determination. But we know it can be done. What's at stake is the best of our country and our Constitution—nothing less than the fabric of our democratic culture.

Chapter Nine

RACIAL PROFILING AFTER SEPTEMBER 11, 2001: NEW REALITY, SAME PROBLEMS

In the aftermath of September 11, discussion of most domestic political issues that had been on the table—education reform, tax cuts, oil drilling in the Arctic National Wildlife Refuge—ceased completely for months. But the issue of racial profiling—which, like these other issues, had been extremely visible, including hearings in the U.S. Senate on August 1, 2001, and continued legislative action in states around the country—did not disappear. In fact, it seemed to gain immediate importance, even as it was dramatically recast.

Before September 11, 2001, a consensus had emerged in our country concerning the issue of racial profiling, a consensus as surprising for its magnitude as for the fact that it involved the always volatile and divisive subject of race relations. *Almost 60 percent* of the American public—not just African Americans and Latinos, but all citizens—said they believed that racial profiling was a widely used police tactic.[1] In survey questions carefully worded to allow respondents to support racial profiling as a "legitimate" law enforcement tool that would catch criminals, *81 percent* of those surveyed said they disapproved of racial profiling and wanted it rooted out of law enforcement.[2] But after September 11, Americans appeared to have rethought racial profiling. In polling after the attacks on the World Trade Center and the Pentagon, over 50 percent of Americans, including members of minority groups who had been most widely victimized by profiling in the past, now said they supported the use of profiling—as long as it was profiling of Middle Easterners and Muslims, at airports.[3]

The reasons for this are not difficult to fathom. As one commentator pointed out in the pages of the *Wall Street Journal,* all of the nineteen suicide hijackers—not some, not most, but *all*—came from a well-defined demographic group: They were young Muslim men from the Middle East. The threat we faced came from Al Qaeda, a group made up largely of Muslims from the Middle East who used a radical interpretation of Islam as the platform for their announced campaign of terror against the United States and the rest of the "infidel" West.

In a heartbeat, everything we'd learned about profiling—its costs and the illusory nature of its crime-fighting benefits, how racial or ethnic characteristics can do a fine job describing known suspects of past crimes but a notoriously poor job of predicting who might perpetrate future crimes—seemed to dissolve. Since the perpetrators were all young Muslim men from the Middle East, the solution seemed obvious: We need to use an ethnic profile at airports that would focus us on young Middle Eastern men. An ethnic profile targeting them wasn't discrimination; it was a sensible antiterrorist measure. Branding everyone who disagreed with her a traitor, syndicated columnist Kathleen Parker gave voice to the common "profiling just makes common sense" feeling when she called racial profiling of Middle Eastern men "a temporary necessity that no patriotic American should protest."[4] And Parker was not alone. Stanley Crouch, African American social critic and columnist for the New York *Daily News* and recipient of a MacArthur Foundation "genius" grant, described his thoughts in language even sharper than Parker's. In a column that ran nationwide[5]—one newspaper titled it "Wake Up: Arabs Should Be Profiled"[6]—Crouch was uncompromising:

"[A]ll those who denounce so-called Arab profiling . . . need to put their faces in a bowl of cold water for a few seconds and wake up . . . [I]f pressure has to be kept on innocent Arabs until those Arabs who are intent on committing mass murder are flushed out, that is the unfortunate cost that they must pay to reside in this nation."

But the unfortunate fact is that instead of making us safer, using racial and ethnic profiling in the struggle against Al Qaeda and its allies will actually damage our antiterrorism efforts. Profiling may seem to be the obvious "commonsense," "rational" answer. But Parker, Crouch, and all those who favor using Arab or Muslim profiling now forget the essential inability of race-based profiles to accurately predict anyone's future involvement in any criminal activity. Using racial or ethnic appearance to identify known suspects in past crimes presents no problem. But as we saw in Chapter Two with the failed hijacker profile of the late 1960s and early 1970s, and in Chapter Four with Drug War "hit rates," using race or ethnicity to try to figure out who might be involved in crimes not yet known is folly. It actually makes police work less effective; officers get fewer bad guys off the street when they use race as a predictive factor than when they use behavior to spot offenders. If we take the time to think clearly about what we learned about racial and ethnic profiling before September 11—a task that is much more difficult than it sounds in a time of real fear—we will see that there are genuine reasons to avoid using this tactic now.

Is It Happening?

The first question we should ask is whether profiling of Arabs and Muslims is in fact happening. Many media reports in 2002 seemed to reflect a widespread belief that the federal government has bent over backward to avoid any accusation of racial or ethnic profiling. For example, an article featured in *Time* on July 15, 2002, on the state of aviation security trumpeted the belief that, as much as airport defenses against terrorism had improved since September 11, what had been done wasn't nearly enough; the measure most urgently—and obviously—needed was ethnic profiling of Arabs and Middle Easterners.[7] Bruce Baumgartner, manager of aviation at Denver International Airport, was among a number of officials at the airport who told *Time* that "more profiling needs to be done, not less."[8]

Although certain officials say that their agencies are not using racial or ethnic profiling and will not do so—Secretary of Transportation Norman Mineta has made a special point of emphasizing this policy in his speeches and public appearances[9]—it is also obvious that ethnic targeting is definitely in use, regardless of official statements and rules. An airport screener at Denver who spoke on condition of anonymity told *Time* that "for me, profiling is the only way to be conscientious in doing the job. I make decisions based on who I wouldn't like to be seated next to on an airplane." Without any hint that his or her method might lend itself to poor antiterrorism enforcement as well as racial and ethnic stereotyping, the screener said that appearance was in fact all-important. "If someone is unkempt and nervous or if they look like they belong on a bus instead of a plane, if they wear a baseball cap backwards, and, without question, if they look to be foreign or of Middle Eastern descent," that person would be stopped and searched.[10]

By early 2002, the effort to focus law enforcement on indicators that a person may be Muslim or Arab had spread from airports to many other settings. For example, federal law enforcement officials now travel the nation offering antiterrorism training to state and local police. In an eerie echo of Operation Pipeline, the DEA program of the 1980s and 1990s in which federal agents trained thousands of state and local police officers to use profiles to spot potential drug dealers and couriers on the highways,[11] federal trainers are again instructing state and local officers, this time in how to use traffic stops as a pretext to spot potential terrorists. And the methods imparted are not at all subtle. "Among the items police are taught to look for besides phony passports and fake or stolen drivers' licenses: prayer rugs and copies of the Koran, Islam's holy book." [12]

But even more troubling, and considerably more far reaching, have been the actions and statements of Attorney General John Ashcroft and the U.S. Department of Justice. In the fall of 2001, Attorney General Ashcroft announced that the department had generated a list of five thousand young men from the Middle East with whom it wished to conduct "voluntary" interviews. (In the spring of 2002, the attorney general expanded the list by adding another three thousand names, bringing the total to eight thousand.) The department had also detained hundreds of Middle Easterners on petty immigration infractions and minor criminal violations. Admittedly, violators of immigration law detained by the Department of Justice have broken the law. But so have literally hundreds of thousands of other people in this country. [13] Yet the government has detained only immigration violators who are members of one narrow group—Muslims and Middle Easterners—and they appear to have been selected for this treatment by virtue of ethnicity.

All of this amounts to racial profiling.

Is This Profiling Legal?

If these antiterrorism tactics do indeed amount to ethnic profiling, a second question arises: Are they legal? To use one example, the "voluntary" questioning of eight thousand men presents a complex set of legal questions. In every discussion of the plan, the attorney general and his deputies were careful to stress that the men were not suspects; they were not being questioned as persons upon whom the veil of suspicion had been cast. Rather, Justice Department officials simply wanted to talk to the men, they said, because they might know something useful—perhaps something they did not even realize was important. [14]

Most of all, department officials stressed that the interviews were strictly voluntary. No one with any misgivings had to talk to them, they said; and because these were voluntary interviews of nonsuspects, there was no need for any of them to retain or seek the advice of counsel, or to be accompanied by counsel during the interviews.[15] Indeed, the November 9, 2001, Department of Justice memorandum to "All United States Attorneys" containing the order to carry out the questioning stresses this very point. "Since the persons to be interviewed are not suspected of involvement in criminal activity, the interviews will be conducted on a consensual basis and every interview subject . . . will be free to decline to answer questions."[16] And it is not hard to understand why the Department of Justice stresses the idea that the interviews are to be voluntary. If true, this would go a long way toward answering critics who might argue that the department was illegally "rounding up" Arabs and Muslims for questioning in ways that the Constitution does not permit.

But the same memorandum throws the actual voluntariness of these questioning sessions, as well as the "nonsuspect" status of the men, into question. First, while carefully stating that the interviews are to be "consensual" and that every individual "will be free to decline to answer," and that the interviews will not ordinarily be conducted at a police station or other law enforcement office, the memorandum points government agents who will conduct the interviews away from using the usual safeguards that accompany police interviews. In an obvious effort to keep the "nonsuspects" from contacting attorneys, the memorandum tells agents to steer clear of the traditional Miranda warnings, which might, the memorandum implies, encourage the interviewees to seek counsel: "As these interviews will not be 'custodial interrogations,' there is no need to seek a waiver of Miranda rights."[17]

The Department of Justice memorandum also raises the specter of the very same tool already most misused against, and feared by, Middle Easterners in the wake of September 11: detention for immigration violations. The existence of these violations, the memorandum implies, would make a good source of leverage against anyone who might decline to answer questions, and it is hard to imagine that a competent agent reading the memorandum would not understand the suggestion:

> While the primary purpose of these interviews is not to ascertain the legality of the individual's immigration status, the federal responsibility to enforce immigration laws, as exercised by [the INS], is an important one. Therefore, if you suspect that a particular individual may be in violation of the federal immigration laws, you should call the INS representative on your Anti-Terrorism Task Force or the INS official at the closest Law Enforcement Support Center.[18]

In other words, this is all voluntary, and none of these people is a suspect, but immigration violations might provide you with what you need to get the individuals to "voluntarily" comply with your "request," or even with what you need to lock them up.

The upshot of all of this is hard to miss. The Department of Justice has obeyed the letter of the law, at least on paper. But the spirit of what it is doing is quite different, and very reminiscent of the War on Drugs: Using the discretion it has in one area of the law—in the War on Drugs, law governing driving and vehicles; in the War on Terror, law governing immigration—as a pretext to make its way around constitutional mandates that would otherwise apply. The parallel is strong, and disconcerting.

WILL IT WORK?

Aside from the existence of profiling and its legality, a third question about the use of racial or ethnic profiling in the antiterrorism effort—one that recalls the central theme of Chapter Four—is surely relevant: Will it work? Will using the fact that a person is Arab, Muslim, or Middle Eastern as part of a profile actually help to make us safe from Al Qaeda terrorists and their murder-

ous intentions? Most people today regard the use of ethnic profiles against Middle Easterners as "just common sense" in the
fight against terrorism. But, as in the War on Drugs and the fight
against crime on the street, this "rational" profiling of Middle
Easterners has little to do with good, solid law enforcement. And
in the end, it will almost certainly blunt our efforts to protect
ourselves against Al Qaeda.

As we saw in Chapter Four, when we use skin color or ethnic
appearance as a proxy for criminality, our law enforcement
agents shift their attention away from what counts—how people
behave—and instead turn their attention to whether people resemble their mental images of what their targets "should" look
like. For example, several of the suicide hijackers behaved suspiciously just prior to their flights on September 11. They bought
one-way tickets, made reservations a relatively short amount of
time before their flights, and they paid for the tickets with large
amounts of cash. Although any one of these behaviors might not
raise any alarm, they become suspicious when a number of them
come together.[19] Other hijackers exhibited suspicious behavior
when they approached flight schools for instruction in flying
commercial jets like Boeing 747s—just flying them, not taking
off or landing.[20] The basis for profiles should be these behaviors—not the color of people's skin or their country of origin. Focusing on the latter takes attention from the former.

The distraction of our enforcement agents from all-important
behavioral clues leads directly to a related point. Profiling is always overinclusive. Even a "good" profile—one that is based on
rigorously analyzed statistics that are culled from plentiful, systematically collected data—will cast suspicion over more innocent people than guilty ones. When we construct a profile using
the wrong kind of characteristic—a racial or an ethnic one as opposed to markers of behavior—we spread our enforcement resources and efforts more thinly than we would otherwise. Even
the FBI does not have unlimited man power; every person FBI
agents must investigate because he "looks like a terrorist" means
that much less in the way of enforcement resources available to

investigate individuals who actually behave suspiciously. And that is a trade-off that makes little sense.

As with other forms of racial profiling, using ethnicity to try to identify terrorists has the added consequence of alienating the very community most able to help with effective law enforcement. If the observation of behavior is one of the pillars of good, solid police work, the collection and analysis of intelligence is surely another. Intelligence in police work is simply the collection and smart use of information—information that tells law enforcement about things in a community that are out of place or out of line, things that seem suspicious, statements and braggadocio that might indicate guilt.

We have heard numerous times since September 11, 2001, how the events of that day represent a massive failure of the intelligence agencies to collect the necessary information, due to a lack of field agents, and an even more egregious failure to "connect the dots" concerning the intelligence that they had in hand. These failures, and the possibility that, as Attorney General Ashcroft said months after the attacks, we may very well still have Al Qaeda "sleeper" cells of Middle Easterners on our soil,[21] obviously make intelligence gathering more crucial than it has ever been. This means that helpful information on this front will almost certainly have to come from those most likely to encounter these "sleeper" members of Al Qaeda: *members of Middle Eastern, Muslim, and Arab communities.* Thus what we need most right now are solid relationships with the Arab and Muslim communities in the United States—relationships based on trust and mutual interest, fostered over time working as partners in fighting crime. But instead of building such solid connections with Middle Eastern communities, we insist on damaging these relationships with mass detentions and questioning.

The exact number of Middle Easterners still detained on petty immigration and criminal violations as of this writing is not known.[22] Reports indicate that over twelve hundred have been detained, with almost eight hundred of those people already deported. Estimates of the number still held as of August 2002 range from eighty-one (according to the Department of Justice) to almost two hundred.[23] If any of these detentions used race and ethnicity as a characteristic to identify particular known suspects in the September 11 crimes, we might find the detention of even such a large number of persons acceptable; using race or ethnic appearance as a way to identify known perpetrators is good police work. Racial or ethnic characteristics are easily observable, and cannot be changed, like clothing or hairstyle. This makes them ideal components of descriptions of specific people suspected of having already committed crime. But this is the only legitimate and effective use of racial or ethnic characteristics in crime fighting.

In the case of the monstrous crimes of September 11, however, all of the known perpetrators are dead. And the physical characteristics of any potential coconspirators who did not die on the planes are unknown. Thus racial and ethnic appearance are being used not to describe known terrorists but to attempt to predict which people could be terrorists—to divine *who might commit acts of terrorism in the future.*

Not surprisingly, all indications as of September 2002—a year later—are that this strategy has yielded nothing, certainly with respect to past crimes. *Not one* individual detained has been found to have any connection to the events of September 11.[24] *Not one* of these detentions yielded any information about the crimes of that day; *not one* person detained was charged with any related offense. The only person charged with any crime in connection with the September 11 hijackings was Zacarias Moussaoui, the alleged "twentieth hijacker," who was arrested in August of 2001—well before the attacks.

The ability of racial profiling to predict and prevent future crimes remains to be seen, and if our past experiences are any guide—using profiles to predict hijackings in the late 1960s and early 1970s—we are extremely unlikely to see any positive results. When John Ashcroft announced that the mass questionings of five thousand young Arab and Muslim men would be extended to another three thousand similar men, the attorney general said that the initial round of interviews had "proven to be valuable sources of information about the would-be terrorists in our midst." [25] But when asked for specifics, Ashcroft refused to give them, arguing that any disclosure might expose "sensitive law-enforcement information." [26] Hundreds detained and thousands questioned is a high price to pay for "yes, it's been helpful, but we can't tell you how."

What we know for sure is that, despite Department of Justice assurances to the contrary, the cost of this approach has been high. These tactics have clearly done deep damage to the relationship between Arab and Muslim communities and federal law enforcement, and to intelligence gathering that depends on these relationships. The questioning and detention did not create bonds between law enforcement and Arab and Muslim communities, as Attorney General Ashcroft asserted; rather, they sowed fear, frustration, and anger. Hussein Ibish, a spokesman for the American-Arab Anti-Discrimination Committee, put it gently, saying, "I don't think it builds trust to interview thousands of people based on a racial profile." [27] Representative John Conyers, whose metropolitan Detroit congressional district contains the largest concentration of Arabs and Muslims in the United States, was more blunt: "The suggestion that Arab and Muslim Americans appreciated being singled out and interrogated is a prime example of the attorney general's wartime propaganda machine in full swing." Although Conyers had found the national leadership of Arab and Muslim organizations willing to help the United States in the war against terrorism, Conyers said that these leaders had repeatedly "expressed to me their outrage" over the questionings. [28]

Such tactics will not foster trust. They will not help build the solid relationships necessary for effective communication and real partnership with Arabs and Middle Easterners. Rather, they will send a clear message to these communities that we regard their members not as our partners in terror prevention, but as potential terrorists—in short, suspects. And that will destroy our ability to gather the crucial intelligence we need to combat terrorism effectively.

All of this explains why a number of high-placed law enforcement professionals quickly rejected the "common sense" of profiling Middle Easterners. Attorney General Ashcroft's "voluntary" questioning of Middle Eastern men met with instant skepticism in many major police departments. Command staff quickly recognized the damage that this questioning would do to their long-term efforts to build crime-fighting partnerships and intelligence links with their Middle Eastern communities.[29] Eight former FBI officials, including former FBI and CIA chief William H. Webster, went on record in the *Washington Post* to voice doubts about the law enforcement value of these tactics. "It's the Perry Mason School of Law Enforcement," according to Kenneth Walton, a former assistant FBI director. The interviews, he said, would likely produce nothing more valuable than "the recipe to Mom's chicken soup."[30] In a profession like law enforcement, in which the unwillingness to question or dissent from command authority is as rare as it is in the military, and in which the reluctance to criticize fellow officers is sometimes called "the blue wall of silence," any public criticism of the attorney general's orders would have been noticeable enough. Questioning of these orders in such a harsh fashion by such high-ranking officials, even former ones, amounts to dissent that is nothing short of astounding.

And these former officials were not alone. Senior intelligence officials—not political appointees, but down-in-the-trenches, "been there done that" professionals now serving the nation—circulated a memorandum early in the fall of 2001, in the aftermath of the attacks, that warned law enforcement and intelligence agents about the dangers of racial and ethnic profiling. Profiling with racial or ethnic characteristics should be avoided at all costs, they said, but not because it was politically incorrect, would generate bad publicity, or might lead to lawsuits. The reasons were much more straightforward: Profiling with these skin-deep characteristics would fail. The only way to succeed was careful observation of suspicious behavior and systematic, straightforward intelligence gathering.[31] "[F]undamentally, believing that you can achieve safety by looking at characteristics instead of behavior is silly," one of the officials told the *Boston Globe*. "If your goal is preventing attacks ... you want your eyes and ears looking for pre-attack behaviors, not characteristics." [32] Sadly, this warning seems not to have penetrated the uppermost levels of the Department of Justice.

A final reason to avoid racial and ethnic profiling in the War on Terror involves the terrorists we will miss. It is easy to forget that prior to September 2001, the largest and most deadly terrorist attack on American soil was carried out not by Muslim Arabs or foreigners from anywhere else in the world, but by homegrown attackers. The Oklahoma City bomber, Timothy McVeigh, and his accomplice, Terry Nichols, were both white male U.S. Army veterans from the American Heartland—McVeigh from a small town in upstate New York, Nichols from Michigan. Yet there was no roundup or mass questioning of white male veterans, and many people would likely have been both surprised and angered if there had been. The unfortunate and unhappy truth is that we simply do not know what the next group of terrorists will look like. Richard Reid, the man accused of trying to destroy an airliner with a bomb in his shoe, and the first Al Qaeda attacker sent to harm us after the events of September 11, is a British citizen not of Middle Eastern or Muslim origin. Jose Padilla, whom Attorney General Ashcroft accused of plotting an attack with a nuclear "dirty bomb," is an American of Hispanic origin and a former Chicago gang member. We saw it in Chapter Four, and it seems that we are seeing it again: Appearance is a poor predictor of behavior.

BACKLASH: THE WAR ON TERROR'S EFFECT ON THE RACIAL-PROFILING DEBATE

In the spring of 2002, a new controversy erupted over racial profiling on the highways of New Jersey. It made national news, with a single idea taking the lead: There was new evidence that showed there had never been, in fact, any racial profiling in New Jersey. The turnabout was so swift—and the evidence for it so thin—that one wonders whether this new evidence would have had the same resonance without the recasting of the racial profiling question in light of the events of September 11, 2001.

Faced with persistent numbers showing that, even after a settlement with the federal government requiring new procedures and systems to combat racial profiling, blacks were still being stopped in numbers disproportionate to their presence on the highway, the New Jersey Attorney General's Office commissioned a study of speeding behavior on the New Jersey Turnpike. Using high-speed photography and radar guns, researchers monitored the speed of vehicles traveling on the road and identified the race of the drivers. An independent panel of evaluators then examined the photos to arrive at the best possible judgment about each driver's race. The study concluded that black drivers on the turnpike were more likely to be speeding than others: Black motorists "are twice as likely to speed as white drivers, and are even more dominant among drivers breaking 90 miles per hour." [33] Blacks were 25 percent of all violators of the speed limit, and were 23 percent of all of those stopped during the study period. [34]

When the study was completed, both the U.S. Department of Justice and the New Jersey Attorney General's Office raised objections to its methodology and its conclusions. [35] But when the study was obtained by the *Bergen Record,* one of the state's largest circulation newspapers, the paper posted the study on its Web site. What happened next was truly unfortunate—a crass distortion of the power of statistics and their meaning in the service of ideology.

Almost as soon as the study hit the press, it was immediately hailed as conclusive evidence that there was not—indeed, that there never had been—any such thing as racial profiling in New Jersey. This was hardly surprising coming from New Jersey's state police themselves and their defenders. According to Kenneth J. McClelland, president of the State Troopers Fraternal Association, the study "proves what we said, that the vast majority of troopers were stopping people because of the way they drove, not because of their race. . . . We feel vindicated by this." [36] But even less personally invested critics, including the Manhattan Institute's Heather MacDonald, latched onto the New Jersey speeding study, quickly declaring "The Racial Profiling Myth Debunked." [37] Given the New Jersey study, she wrote, "the evidence shows that systematic racial profiling by police does not exist." [38]

The problem with this conclusion is that it simply isn't supported by the data in the New Jersey speeding study, even assuming the correctness of the study's methodology. First, as discussed in Chapter Two, even the most cursory glance at any state's vehicle code reveals an almost endless variety of possible moving violations,[39] along with a seemingly limitless number of offenses based not on driving itself but on the condition and equipment in the vehicle.[40] Speeding is only one possible violation among many. Indeed, of the 1,084 stops on Interstate 95 in Florida by Sheriff Bob Vogel's officers discussed in Chapter Three, only 155, or about 15 percent, were for speeding. Most were for a variety of other offenses, such as following too closely (237, or about 22 percent), swerving (253, or 23 percent), burned-out license tag illumination bulbs (71, or about 7 percent), improper license tags (46, or about 4 percent), failure to signal lane change, or unsafe lane change (67, or 6 percent), or other unknown or miscellaneous violations (255, or 23 percent). In other words, speeding was not the largest category of stops, or even the second or third largest; it represented less than one seventh of all of the stops.[41] Clearly, then, even accepting the New Jersey study's conclusions, something else—not driving behavior—is responsible for the disproportionate number of highway stops of African American drivers. And the obvious answer is police discretion. Because everyone violates some aspect of the incredibly detailed traffic code during even the shortest drive, police *decide* whom they should stop. John Lamberth's studies in New Jersey drive this point home. Lamberth found that police officers assigned to use radar from inside a closed van to pick out speeding cars without viewing the cars or the drivers stopped a percentage of black drivers very nearly mirroring the percentage of black drivers on the road—about 18 percent. Racial disproportions became glaring, however, when he looked at general patrol units—those police officers that are assigned not to find traffic violators but to look for crime generally. These officers would see the drivers and, using their *discretion* about whom to stop, would use traffic enforcement as a pretext to pull drivers over and "fish" for evidence of crime. For these units, the proportion of black drivers stopped doubled—to 36 percent.[42]

Beyond police stops, even stronger evidence from New Jersey shows that race and ethnic appearance play a role in deciding *which of those stopped drivers police decide to search.* Recall that a traffic offense alone does not give a police officer the right to search a car. To do that, the officer must observe something that gives him probable cause to believe a crime is afoot. Failing that, an officer may simply ask for the driver's consent for a search. And, according to the U.S. Supreme Court, police need no probable cause, fact-based suspicion, or any evidence at all to ask.[43] (New Jersey's own highest court restricted the use of consent searches in the state in 2002, finding that they had played a key role in racial profiling.)[44] So it is no surprise that consent searches have been the primary tool police use to search the drivers they stop. Because no evidence is needed for consent searches, patterns in these searches, more than in traffic stops themselves, represent the clearest possible picture of how officers exercise their discretion. Whether a driver was speeding, of course, has nothing to do with this.

The evidence concerning how some members of the New Jersey State Police exercise this discretion to perform consent searches remains powerfully damning. For example, in 2000, searches by troopers at the Moorestown station—a center of much of the profiling activity in prior years—showed a clear racial pattern. Blacks made up 53 percent of all those drivers subjected to consent searches and Latinos were 25 percent, whereas whites were only 19 percent. For blacks and Latinos, these percentages were far higher than their representation among drivers on the road or even among drivers stopped.[45]

Just as troubling, this exercise of discretion continues despite evidence that the use of race or ethnicity to decide who is suspicious and therefore worth stopping and searching is not an effective police tactic. The same statistics from the Moorestown station indicated that when troopers stopped and searched blacks, they got a lower rate of return—that is, they found drugs, guns, or evidence of other crime much less often—than they did for whites. In other words, the hit rates—the rates at which the searches succeed in finding contraband or criminals—do not support profiling. The hit rate for searches of whites, 25 percent, was nearly twice as high as the hit rate for searches of blacks, 13 percent. And the white hit rate was five times higher than the hit rate for Latinos, which was just 5 percent.[46]

Perhaps most curious of all, MacDonald and others who want to dismiss the existence of racial profiling apparently don't see that the New Jersey speeding study does nothing to explain other evidence that comes straight from the source: state officials and troopers themselves. In a report released by New Jersey's attorney general in 1999, the state publicly admitted that the accusations it had fought so bitterly for so many years were in fact true: Racial profiling was "real, not imagined."[47] The report went on to detail significant statistical evidence that showed that racial profiling by the New Jersey State Police was indeed something that happened, not something made up. (MacDonald has dismissed these admissions as nothing but politically inspired poppycock wrapped in political correctness.)[48] But when the state released ninety thousand pages of documents in late 2000 about the subject, these records showed in black and white that the admission in the attorney general's report had not only been accurate, but was actually the conclusion that many state officials had harbored for years, even as they publicly disputed it and vehemently fought it in the courts. As discussed in Chapter Three, the New Jersey State Police themselves were quite aware of the reality. In an internal memorandum dated October 4, 1996, roughly the same time that state police officials were denouncing a judge's finding that New Jersey State Police had indeed engaged in racially biased use of traffic stops, the bureau chief of State Police Internal Affairs stated that an examination of internal data actually showed that "the percentage of minorities stopped by both minority and nonminority troopers were dramatically higher than the 'expert' testified in" that same case. In another internal memorandum to the superintendent of the State Police, a member of the force said that examination of the data showed that "at this point, we are in a very bad spot . . . the [U.S.] Justice Department has a very good understanding of how we operate and the types of numbers they can get their hands on to prove" a case against the State Police.

And, in perhaps the most shocking revelation, in court proceedings in January of 2002, the two troopers involved in the most notorious profiling incident on the turnpike—the shooting of four young unarmed black men in a van who were pulled over on their way to a basketball camp—freely admitted that they had used racial profiling. Indeed, they said that they had been trained to focus on blacks and Latinos and ordered to use these techniques by their superiors. As reported by the *New York Times,* the New Jersey troopers "publicly acknowledged today for the first time that they had stopped the vehicle because its occupants were black and Latino. The troopers said their supervisors had trained them to focus on black- and brown-skinned drivers because, they were told, they were more likely to be drug traffickers." [49]

The bottom line seems clear. Even if blacks speed more often than whites, this does not mean profiling is either acceptable or effective. And it certainly does not mean that profiling is a myth, a tactic that never existed. But the widespread circulation of the study and the unquestioning willingness of the media to give it full credence as proof of a point it does not support may show—frustratingly—that the acceptability of racial profiling as an antiterrorism tool has changed the public discussion for purposes of domestic crime fighting as well—despite all that we have learned about racial profiling's failures, and its costs.

Chapter Ten

CONCLUSION:
A SELF-FULFILLING PROPHECY
AND THE FUTURE

We now know that racial profiling does not help us fight crime. It is not, to use the terms employed by its proponents, a "rational" or "commonsense" response to the nature of crime in our society. And it does great damage to individuals, to the social fabric of our country, to the rule of law, and to the entire legal and criminal justice system. This damage extends to the very core of our system, corroding its most basic principles. One of these is the presumption of innocence, which occupies a central place in our criminal justice system. In Anglo-American law, the state must shoulder the burden of proving beyond a reasonable doubt any allegation that a citizen has committed a crime. This idea is reflected in the constitutional principles that govern policing, particularly the Fourth Amendment. The Fourth Amendment prohibits unreasonable searches and seizures and requires warrants based on probable cause. The basic idea is that police generally need a reason—something concrete that leads them to suspect a particular individual of involvement in crime—before detaining a person for any length of time or searching someone. Without a reason, police officers generally cannot demand that an individual explain himself—what he's doing, where he's going, why, or anything else. Profiling turns this idea on its head. Instead of the police officer needing justification to inquire of the citizen, the citizen must justify himself to the police officer.

The Supreme Court has in every practical sense turned a blind eye to the use of race as a central factor in focusing police suspicion and activity. This leaves police free to use race as one factor, or even *the* factor, that determines whether officers should stop, question, and search someone. In other words, the law allows police to use membership in a particular racial or ethnic group as a proxy for a greater propensity to commit crimes. Police can use skin color as evidence of criminal involvement, even without any other evidence that points in that direction. This means, in clear and unequivocal terms, that *skin color itself has been criminalized*. This approach to law enforcement stigmatizes every African American, Latino, Asian, or member of any other minority group whose unchangeable personal characteristics, like black or brown skin, or the physical features of Asians, become physical markers of criminality, more indelible than any scarlet letter.

When police use race or ethnic appearance to focus their suspicions, hit rates tell us that blacks and Latinos are arrested for violating drug and gun possession laws at lower rates than whites. When racial profiling continues despite these hard facts, it becomes a self-fulfilling prophecy. As Professor William Stuntz explains, when police enforce drug and gun laws, "whom they catch depends on where they look." If a police officer assumes people of color are more likely to commit crimes because he knows that African Americans and Latinos are overrepresented among people arrested and imprisoned, and he therefore investigates people of color more frequently as a result, his theory and preexisting beliefs will be confirmed. Of the drivers and pedestrians he stops and searches, most will be black or brown. Not surprisingly he will then end up arresting primarily black and brown individuals. He never stops to think about the *rate* at which he finds illegal behavior among this group versus the *rate* he might find it among a similar number of white drivers and pedestrians. Indeed, it has never occurred to him that he might find illegal behavior *more often* among a similar number of whites (as the data consistently show). And the officer would almost never have any information about the success rates of search activity, since police departments almost never collect data on this. His choice of where to look for criminal activity is informed by his own and society's biases. At the end of the day, he has his arrests, so why stop to examine his premises?

When we use race as a way to predict who might be a criminal, because we believe the statistics bear this out, a funny thing happens. The prophecy is fulfilled; the theory works. We arrest more blacks and Latinos, convict more blacks and Latinos, and jail more blacks and Latinos. As we go round and round this circle, we never notice facts that lie just outside our vision. And we never ask ourselves questions—because we have the answers we need already.

Whatever the cost of profiling is, it does not create any benefit for law-abiding blacks that they could not get with an even-handed enforcement policy that did not use race as a proxy characteristic for greater propensity to commit crimes. If profiling doesn't work—does not, in fact, make for better law enforcement—the benefits to anyone, let alone to African Americans who have to put up with its substantial downsides, are illusory.

All of this is thrown into sharp relief by the 2000 Census, which showed that the United States has never been more diverse.[1] These new figures, especially those that show the astonishing growth in the population of Latinos in America, carry important implications for law enforcement as well as for many other aspects of our lives. As our nation's compexion changes—not just in our cities, but in our suburban and rural areas as well—police may increasingly be tempted to turn to the "rational," "commonsense" approach of profiling to help them target "likely criminals." At the same time, as minority populations grow, profiling becomes an even less accurate way to enforce the law—even more overinclusive than it is now. And the social and legal cost of racial profiling will expand, with alienation from the police and the law, distrust of the legal system, and fear of police contacts spread across a larger and growing group of citizens. All of us, *but especially law enforcement,* have a substantial and important stake in coming to grips with racial profiling and in dealing with it straightforwardly, honestly, and directly.

Fortunately, there are alternative ways to enforce the law, outlined in this book, that do not use racial profiling and that are more powerful and effective methods of fighting crime. Cities and police departments that turn to these methods will move themselves away from practices that harm and humiliate a substantial portion of their citizenry and toward a system based on accountability. Accountability is a bedrock principle for every institution that is part of a democracy; government by, for, and of the people means that every part of the government must be responsive to the people. That requires information, so that the public can make intelligent and informed judgments, and it requires responsiveness of the institutions to the public. Accountability is a necessity for police departments no less than for other institutions in our democracy, and the strategies outlined here can help build this important principle into policing, as they help address racial profiling and all of the damage, danger, and cost it carries with it.

In the end, we must take a broader view of racial profiling and of all the difficult problems that our society must cope with at the intersection of race and criminal justice. Racial profiling is often seen as an African American problem, or perhaps as a minority problem. But we must come to see it as something more. Racial profiling is a problem for every American who believes in fairness and equal treatment under the law. It is a problem for every citizen, for every lawyer, for every judge, for every police officer and every police chief—for every person who believes that just and equal treatment for each individual is part of the birthright of every American.

Carved into the stone above the door to the Supreme Court of the United States are four words: "Equal Justice Under Law." That ideal is a part of our heritage that is as precious as any other. To be sure, we have not always lived up to this principle. But in addressing racial profiling, we have the opportunity to move toward it.

NOTES

CHAPTER ONE: PROFILES IN INJUSTICE: AMERICAN LIFE UNDER THE REGIME OF RACIAL PROFILING

1. Segeant Rossano Gerald, interview with author, 12 September 2000.

2. Ziva Branstetter, "OHP Pays $75,000 to Settle Lawsuit," *Tulsa World,* 17 May 2001.

3. Judge Filemon B. Vela, interview with author, 30 August 2000.

4. Jim Yardley, "Some Texans Say Border Patrol Singles Out Too Many Blameless Hispanics," *New York Times,* 26 January 2000, sec. A, p. 17.

5. Ibid.

6. Davan Maharaj, "Rights Suit Involving Police Photos Is Settled," *Los Angeles Times,* 12 December 1995, p. 1 (detailing incident, lawsuit, and settlement); Daniel Tsang, "Is 'Innocent Until Proven Guilty' a Lost Principle?" *Los Angeles Times,* 30 August 1993, sec. B, p. 5 (describing incident and picturing girls in clothing similar to what they were wearing when the police stopped them). Some reports also indicated that a third Asian girl was also present.

7. Mark Nye (detective, Westminster (California) Police Department), "Asian Gangs in Little Saigon: Identification and Methods of Operation," quoted in Daniel Tsang, "Is 'Innocent Until Proven Guilty' a Lost Principle?" *Los Angeles Times,* 30 August 1993, sec. B, p. 5.

8. Robert Wilkins, interview with author, 21 July 1999; see also Complaint, *Wilkins* v. *Maryland State Police et al.,* Civ. No. MJG-93-468 (D. Md. 1993).

CHAPTER TWO: PROFILING PAST AND PRESENT, AND HIGH DISCRETION POLICE TACTICS

1. McGinley and Downs, "Airport Searches and Seizures—A Reasonable Approach," *Fordham Law Review* 41 (1972): 293, 294–95.

2. Wayne R. LaFave, *Search and Seizure: A Treatise on the Fourth Amendment,* vol. 4 (St. Paul, Minn.: West Publishing, 1996), 619.

3. Ibid., 619, n. 5.

4. Ibid.

5. FAA Press Release No. 72–26 (Feb. 6, 1972); see also 14 C.F.R. sec. 121.538 (1973).

6. Paul Wilkinson, *Terrorism and the Liberal State,* 2d ed. (New York: New York University Press, 1986), p. 228, table 9.

7. Ibid.

8. See for example, John Douglas with Mark Olshaker, *Mindhunter, Inside the FBI's Elite Serial Crime Unit* (New York: Scribner, 1995); Robert K. Ressler, Ann W. Burgess, and John E. Douglas, *Sexual Homicide, Patterns and Motives* (Lexington, Mass.: Lexington Books, 1988).

9. John Douglas with Mark Olshaker, *Mindhunter, Inside the FBI's Elite Serial Crime Unit* (New York: Scribner, 1995). (Book's back-cover photo caption reads, "John Douglas with Scott Glen on the set of *The Silence of the Lambs.* Glenn plays Jack Crawford, a character inspired by Douglas's life and career.")

10. *Profiler* premiered on NBC in September 1996. Its main character, Dr. Sam Waters, is a brilliant forensic psychologist with the ability to "think" in pictures and visualize a crime through the eyes of both the victim and the perpetrator of the crime. The NBC web site and no fewer than fourteen different fan web sites were dedicated to the show as of June 2001.

11. John Marcello, "Q: Is Public Concern About Federal Police Using Racial Profiling Justified?" *Insight on the News,* July 19, 1999.

12. 490 U.S. 1 (1989).

13. Ibid.

14. Sheriff Bob Vogel, interview by author, 3 July 2000.

15. Vogel, interview; see also Gary Webb, "DWB," *Esquire,* April 1999.

16. *U.S.* v. *Smith,* 799 F. 2d 704 (11th Cir. 1986).

17. Gary Webb, "DWB," *Esquire,* April 1999.

18. James Q. Wilson and George L. Kelling, "Broken Windows: The Police and Neighborhood Safety," *Atlantic Monthly,* March 1982.

19. Ibid., 20.

20. Ibid., 4.

21. Ibid., 23.

22. Police Strategy No. 5, "Reclaiming the Public Spaces of New York" (1994).

23. Police Strategy No. 1, "Getting Guns off the Streets of New York" (1994).

24. Police Strategy No. 5, "Reclaiming the Public Spaces of New York," 7.

25. See, e.g., "Respectful and Effective Policing: Two Examples in the South Bronx," Vera Institute of Justice, March 1999, p. 1 ("Stopping people on minor infractions made it riskier for criminals to carry guns in public").

26. Another way to say this is that people respond not so much to facts as they do to symbols and emotions.

27. There is considerable research on all of these points. For excellent discussions and summaries of the state of contemporary research on these aspects of memory and thinking, see Daniel L. Schacter, *The Seven Sins of Memory* (Boston: Houghton Mifflin, 2001), 9–10: "Stereotypical biases influence memories and perceptions in the social world. Experience with different groups of people leads to the development of stereotypes that captures their general properties, but can spawn inaccurate and unwarranted judgments about individuals" and p. 155: "The problem [with stereotypical biases] arises because people are sometimes willing to act on these biases in cases in which they are entirely unwarranted, resulting in what [researcher Mahzarin] Banaji calls 'guilt by association' rather than 'guilt by behavior': individuals are perceived negatively based on their membership in a group rather than because of their specific behaviors or attributes."

28. Ibid., 156: A person with biased views of racial or ethnic minorities "would be more likely to remember stereotypical features of an African American's behavior than a less prejudiced person, and less likely to remember behaviors that don't fit the stereotype. This tendency can create a self-perpetuating cycle in which a stereotype biases recall of congruent incidents, which in turn strengthens the stereotypical bias. . . . When events unfold in a way that contradicts our expectations based on stereotypes and related knowledge of the world, we may be biased to fabricate incidents that never happened in order to bring our memories in line with our expectations." Some communications theorists call this selective exposure to information, which asserts that people attend only to parts of communications that fit well into their value systems and what they already believe. Information that causes them to experience dissonance is subconsciously disregarded. See, e.g., David O. Sears and Jonathan L. Freedman, "Selective Exposure to Information: A Critical Review," *Public Opinion Quarterly* (1967): 161, 164; Behavior Sciences Subpanel, President's Science Advisory Committee, "Report to the President," *Behavioral Science* 7 (1962): 277: "[I]ndividuals engage in selective exposure. . . . If a new piece of information would weaken the existing structure of their ideas and emotions, it will be shunned . . . [and] if it reinforces the structure, it will be sought out"; John L. Cotton, "Cognitive Dissonance in Selective Exposure," in eds., Dillman and Bryant, *Selective Exposure to Communication* 11–33 (Hillsdale, N.J.: Erlbaum Associates 1985), summarizing research on how humans limit exposure to new information in order to decrease cognitive dissonance.

29. Jennifer K. Robbennolt and Mark S. Sobus, "An Integration of Hindsight Bias and Counterfactual Thinking: Decision-Making and Drug Courier Profiles, *Law and Human Behavior* 21(1997): 539, 540–41; Daniel

L. Schacter, *The Seven Sins of Memory,* 147: "Hindsight bias, then, is ubiquitous: people seem almost driven to reconstruct the past to fit what they know in the present. In light of the known outcome, people can more easily retrieve incidents and examples that confirm it."

30. *U.S. v. Hooper,* 935 F. 2d 484 (2d Cir. 1991).

31. Lewis Carroll, *Through the Looking Glass* (1872).

32. *U.S. v. Hooper,* 935 F. 2d 484, 499 (Pratt, dissenting), quoting *U.S. v. Sokolow,* 831 F. 2d 1413, 1418 (9th Cir. 1987), revised 490 U.S. 1 (1989).

33. Ibid.

34. Ibid., 499–500.

35. David Cole, *No Equal Justice: Race and Class in the American Criminal Justice System* (New York: The New Press), 48–49.

36. E.g., N.M. Stat. Ann., sec. 66-7-305 (Michie 1994) (prohibits driving "at such a slow speed as to impede the normal and reasonable movement of traffic"; 18 D.C. Mun. Regs., sec. 2200.10 (1995).

37. Utah Code Ann., sec. 41-6-69 (1993).

38. E.g., Md. Code Ann. Transp. II, sec. 21-604 (d) (signal must "be given continuously during at least the last 100 feet"); N.M. Stat. Ann. sec. 66-7-325B (Michie 1994) (same); Ohio Rev. Code Ann., sec. 4511.39 (Banks-Baldwin 1993) (same); S.C. Code Ann., sec. 56-5-2150 (b) (Law Co-op. 1991) (same).

39. E.g., Md. Code Ann. Transp. II, sec. 21-604 (e) (1992) ("If there is an opportunity to signal, a person may not stop or suddenly decrease the speed of a vehicle until he gives an appropriate signal"); N.M. Stat. Ann., sec. 66-7-325C (Michie 1994) ("No person shall stop or suddenly decrease the speed of a vehicle without first giving an appropriate signal"); S.C. Code Ann., sec. 56-5-2150 (c) (Law Co-op. 1991) (same).

40. E.g., Md. Code Ann. Transp. II, sec. 22-204 (a) (1992) ("[E]very motor vehicle . . . shall be equipped with at least 2 tail lamps mounted on the rear, which . . . shall emit a red light plainly visible from a distance of 1000 feet to the rear"); N.D. Cent. Code, sec. 39-21-04(1) (1987) (same); S.C. Code Ann., sec. 56-5-4510 (Law Co-op. 1991) (same, except that red lights must be visible from a distance of 500 feet).

41. E.g., Md. Code Ann. Transp. II, sec. 22-204 (f) (1992) (requiring a "white light" that will illuminate the rear registration plate "and render it clearly visible from a distance of fifty feet"); N.D. Cent. Code, sec. 39-21-04(3) (1987) (same); S.C. Code Ann., sec. 56-5-4530 (Law Co-op. 1991) (same).

42. E.g., Ohio Rev. Code Ann., sec. 4513.241 (A), (D) (Anderson 2001), "Restrictions on use of tinted glass and other vision obscuring materials" ("The director of public safety, in accordance with Chapter 119 of the Revised Code, shall adopt rules governing the use of tinted glass, and the use of transparent, nontransparent, translucent, and reflectorized materials in or on motor vehicle windshields, side windows, sidewings, and rear windows that prevent a person of normal vision looking into the motor vehicle from seeing or identifying persons or objects inside the motor vehicle. . . .

No person shall install in or on any motor vehicle, any glass or other material that fails to conform to the requirements of this section or of any rule adopted under this section").

43. E.g., Md. Code Ann. Transp. II, sec. 22-405.5 (b) (1992) (tire considered unsafe if tread wear indicators are "flush with the tread at any place on the tire" or in absence of tread wear indicators, do not meet precise measurements at three locations on the tire); S.C. Code Ann., sec. 56-5-5040 (Law Co-op. 1991) (tires "shall be in a safe operating condition").

44. E.g., S.C. Code Ann., sec. 56-5-5350 (a) (Law Co-op. 1991) ("No person shall drive . . . any vehicle . . . unless there shall be in effect and properly displayed thereon a current certificate of inspection").

45. E.g., Ohio Rev. Code Ann., sec. 4511.22 (A) (Anderson 2001) ("No person shall stop or operate a vehicle . . . at such a slow speed as to impede or block the normal and reasonable movement of traffic, except when stopping or reduced speed is necessary for safe operation or to comply with law").

46. Gary Webb, "DWB," *Esquire,* April 1999 ("Since it's nearly impossible for drivers to go ten feet without violating some obscure ordinance [former Florida Highway Patrol officer and Volusia County, Florida, Sheriff Robert], Vogel would simply tag along and wait for it to happen").

47. Lawrence F. Tiffany, et al., Detection of Crime: Stopping and Questioning, Search and Seizure, Encouragement and Entrapment (Boston: Little, Brown, 1967), 131.

48. *Schneckloth* v. *Bustamonte,* 412 U.S. 218 (1973); *Ohio* v. *Robinette,* 519 U.S. 33 (1996); see also *Illinois* v. *Rodriguez,* 497 U.S. 177 (1990) (centering on the issue of third-party consent given by someone with apparent, but not actual, authority).

49. *Schneckloth,* 412 U.S. 220 (stop was for a traffic offense, of which there would be no evidence in car to search for; police testified that no one was under arrest and interaction was "congenial" when consent was requested and given); *Robinette,* 519 U.S. 36 (defendant stopped for speeding; license was checked by computer, finding no previous violations; license was returned, with a verbal warning, all before consent was requested and then given).

50. Ibid., pp. 39–40 ("unrealistic" to require police to inform those detained and now free to go that they can do so); *Schneckloth,* 412 U.S. 227–28 (labeling consent searches "valuable" and "wholly legitimate" crime-fighting tools).

51. *Schneckloth,* 412 U.S. 231–32.

52. *Robinette,* 519 U.S. 39–40.

53. Illya D. Lichtenberg, "Voluntary Consent or Obedience to Authority: An Inquiry into the Consensual Police-Citizen Encounter" (Ph.D., diss., Rutgers University, 1999).

54. Ibid., 160–64 (sources of data were from settlement of litigation involving Maryland State Police and covered all stops by agency followed by searches by consent or with canines between January 1, 1995, and June 30,

1997, and from all stops in which the Ohio Highway Patrol requested consent to search between 1987 through 1991 ("Ohio 1") and 1995 through May 1997 ("Ohio 2").

55. Ibid., 199–200.

56. Ibid. (more than 8,100 people of the 9,028 asked granted consent, for a rate of 89.3 percent).

57. See, e.g., Stanley Milgram, Obedience to Authority: An Experimental View (New York: Harper & Row 1974) (discussing Milgram's experiments in which a subject is told to administer electric shocks to a "learner"; though the "learner" was a confederate of Milgram and no actual shocks were given, the subject was led to think exactly the opposite. Approximately two-thirds of all of the subjects administered "shocks" at the "maximum level of 450 volts, despite obvious clues that they were causing the "learner" great pain. In another set of experiments, Leonard Bickman tested whether passersby would comply with commands at higher rates when ordered to do some small task when the person giving the order was wearing a uniform. Leonard Bickman, "The Social Power of a Uniform," *Journal of Applied Social Psychology* 4 (1974): 47, 49. Compliance rates in Bickman's experiments increased markedly when the order was given by a person in a uniform—even in a *milkman's* uniform. When the person wore a uniform that resembled a police officer's, compliance rates were even higher—almost three times the rate of compliance for a command given by someone wearing either "civilian" clothing or the milkman's uniform.

58. Ibid., 201–7 (though females consented at slightly higher rates than males, difference was not statistically significant).

59. Ibid., 207–13 (age affects consent rate only slightly, and in the opposite direction than what the Supreme Court predicted in *Schneckloth*, e.g., "the youth of the accused" making citizens more likely to consent, 412 U.S. 226, when in fact younger people are slightly less likely to consent than older ones).

60. Ibid., 213–19 (difference in rates of consent between racial groups were statistically insignificant). The one exception seems to be Hispanics, who seem to consent at higher rates. Lichtenberg speculates that this may be due to their experiences and attitudes regarding police in their native countries and cultures in Central and South America, where the judicial system is viewed as "inquisitorial." Ibid., 219–21. Another interesting aspect of Lichtenberg's findings is that they may contradict some scholarship that implies that the situations of African Americans confronting the police are much different than that of whites, so that the "reasonable person" so often supposed by the Supreme Court in these encounters simply must be conceptualized differently when a black citizen is involved. See, e.g., Tracey Maclin, "Black and Blue Encounters—Some Preliminary Thoughts About Fourth Amendment Seizures: Should Race Matter?" *Valparaiso University Law Review* 26 (1991): 243 (arguing that race should be considered in the context of police stops of black citizens, because the interaction is qualitatively different than an interaction with a white person). At least in the con-

text of consent searches, race does not seem to matter; whites, blacks, and everyone else give consent at about the same high rate.

61. Ibid., 231–37.

62. 470 U.S. 675 (1985).

63. Ibid., 686 (the question is "whether the police diligently pursued a means of investigation . . . during which time it was necessary to detain the defendant").

64. E.g., *Horton* v. *California,* 496 U.S. 128 (1990) (allowing seizure of objects seen in plain view during otherwise legitimate police activity, if seen from a vantage point that officers have a right to be present at, and if it is immediately apparent that the object seen is contraband).

65. *Berkemer* v. *McCarty,* 468 U.S. 420 (1984) (given noncustodial and public nature of car-side questioning, police may question motorists after a traffic stop without administering Miranda warnings).

66. *Pennsylvania* v. *Mimms,* 434 U.S. 106 (1977) (allowing police to order driver out of vehicle without any individual suspicion of any kind in order to help insure the officer's safety).

67. *Maryland* v. *Wilson,* 519 U.S. 408 (1997) (same as to passengers of vehicles).

68. 462 U.S. 696 (1983).

69. Ibid., 707.

70. Ibid.

71. Ibid.

72. *Berkemer* v. *McCarty.*

73. I assume here for purposes of discussion that none of these things would give rise to probable cause to search; if that were true, there would be no need to request consent for a search.

74. See discussion of *Sharpe.*

75. Lichtenberg, 251.

76. Ibid., 260–75, 275.

77. Priar and Martin, "Searching and Disarming Criminals," *J. Crim. L. C.* (1954): 45; *Public Science* (1954): 481.

78. Eliot Spitzer, attorney general of the state of New York, "The New York City Police Department's 'Stop and Frisk' Practices: A Report to the People of the State of New York," 1 December 1999. The report notes that despite the large number of stop-and-frisk reports it surveys, there is reason to think that these represent only part of all those stops and frisks actually performed.

79. Remo Franceschini and Peter Knobler, *A Matter of Honor: One Cop's Lifelong Pursuit of John Gotti and the Mob* (New York: Simon & Schuster, 1993).

80. Ibid., 36.

81. Ibid.

82. See N. Y. Code Crim. Proc., sec. 180-a, which provided: "1. A police officer may stop any person abroad in a public place whom he reasonably suspects is committing, has committed or is about to commit a felony

or any of the offenses specified . . . and may demand of him his name, address and an explanation of his actions. 2. When a police officer has stopped a person for questioning pursuant to this section and reasonably suspects that he is in danger of life or limb, he may search such person for a dangerous weapon"), quoted in *Sibron* v. *New York,* 392 U.S. 40, 43–44 (1968).

83. *Terry* v. *Ohio,* 368 U.S. 1 (1968).

84. 449 U.S. 411 (1981).

85. Ibid., 417–18.

86. Ibid., 418.

87. *Minnesota* v. *Dickerson,* 508 U.S. 366, 373 (1993).

88. See the cases collected in David A. Harris, *"Frisking Every Suspect: The Withering of Terry, University of California Davis Law Review* 28, (1994): 1, 24, n. 128.

89. *U.S.* v. *Oates,* 560 F. 2d 45, 62 (2d Cir. 1977).

90. See the cases collected in David A. Harris, *"Frisking Every Suspect: The Withering of Terry," University of California Davis Law Review* 28, (1994): 1, 24, n. 133, 134.

91. Ibid., nn. 136–37.

92. *Richards* v. *Wisconsin,* 520 U.S. 385, 393–94 (1997) (rejecting a per se exception to the "knock and announce" rule for narcotics cases because categorical judgments skirt the Fourth Amendment's requirement of individual suspicion, and "the reasons for creating an exception in one category [of Fourth Amendment cases] can, relatively easily, be applied to others," so that the exception swallows the rule); *Florida* v. *J.L.,* 529 U.S. 266, 273 (2000) (categorical "firearms exception," always allowing frisks for any tip or report involving a firearm, would not satisfy the Fourth Amendment).

93. 508 U.S. 366 (1993).

94. Ibid., 368–69.

95. Justice Scalia quoted this phrase, from Proverbs 28:1, in *California* v. *Hodari D.,* 499 U.S. 621, n. 1 (1991). Justice Scalia did not use the full phrase. It reads: "The wicked flee when no man pursueth, but the righteous are as bold as a lion."

96. Proverbs 22:3. The quoted language comes from Justice Stevens's dissenting opinion in *Illinois* v. *Wardlow,* 528 U.S. 119, 129, note 3. Stevens cites no source for his version of this quote, but the sense is the same as in the most common versions. E.g., The Holy Bible, Authorized King James Version 473 (Chicago: Consolidated Book Publishers, 1973) ("A prudent man foresees the evil, and hideth himself: but the simple pass on and are punished"); The Jerusalem Bible, Reader's Edition 839 (Garden City, New York: Doubleday and Company, 1968) ("The discreet man sees danger and takes shelter, the ignorant go forward and pay for it.")

97. Courts have differed over this point. See, e.g., *State* v. *Anderson,* 155 Wis. 2d 77, 454 N.W. 2d 763 (Wis. 1990) (flight alone is sufficient); *Platt* v. *State,* 589 N.E. 2d 222 (Ind. 1992) (same); *State* v. *Hicks,* 241 Neb. 357, 488 N.W. 2d 359 (1992) (flight is not enough); *State* v. *Tucker,* 136

N.J. 158, 642 A. 2d 401 (1994) (same); *People* v. *Shabaz,* 424 Mich. 42, 378 N.W. 2d 451 (1985) (same); *People* v. *Wilson,* 784 P. 2d 325 (Colo. 1989) (same).

98. See, e.g., *State* v. *Jones,* 450 So. 2d 692, 694-95 (La. Ct. App. 1984) (presence in high-crime area at night and briskly walking away when police approached is enough for reasonable suspicion), rev'd in part on other grounds, 456 So. 2d 162 (La. 1984); *State* v. *Belton,* 441 So. 2d 1195 (La. 1983) (reasonable suspicion existed to stop a defendant who fled when police approached a bar where narcotics are sold), cert. denied, 466 U.S. 953 (1984); *State* v. *Stinnnett,* 760 P. 2d 124, 127 (Nev. 1988) (defendant's presence in huddled group of men in high-drug area and running away when he saw police amounted to reasonable suspicion); *State* v. *Butler,* 415 S.E. 2d 719, 722-23 (N.C. 1992) (defendant's presence on drug corner and fact that defendant "immediately turned and walked away" amounted to reasonable suspicion); *State* v. *Andrews,* 565 N.E. 2d 1271, 1273-74 (Ohio 1991) (defendant's presence in high-crime area and his running from the direction of a police car was enough for experienced officer to form reasonable suspicion). To be sure, there are examples to the contrary. See, e.g., *People* v. *Aldridge,* 674 P. 2d 240, 243 (Cal. 1984) (flight is insufficient alone to justify a *Terry* stop); *People* v. *Wilson,* 784 P. 2d 325, 326-27 (Colo. 1989) (defendant's presence in drug area and flight from police insufficient for reasonable suspicion); *Watkins* v. *State,* 420 A. 2d 270, 274 (Md. Ct. App. 1980) (flight alone not necessarily indicative of criminal activity); *People* v. *Posnjak,* 72 A. 2d 966 (N.Y. App. Div. 1979) (defendant's presence with others at scene of crime, and fact that he walked away, was insufficient for reasonable suspicion). The point is that this is a widespread police practice, even if it is not accepted everywhere.

99. 423 S.E. 2d 723 (1992).

100. Ibid.

101. Ibid.

102. 528 U.S. 119, 120 S. Ct. 673 (2000).

CHAPTER THREE: PROFILING UNMASKED: FROM CRIMINAL PROFILING TO RACIAL PROFILING

1. *Operation Pipeline,* produced by the Drug Enforcement Administration and the New Mexico State Police, 45 minutes (1986) videocassette. Credits say that the video was financed by the DEA; it purports to teach tactics and techniques for highway traffic stop drug interdiction developed by the New Jersey State Police and the New Mexico State Police.

2. William Buckman, interview by author, 21 September 2000.

3. According to the *New York Times,* the Department of Justice's Civil Rights Division reviewed DEA procedures, including Operation Pipeline training, in 1997, well after a New Jersey judge found overwhelming evidence of profiling. Federal officials say that the review concluded that the

Pipeline "program was sound and that the Drug Enforcement Administration did not encourage or teach profiling." David Kocieniewski, "U.S. Wrote Outline for Race Profiling, New Jersey Argues," *New York Times,* 29 November 2000, A1.

4. Ibid.

5. *Operation Pipeline,* a report prepared by the California Legislature's Task Force on Government Oversight.

6. David Kocieniewski, A1.

7. Ibid.

8. Ibid.

9. Ibid.

10. Ibid.

11. David Kocieniewski and Robert Hanley, "Racial Profiling Was the Routine, New Jersey Finds," *New York Times,* 28 November 2000, A1.

12. *Operation Pipeline.*

13. Ibid., 5.

14. Ibid.

15. Ibid., 2.

16. Ibid., 6.

17. President's Commission on Law Enforcement and Administration of Justice, *Task Force Report: The Police* (Washington, D.C.: GPO, 1967), 183–84.

18. Mark Hosenball, "It's Not the Act of a Few Bad Apples: A Lawsuit Shines the Spotlight on Allegations of Racial Profiling by New Jersey State Troopers," *Newsweek,* 17 May 1999, 34.

19. Report of John Lamberth (Defendant's Expert), *Revised Statistical Analysis of the Incidence of Police Stops and Arrests of Black Drivers/Travelers on the New Jersey Turnpike Between Interchanges 1 and 3 from the Years 1988 Through 1991,* at 2. Lamberth's report is relied upon and quoted at length in *State* v. *Pedro Soto,* 734 A. 2d 350 (N.J. Super. Ct. Law. Div. 1996).

20. *State* v. *Pedro Soto,* 734 A. 2d 350 (N.J. Super. Ct. Law. Div. 1996).

21. The state presented its own statistical expert, but Judge Francis found his testimony flawed and wholly unpersuasive.

22. See Lamberth report, 2–3.

23. Ibid., 3–6.

24. Ibid., 6–9.

25. Ibid., 26.

26. *Soto,* 734 A. 2d 354.

27. Gil Gallegos, interview by author, 6 September 2000.

28. Lamberth report, 20.

29. Ibid., 21.

30. Ibid., 25.

31. Ibid., 26, 28.

32. *Soto,* 734 A. 2d 359.

33. Memorandum from Sergeant Thomas Gilbert to Superintendent Carl Williams, head of state police. The memo is undated, but various news

organizations have stated that it was sent in 1997. E.g., Joe Donohue, "Memos Cast New Doubts on Verniero," *Newark Star-Ledger,* 13 October 2000.

34. Kathy Barrett Carter and Michael Raphael, "State Police Reveal 75% of Arrests Along Turnpike Were of Minorities," *Newark Star-Ledger,* 10 February 1999.

35. Joe Donohue, "Trooper Boss: Race Plays a Role in Drug Crimes," *Newark Star-Ledger* 28 February 1999.

36. Asked about profiling at a March 3 news conference at the National Press Club, Whitman said, "What proof do we have that it does exist? . . . One person makes an allegation."

37. Peter Verniero and Paul Zoubek, *Interim Report of the State Police Review Team Regarding Allegations of Racial Profiling,* 29 April 1999, at 4.

38. Ibid., 26. Blacks were 27 percent, Hispanics 6.9 percent, and Asians 3.9 percent. The data represented all of the stops done by troopers from the Moorestown and Cranbury barracks—the very same units and geographic area from which John Lamberth drew his data in *Soto*. The Task Force's statistics on stops by officers from the Moorestown and Cranbury stations included more than eighty-seven thousand stops.

39. Ibid., 34.

40. Ibid., 27. Of all drivers searched by officers from the Moorestown and Cranbury barracks, those that were alleged to be profiling in the *Soto* case, 53.1 percent were black and 24.1 percent were Hispanic.

41. Ibid., 33–34.

42. Mark Pazniokas, "Discrimination Often Hard to Prove," *Hartford Courant,* 2 May 1994, A11 ("[V]ictims are reluctant to sue" and "shrug off the [racially biased] stops as an annoying fact of life").

43. Complaint, *Wilkins v. Maryland State Police et al.,* Civil No. MJG-93-468 (D. Md. 1993).

44. Michael Fletcher, "Driven to Extremes; Black Men Take Steps to Avoid Police Stops," *Washington Post,* 29 March 1996, A1.

45. Settlement Agreement, *Wilkins v. Maryland State Police,* Civil No. MJG-93-468 (D. Md. 1995).

46. Report of Dr. John Lamberth (plaintiff's expert), *Wilkins v. Maryland State Police et al.,* Civil No. MJG-93-468 (D. Md. 1996).

47. Ibid., 4–5.

48. Ibid., 4, 6.

49. Ibid., 6.

50. Ibid., 6–7.

51. Ibid., 9.

52. Ibid., 9–10.

53. Henry Pierson Curtis, "Statistics Show Pattern of Discrimination," *Orlando Sentinel Tribune,* 23 August 1992, A11.

54. Ibid.; Jeff Brazil and Steve Berry, "Color of Driver Is Key to Stops in I-95 Videos," *Orlando Sentinel Tribune,* 23 August 1992, A1.

55. Ibid.

56. Ibid.

57. Henry Pierson Curtis, n. 91, p. A11 (during five days of sampling, "about 5 percent of the drivers of 1,120 vehicles counted were dark skinned").

58. Ibid.; Jeff Brazil and Steve Berry, n. 92, A1 ("Almost 70 percent of the motorists stopped were black or Hispanic, an enormously disproportionate figure because the vast majority of interstate drivers are white").

59. Henry Pierson Curtis, n. 91.

60. Ibid.

61. Jeff Brazil and Steve Berry, n. 92, A1 (Average length of stop in minutes: minority drivers, 12.1, white drivers, 5.1).

62. Jeff Brazil and Steve Berry, n. 92, A1 (of 507 searches shown by the tapes, four out of five were of cars with black or Hispanic drivers; note, however, that these numbers do "not include 78 possible searches/incomplete video").

63. Ibid.

64. Ibid.

65. Ibid.

66. Ibid.

67. Ibid. Eighty-nine seizures of cash and thirty-one drug arrests, respectively. Note also that almost 87 percent of stops were in the southbound lanes, "where any drug traffickers would more likely be carrying cash to Miami," and "[o]nly 13 percent of stops were in the northbound lanes, where the catch would more likely be drugs." Ibid.

68. Ibid.

69. Ibid.

70. Steve Berry, Drug Squad's I-95 Tactics Going On Trial, The Orlando Sentinel Tribune, Jan 6, 1995, at A1; I-95 Cash-Seizure Stops, The Orlando Sentinel Tribune, June 10, 1995, at D3 (first case denied class action status in both).

71. *Nater et al.,* v. *Vogel,* 106 F. 3d 415 (11th Cir. 1997).

72. "Illegal Searches Used in Illinois, Suit Alleges," *New York Times,* 4 September 1994 (suit filed after "hundreds of complaints from motorists"); Andrew Fegelman, "State Police Sued in Stops of Minorities, *Chicago Tribune,* 31 August 1994 (Chavez's suit "echo[ed] complaints the organization has received from motorists for six years"); "Profiles in Prejudice," *St. Louis Post-Dispatch,* 19 September 1994, 6B.

73. "Illegal Searches," *New York Times.*

74. Illinois Drug Searches Prompt Lawsuit By ACLU, *Orlando Sentinel Tribune,* 1 September 1994, A12.

75. Fourth Amended Complaint, *Peso Chavez et al.* v. *Illinois State Police,* No. 94 C 5307, U.S. District Court, N.D. Ill., E. Div., pars. 23, 24 (hereinafter Fourth Amended Complaint).

76. Ibid., par. 25.

77. Ibid., par. 26.

78. Complaint, par. 22; Sam Vincent Meddis, "Suit Says Suspect 'Profiles' Are Racist," *USA Today,* 1 September 1994, 3A.

79. Fourth Amended Complaint, par. 29.

80. Ibid., pars. 30, 31.

81. Ibid., pars. 32, 33.

82. Ibid., par. 33.

83. Ibid., par. 33.

84. Sam Vincent Meddis, 3A.

85. Fourth Amended Complaint, pars. 39–129. Many of these plaintiffs were stopped by the Illinois State Police more than once.

86. *Chavez* v. *Ill. State Police,* Nos. 99-3691 and 00-1462, slip opinion (7th Cir. 2001), (minorities failed to show that police program's alleged racial profiling violated equal protection as statistical data failed to show a discriminatory effect, and there was no evidence that state police department encouraged racial profiling).

87. Patrick O'Driscoll, " 'Drug Profile' Lawsuit Settled," *Denver Post,* 10 November 1995, Al.

88. Robert Jackson, "Eagle County Must Pay for Stopping Motorists," *Rocky Mountain News,* 10 November 1995, 4A ("Of the 402 people stopped between August 1988 and August 1990 on I-70 between Eagle and Glenwood Springs, none was ticketed or arrested for drugs").

89. Patrick O'Driscoll, A1.

90. Ibid.

91. Ibid.

92. Ibid.

93. Robert Jackson, 4A.

94. Patrick O'Driscoll, A1.

95. Patrick O'Driscoll, A1. For a criminal case in which a suppression motion grew out of the Eagle County deputies' use of pretextual stops, see *U.S.* v. *Laymon,* 730 F. Supp. 332 (D. Colo. 1990), in which the court found that the Eagle County deputy involved had used a traffic stop as a pretext and, therefore, the consent that followed the stop was not valid.

96. Patrick O'Driscoll, at A1.

97. Ibid.

98. Robert Jackson, n. 152, 4A.

99. David A. Harris, "The Stories, The Statistics, and the Law: Why Driving While Black Matters," *Minnesota Law Review* 84 (1999): 265, 281.

100. Ibid., 283–84.

101. Ibid., 285–87.

102. Ibid., 286–88.

103. Ibid., 288.

104. Kevin Johnson, "Ohio Report Finds Blacks More Likely to Get Tickets," *USA Today,* 1 June 1999, 3A (quoting Columbus police official as asserting that findings must be invalid in Columbus, and arguing that study's author is "a professor with an agenda").

105. Albert J. Meehan, "The Impact of Mobile Data Terminal (MDT)

Information Technology on Communication and Recordkeeping in Patrol Work," *Qualitative Sociology* 21(1998): 225–54.

106. Albert J. Meehan and Michael Ponder, "Race and Place: The Ecology of Racial Profiling of African American Motorists" (Dept. of Sociology and Anthropology, Oakland University, Rochester, Michigan, unpublished manuscript, 2001).

107. High rates of African American MDT queries are "potentially a more serious issue than actual stops. It means that black motorists are subject to surveillance at a much higher rate than recorded stops and/or tickets show. Thus in our view, racial profiling is better measured by the extent to which the police disproportionately surveil African Americans when on patrol." Traffic stop and search studies "overlook a crucial step in the decision-making process: *the police scan that universe of drivers in a more purposeful than random manner*"; ibid., 6–7.

108. The researchers say that this made their study quite accurate. In fact, the way it was constructed, it would underestimate the bias present; "racial profiling indicated by our data may actually be higher but not lower than we report"; ibid., 18.

109. Ibid., 10.

110. Ibid., 11.

111. Ibid., 11–12.

112. Ibid., 30.

113. Joseph Neff and Pat Stith, "Highway Drug Unit Focuses on Blacks," *Raleigh News and Observer*, 28 July 1996, sec. A, p. 1; "Who's Being Stopped," *Raleigh News and Observer*, 19 February 1999, sec. A, p. 14.

114. Amber Arellano, "Racial Profiling's Gray Area," *Detroit Free Press*, 1 June 2000, 1-A.

115. James Walsh and Dan Browning, "Presumed Guilty Until Proven Innocent," *Minneapolis Star Tribune*, 23 July 2000.

116. Andrew Garber, "Seattle Blacks Twice as Likely to Get Tickets," *Seattle Times*, 14 June 2000, A1.

CHAPTER FOUR: THE HARD NUMBERS: WHY RACIAL PROFILING DOESN'T ADD UP

1. Marshall Frank, "Racial Profiling: Better Safe Than Sorry," *Miami Herald*, 19 October 1999.

2. Marshall Frank, "Is the Practice of Pulling People Over Simply Because of Their Race an Urban Myth—or an Ugly Reality?" *Asheville Citizen Times*, 16 July 2000, 9.

3. John Marcello, "Q: Is Public Concern About Federal Police Using Racial Profiling Justified?" *Insight on the News*, 19 July 1999, 24.

4. Officials Trying to Determine If Racial Profiling Tactics Are Being Employed By Federal Law Enforcement Officials, National Public Radio broadcast, 10 June 1999.

5. Randall Kennedy, *Race, Crime, and the Law* (New York: Pantheon Books, 1997).

6. Randall Kennedy, "Suspect Policy," *The New Republic,* 13 September 1999.

7. Heather Mac Donald, "The Myth of Racial Profiling," *City Journal* 11, no. 2 (Spring 2001).

8. Amitai Etzioni, "Another Side of Racial Profiling," *USA Today,* 21 May 2001, 15A.

9. Marc Mauer, *Young Black Men and the Criminal Justice System: A Growing National Problem* (Washington, D.C.: The Sentencing Project, 1990).

10. Marc Mauer and Tracy Huling, *Young Black Americans and the Criminal Justice System: Five Years Later* (Washington, D.C.: The Sentencing Project, 1995).

11. U.S. Department of Justice, Bureau of Justice Statistics, National Crime Victimization Survey, "Criminal Victimization in United States, 1999, Statistical Tables," table 91, obtained at http://www.ojp.usdoj.gov/bjs/, 17 March 2001.

12. Ibid.

13. See William Stuntz, "Race, Class, and Drugs," *Columbia Law Review* 98 (1998): 1795, 1803.

14. Ibid., 1819.

15. John Kitsuse and Aaron Cicourel, "A Note on the Use of Official Statistics," Social Problems (Fall 1963).

16. Delbert Elliot, "Lies, Damn Lies, and Arrest Statistics," (Sutherland Award presentation to the American Society of Criminology, Boston, Mass., November 1995), 1.

17. Jodi Wilgoren, "Police Profiling Debate Hinges on Issue of Experience vs. Bias," *New York Times,* 9 April 1999, B1.

18. These numbers—both almost 30 percent—seem high; a three in ten hit rate seems much better than what one would expect. See Jeffrey Goldberg, "The Color of Suspicion," *New York Times Magazine,* 20 June 1999 (quoting Los Angeles Police Chief Bernard Parks as saying that a three in ten hit rate "would get you into the Hall of Fame." But the explanation may lie in the fact that the Maryland numbers provided to the court included only cars that were both stopped and searched. In other words, by the time the police searched, they had in effect screened out all the candidates that seemed unlikely to be carrying contraband, and they concentrated only on those whom they decided were most likely to be concealing drugs or other evidence.

19. *Summary of Troop D Consent Searches for 2000,* document released by New Jersey State Police in April 2001 hearings. For the Moorestown station, which did most of the searches in Troop D, the numbers indicated that blacks were 53 percent of those searched and Hispanics 25 percent of those searched; whites were 19 percent. For the Cranbury station, which had the next highest number of searches, blacks were 44 percent of searches and Hispanics 24 percent, for a total of 68 percent.

20. *Moorestown Station Consent to Search Seizures for Whites, Blacks, and Hispanics,* documents released by New Jersey State Police in April 2001 hearings.

21. Matthew T. Zingraff, et al., "Evaluating North Carolina State Highway Patrol Data: Citations, Warnings, and Searches in 1998" (report submitted to the North Carolina Department of Crime Control and Public Safety and North Carolina State Highway Patrol, 1 November 2000), p. 19, table 11; p. 21, table 14.

22. Eliot Spitzer, attorney general of the state of New York, "The New York City Police Department's 'Stop & Frisk' Practices: A Report to the People of the State of New York," 1 December 1999, 111.

23. Ibid., p. 115, table IB. 2.

24. Albert J. Meehan and Michael Ponder, "Race and Place: The Ecology of Racial Profiling African American Motorists" (Department of Sociology and Anthropology, Oakland University, Rochester, Michigan, unpublished manuscript, 2001).

25. Ibid., 36–37.

26. Ibid., 38.

27. U.S. Customs Service, *Personal Searches of Air Passengers Results: Positive and Negative, Fiscal Year 1998.*

28. Figures on air travel by minorities are hard to come by, but we can make some educated guesses. According to the Travel Industry Association of America, African Americans and Latinos travel less than other Americans and are less likely to travel by air than others. Thirty-two percent of U.S. households take at least one trip per month; by way of comparison, 26 percent of African American households and 27 percent of Latino households travel each month. African Americans travel more often by bus, train, and rental cars than others, and loss often by air. Travel Industry Association of America, "The Minority Traveler," accessed 6 June 2001, at http://www.tia.org/travel/summMinority00.asp. Although African Americans now take ninety million personal trips per year, blacks remain less likely to fly than whites. David Johnson, African Travel Hits New Heights," accessed 6 June 2001, at http://www.africana.com/DailyArticles/index_20000103.htm.

29. U.S. Customs Service, 1.

30. There is another view of hit rates, based on econometrics, which argues that similar hit rates for blacks and whites actually indicate that there is *no* racial discrimination. As expressed by several econometricians from the University of Pennsylvania in a 1999 paper, John Knowles, Nicola Persico, and Petra Todd, "Racial Bias in Motor Vehicle Searches: Theory and Evidence," *Journal of Political Economy* 109 (February 2001):203, this view takes as its underlying assumption that statistics indicating whom police decide to search can show one of two things: racial prejudice, which would reveal itself in numbers that show more blacks searched, or statistical discrimination, in which police care not about the race of those they stop but simply look to maximize the return on their effort. Police are rational maximizers, the Penn econometricians argue; they want the biggest bang for

the buck when they decide to stop and search drivers. Therefore, they do what they believe is rational to get to the same hit rate for everyone. This may mean more blacks get stopped, but that the resulting hit rate is the same for both blacks and whites indicates that police have reached an equilibrium point with regard to their decision to search. The Penn econometricians tested this hypothesis against the data for the Maryland State Police from 1995 to 1999. They assumed that police were deciding to search all drivers based on the same list of neutral, nonracial criteria—for example, the presence of CB radios, cellular telephones, radar detectors, tinted windows, religious paraphernalia, or maps. Id. at C, "Observable Indicators of Criminal Activity"; communication between the author and Nicola Persico, 14 March 2001 (to the question whether the "observable indicators" are the same criteria used to evaluate suspiciousness for both races, "the answer is yes. These are signs that the police manual suggests as indicative, or suggestive, of criminal activity") (copy on file with the author). The fact that police find contraband (mainly drugs) at the same rates for blacks and whites means, they said, that they have equally good suspicions for blacks and whites; it's just that more blacks meet the criteria for suspiciousness, and so more of them are searched to produce this same hit rate. They concluded that, having reached the equilibrium point—a very similar hit rate for blacks and whites, though far more blacks were searched—meant that police were practicing not racial discrimination, but rational and efficient statistical discrimination. For Hispanics searched, however, the hit rate was far lower than for whites—meaning that police were searching greater numbers of comparatively unsuspicious Hispanics because of their ethnicity. In other words, police in Maryland were, in fact, practicing ethnic discrimination against Hispanics, not rational law enforcement based on statistical discrimination. All in all, the data showed that, at least for African Americans, the way that Maryland police were deciding which drivers to search exhibited evidence of efficient, rational law enforcement. On closer examination, the idea of statistical discrimination at a kind of rational equilibrium proves unpersuasive—an attractive, well-assembled house of cards. First, like many economic models, the econometric model relies on a number of assumptions about people that may or may not resemble the real world. For example, the researchers who examined the Maryland State Police data assumed that police officers are taking rational actions to maximize their hits per stops. While this may make sense on the surface, many other factors could also be at work. Have supervisors guided or ordered officers to stop certain kinds of people, regardless of how individuals in these groups may stack up vis-à-vis the criteria of suspiciousness? (This may sound paranoid or farfetched—until one considers that there was *written* evidence of exactly this kind of targeting uncovered in the Maryland case.) Are police officers perhaps not operating on the basis of the criteria of suspiciousness but instead on intelligence they have gathered? As for those found with drugs, the researchers assume that they make rational calculations based at least in part on the risk of getting caught in deciding whether to transport drugs in their cars. Again, this seems reasonable, but it is far from clear that a person carrying a small amount of marijuana (the most common drug found, according to the data) makes any kind of assessment of the risk, or indeed thinks much about it at all before driving. And even those drivers carrying larger, "courier-level" amounts may not make any elaborate assessments of the risk. Whereas risk is perhaps part of the calculation for the traffickers themselves—those owning the cocaine and paying for drivers to transport it—those actually driving vehicles with drug loads in them likely have a completely different outlook. And, comparing the relatively few stops made to the millions of cars on the road every day, the real risk of getting stopped and searched is actually quite low; it is a comparatively rare event. Thus there is little reason to think that any risk assessment goes on in the formal way that the econometric model contemplates. Second, these kinds of models present us with a false dichotomy: either the data show racial discrimination and prejudice, or they show neutral, statistical discrimination. In reality, of course, a conclusion that the data show "just" statistical discrimination fails to take into consideration that both racial and statistical discrimination could be present. In fact, a finding of statistical discrimination could mask racial discrimination quite easily. In other words, statistical discrimination may only hide racial discrimination instead of serving as a true alternative explanation; racial discrimination could very well be present, simply masquerading as something else. Thus the "either/or" typology could be little more than an illusion that hides what is really important. Third, the econometric model does not really describe accurately what is happening when police stop drivers and decide to search them. According to sociologist and criminologist Joseph E. Jacoby, there is no reason that differential numbers of searches of whites and blacks that yield the same hit rate could be a rational approach to law enforcement. Since the hit rates for blacks and whites are the same, Jacoby says, only two possibilities exist to explain the much larger number of searches of blacks. One is racial discrimination. The other is a real association between being black and the observable characteristics of criminal activity that the Penn econometricians have assumed are applied equally to blacks and whites, "combined with the incorrect assumption by the police that these 'observable characteristics' are associated with illegal behavior." In other words, Jacoby says, police assert that they stop a disproportionate number of black drivers not because they are black but because black motorists are more likely to be suspicious. "Assuming that the police are accurate, the fact that (searches) of blacks produce no higher a percentage of hits than (searches) of whites suggests that the 'observable characteristics' are more strongly associated with race than with criminality." Communication between the author and Joseph E. Jacoby, Bowling Green State University, 12 March 2001 (copy on file with the author). The so-called observable characteristics of criminality thus turn out to be unhelpful at best and downright racially biased at worst. Albert J. Meehan and Michael Ponder, whose MDT data studies showed high rates of racial profiling, drew similar conclusions. The hit rates for blacks were higher than those for whites in their study, they said, but only slightly; in fact, the hit rates for both groups were remarkably low, and together were almost no different than hit rates for randomly selected cars. See Meehan and Ponder. But even knowing that black hit rates for MDT queries were higher than those for whites proves nothing about the efficiency or success of profiling. Ibid. Fourth, the Penn econometricians seem to assume that blacks and other minorities are carrying drugs at a rate higher than that of whites. It is because they are searched in disproportionate numbers, the Penn econometricians have argued, that some percentage of these minority citizens is discouraged from carrying drugs, resulting in the equal hit rate for the races. Thus racial targeting is, indeed, an efficient law enforcement tactic. There are two problems with the cold logic of these arguments. There is absolutely no evidence presented for the assumption that African Americans, Hispanics, or other minorities are overrepresented among those guilty of drug possession or involved in the narcotics trade. Neither the Penn econometricians nor Professor John J. Donohue of Stanford University supply any evidence to show that their assumptions are anything other than assumptions. Thus the analysis arrives at the conclusion—it is statistically efficient policing to target minorities—by bringing in an unproved assumption through the back door. But even assuming there *was* some evidence to support their assumption, and that they are correct that this shows efficient, statistically based policing, a more fundamental problem remains. The Fourteenth Amendment to the U.S. Constitution requires that each and every citizen enjoy the equal protection of the laws; it does not permit racially or ethnically discriminatory enforcement of the laws just because it may be statistically efficient. David Rudovsky, a senior fellow at the University of Pennsylvania Law School who has handled a number of important cases involving racially unequal law enforcement, says the very idea of allowing discriminatory policing because it is efficient is almost diametrically opposed to the entire basis of how the Constitution requires the government to enforce the law. If statistics demonstrated that African Americans committed more robberies, Rudovsky says, the Fourteenth Amendment would never tolerate a statute that said that whites convicted of robbery could be sentenced to up to five years in prison, but that blacks, whom we need to discourage from committing robbery because they commit more than their share of it, could be sentenced to up to ten years. That, he says, is precisely what the econometric model would have us do— wrap the law around an efficiency-based model, which is concerned not with individual justice but with statistics based on unproved assumptions. Interview with David Rudovsky, 21 March 2001. (Perhaps this is why the Penn econometricians end their article with a section that concedes that, even though they feel statistical discrimination is an efficient way to police, it lacks fairness, and hence its unfairness may make it an unattractive way of enforcing the law.)

Fifth, the Penn econometricians' work analyzes data from Maryland, in which the hit rates for African Americans and whites were roughly equal. Recall that their data also contained hit rates for Hispanics, and that those hit rates were much lower than hit rates for whites. This, they said, showed that there was in fact discrimination taking place that had no statistical justification. This is a telling insight; if it is true, it means that hit rates do, indeed, show how widespread profiling-type discrimination is. Because while in Maryland hit rates for African Americans and whites measure up equally, in most other cases hit rates for minorities are *lower* than for whites. Recall that in the data from U.S. Customs searches in 1998, hit rates for blacks were lower than for whites; hit rates for Hispanics were dramatically lower. In New York City stops and frisks, we see the same pattern, with lower hit rates for both blacks and Hispanics than for whites. If the Penn econometricians applied the same kind of analysis to these data, they would conclude that racial discrimination exists in these stops and searches—just as they did for the Hispanic data in Maryland.

31. Heather MacDonald, "The Myth of Racial Profiling," *City Journal* 11, no. 2 (Spring 2001). MacDonald fails to mention that in all of the statistical examinations of hit rates except one, hit rates were lower for minorities than whites; in just one—Maryland—were the rates the same.

32. *Contacts Between Police and the Public,* U.S. Department of Justice, Bureau of Justice Statistics, March 2001.

33. Ibid., p. 22, table 14.

34. Peter Verniero and Paul Zoubek, "Interim Report of the State Police Review Team Regarding Allegations of Racial Profiling," 20 April 1999, 28.

35. Illya D. Lichtenberg, "Voluntary Consent or Obedience to Authority: An Inquiry Into the 'Consensual' Police-Citizen Encounter" (Ph.D. diss., Rutgers University School of Criminal Justice, October 1999), 170–71 (copy on file with the author).

36. Ibid., 177.

37. Peter Verniero and Paul Zoubek, 37.

38. Eliot Spitzer, 91 ("comments by some police officials that [stop and frisk forms] are not filled out in every 'mandated' circumstance").

39. *Ohio v. Robinette,* 519 U.S. 33 (1996).

40. Press Release, "Attorney General Betty Montgomery Hails U.S. Supreme Court Decision as a Victory for Ohio Law Enforcement," 18 November 1996.

41. Memorandum from Staff Lieutenant W. D. Healy, TDIT Unit Coordinator, to Major R. N. Rucker, 11 December 1995, A-3.

42. Telephone interview with Todd Boyer, Office of the Ohio Attorney General, 13 December 1996.

43. William J. Stuntz, "Race, Class, and Drugs," *Columbia Law Review* 98 (1998): 1795, 1799, 1821.

CHAPTER FIVE: THE COSTS OF RACIAL PROFILING: CASUALTIES AND COLLATERAL DAMAGE

1. Larry Sykes, interview by author, 27 June 2000.
2. Hugh Grefe, interview by author, 27 June 2000.

3. Interview by author, 1 October 1998. Michael asked that his last name not be used.

4. "America in Black and White: Fitting the Profile," *Nightline,* broadcast ABC News, 3 April 1998.

5. Ronald Weitzer, "Racialized Policing: Residents' Perceptions in Three Neighborhoods," *Law and Society Review* (2000): 129.

6. Janis Sanchez-Hucles, "Racism: Emotional Abusiveness and Psychological Trauma for Ethnic Minorities," *Journal of Emotional Abuse,* (1998): 69.

7. Dr. Janis Sanchez-Hucles, interview by author, 20 October 2000.

8. Vivian Martin, " 'Driving While Black' Is Part of the Burden of Being Black," *Baltimore Sun,* 13 July 1999, 11A.

9. Hugh F. Butts, "Psychoanalytic Perspectives on Racial Profiling," *Journal of the American Academy of Psychiatry and Law* (1999): 633.

10. Ibid.

11. Michael Fletcher, "Driven to Extremes: Black Men Take Steps to Avoid Police Stops," *Washington Post,* 29 March 1996, A22.

12. Ibid.

13. Emmanuel Key, interview by author, 6 November 1998.

14. U.S. Department of Justice, Bureau of Justice Statistics, *Contacts Between Police and the Public* (Washington, D.C.: GPO, 2001).

15. Ibid., 13.

16. Ibid., 18 (police searched 11 percent of black drivers, 11.3 percent of Hispanic drivers, but only 5.4 percent of white drivers).

17. Ibid., 22.

18. Ibid., 17.

19. Key, interview.

20. *Shelly* v. *Kramer,* 334 U.S. 1 (1948).

21. George C. Galster, "Polarization, Place, and Race," *North Carolina Law Review* 71 (1993): 1421, 1430–31.

22. Ibid., table 9.

23. William J. Stuntz, "Race, Class, and Drugs," *Columbia Law Review* 98 (1998): 1795, 1810.

24. Eric Schmitt, "Analysis of Census Finds Segregation Along with Diversity," *New York Times,* 4 April 2001, A15 (even as the nation as a whole became more diverse, "adopting a slightly darker hue, whites, blacks, Asians, and Hispanics still tend to live apart"); Eric Schmitt, "Segregation Growing Among U.S. Children," *New York Times,* 5 May 2001, 28 (census data show that white and black children live in ever more segregated neighborhoods, especially in the Midwest and Northeast).

25. James Banks, interview by author, 30 October 1998.

26. Complaint, *Suron Jacobs* v. *Village of Ottawa Hills et al.,* CI99-1386.

27. Eric Schmitt, "The Fire Next Time: Finding Embers in the Ashes," *New York Times,* 6 May 2001, sec. 4, p. 1 (2000 Census shows that "economic geography has been changing . . . job growth tends to be greatest in

the suburbs, often hard to reach on mass transit"; this has meant "progressive decentralization of jobs," especially those paying a decent wage and requiring only modest skills); George Galster, "Polarization, Race, and Place," *North Carolina Law Review* 71(1993): 1421, 1432.

28. Diane Frederick, "Police Case in Carmel Is Settled for $100,000; Plaintiff Was Trooper Who Accused the City of Racist Traffic Stop," *Indianapolis Star,* 23 April 1998.

29. Ibid.

30. Mary Ellen O'Toole, *The School Shooter: A Threat Assessment Perspective,* Federal Bureau of Investigation, U.S. Department of Justice (Washington, D.C.: GPO, 2000). (O'Toole is a supervisory special agent at the FBI.)

31. Ibid., 12.

32. Ibid., 6–7.

33. Ibid., 1–3.

34. The author attended this meeting as a participant.

35. Saul Green, interview by author, 30 August 1999.

36. "U.S. Attorneys Caution Sons About Police; Youths Warned They May Be Stopped Because of Race," *Richmond Times Dispatch,* 2 June 1999, A2.

37. Ibid.

38. Ibid.

39. Ibid.

40. Federal News Service, "Attorney General Janet Reno's Address to the National Press Club," 15 April 1999.

41. Debra Ramirez, interview by author, 14 August 2000.

42. John Solomon, interview by author, 28 June 2000.

43. Officer Ova Tate, interview by author, 28 August 1998.

44. Diana Jimenez, interview by author, 17 November 2000.

45. Tammerlin Drummond, "Coping with Cops," *Time,* 3 April 2000.

46. 100 Blacks in Law Enforcement, "What to Do When Stopped by Police" Information Kit, at http://members.tripod.com/blacksnlaw/, 6 November 2000.

47. Rossano Gerald, interview by author, 12 September 2000.

48. Harland C. Stonecipher, interview by author, 17 November 2000.

49. E.g., "200 Best Small Companies," *Forbes,* 1 November 1999 (Pre-Paid Legal ranks number 13); "200 Best Small Companies," *Forbes,* 2 November 1998 (Pre-Paid Legal ranks number 5); *Equities,* July/August 1999 (ranked as 33rd fastest growing company); "Legal Protection in the Bank," *Black Enterprise,* July 1997 (describing company as a provider of essential legal services on an affordable basis); "Top 50 Stock Picks for the '90s," *Money,* August 1998 (ranking Pre-Paid Legal number 13).

50. The company's stock ticker symbol is PPD.

51. Marilyn Thompson, interview by author, 3 November 2000. Thompson national media director for Pre-Paid Legal, Inc., says that the corporation has no marketing plan that calls for marketing Legal Shield to

African Americans or other minorities; she says that it is a product that every American should have because "police stop and arrest people of all kinds for no reason. I have friends this has happened to. I tout it to all my clients down here [in Oklahoma], and they're almost all white." Thompson said that she was aware that Tony Brown, the New York–based journalist, sold Pre-Paid Legal products and marketed them directly to African Americans. She said she thought that other "associates" did too, but she refused to supply any further information.

52. Leon Wynter, "Police Abuse Gives Insurer an Opportunity," *Wall Street Journal,* 3 November 1999, B1 ("If Abner Louima had a Legal Shield card and showed it on the way to the bathroom, I believe [the assault on him] would never have happened").

53. Web site for Allen L. Thomas. The "Asian man in New York" may refer to Amadou Diallo, an African man who was shot forty-one times by New York City Police.

54. Leon Wynter, "Police Abuse."

55. Tony Brown and Harland Stonecipher, "Solid Evidence That a 'Shield' is Needed" 7 December 1999.

56. Marilyn Thompson interview.

57. Martha L. Henderson et al., "The Impact of Race on Perceptions of Criminal Injustice," *Journal of Criminal Justice* 25 (1997): 447.

58. Ibid., 453–54, table 3.

59. Ibid.

60. Darrell West, "Race, Gender, and Providence Courts," Brown Policy Report, August 2000, published at http://www.insidepolitics.org/policyreports/CTREP800.html. (West is the director of the Taubman Center for Public Policy, at Brown University.)

61. Saul Green interview.

62. *Criminal Victimization and Perceptions of Community Safety in 12 Cities,* U.S. Department of Justice, Bureau of Justice Statistics, and Office of Community Oriented Policing Services (Washington, D.C.: GPO, 1998), p. 25, tables 33, 34.

63. Ibid.

64. "Attitudes Toward Fair Treatment of Persons of Different Races by Police in Own Community, by Demographic characteristics, U.S., 2000, Sourcebook of Criminal Justice Statistics Online," at http://www.albany.edu/sourcebook/1995/pdf/t228.pdf, table 2.28.

65. "Perceptions of Black and White Americans Continue to Diverge Widely on Issues of Race Relations in the U.S.," Gallup News Service, 28 February 2000.

66. Frank Newport, "Racial Profiling Seen as Widespread, Particularly Among Young Black Men," Gallup Poll, 9 December 1999.

67. Ibid.

68. Ibid.

69. "Respondents Reporting Fear That the Police Will Stop and Arrest Them When Innocent, by Demographic characteristics, U.S., 2000, Source-

book of Criminal Justice Statistics Online," at http://www.albany.edu/
sourcebook/1995/pdf/t229.pdf, table 2.29.

70. DecisionQuest and the National Law Journal, *2000 Annual Juror Outlook, Third Annual Juror Outlook Survey,* 22–24 September 2000.

71. Frank Newport, "Racial Profiling."

72. Ibid.

73. "Standard Enforcement—A Michigan Perspective," EPIC/MRA, Lansing, Michigan, January 2000.

74. "Politics in the Judiciary," (panel discussion at the University of Toledo College of Law, Toledo, Ohio, with Judge James Carr, Justice Joseph Baca, and Judge Eric Clay, 20 October 2000).

75. Lucas Miller, "The Diallo Verdict: A Cop's View," *Slate,* 26 February 2000 (viewed at http://slate.msn.com/dispatches/00-02-25/dispatches.asp).

76. David Rohde, "Juror's Trust in Police Erodes in Light of Diallo and Louima," *New York Times,* 9 March 2000.

77. Jeffrey Rosen, "One Angry Woman," *New Yorker,* 24 February, 3 March 1997, 54, 64.

78. Ibid.

79. Paul Butler, "Racially Based Jury Nullification: Black Power in the Criminal Justice System," *Yale Law Journal* 105 (1995): 677.

80. *U.S.* v. *Leviner,* 31 F. Supp. 2d 23 (D. Mass. 1998).

81. Ibid., 24.

82. Ibid., 33, n. 26.

83. Ibid., 33.

84. Ibid., 31, 34.

85. See chapter 3.

CHAPTER SIX: IT'S NOT JUST DRIVING WHILE BLACK: HOW PROFILING AFFECTS LATINOS, ASIANS, AND ARABS

1. Henry Louis Gates, "Thirteen Ways of Looking at a Black Man," *New Yorker,* 23 October 1995, 59 (constant stops by police is what "many African-Americans know as D.W.B.: Driving While Black"); Michael Fletcher, "Driven to Extremes: Black Men Take Steps to Avoid Police Stops," *Washington Post,* 29 March 1996, A1 (black men are stopped so often by police that they say they are stopped for the offense one of them "calls DWB—driving while black").

2. Davan Maharaj, "Rights Suit Involving Police Photos Is Settled," *Los Angeles Times,* 12 December 1995, 1 (Orange Co. ed.) (federal lawsuit involving police detention and taking of photos of young Asians as suspected gang members based on appearance and attire settled); Daniel C. Tsang, "Is 'Innocent Until Proven Guilty' a Lost Principle?," *Los Angeles Times,* 30 August 1993, B5 (Asian youth identified by police as gang members based on clothing and Asian appearance); see also chapter 1.

3. *U.S.* v. *Ramsey,* 431 U.S. 606, 616 (1977).

4. Ibid.

5. Ibid., 546–47.

6. Ibid., 563–64.

7. Ibid., n. 17.

8. *U.S.* v. *Brignoni-Ponce,* 422 U.S. 873 (1975).

9. Ibid., 883–48.

10. Ibid., 886.

11. Ibid.

12. Ibid., 880.

13. Ibid., 886–87.

14. Edwin Harwood, "Arrest Without Warrant: The Legal and Organizational Environment of Immigration Law Enforcement," *U.C. Davis Law Review* 17, (1984): 505, 531.

15. U.S. Census Bureau, "Resident Population Estimates of the United States by Sex, Race, and Hispanic Origin: April 1, 1990 to July 1, 1999, with Short-Term Projection to November 1, 2000, August 25, 2000"; www.census.gov/population/estimates/nations/intfile3-1.txt; "Hispanic and Asian Populations Expand," *New York Times,* 30 August 2000, A15.

16. U.S. Census Bureau, "1990 to 1999 Annual Time Series of State Population Estimates, Race and Hispanic Origin" (Washington, D.C.: GPO, 2000).

17. "Hispanic and Asian Populations Expand," *New York Times,* 30 August 2000, A 15.

18. Mark Finnegan, interview by author, 15 May 1998.

19. 8 U.S.C. sec. 1304 (e).

20. Complaint, *Farm Labor Organizing Committee et al.,* v. *Ohio State Highway Patrol,* No. 3:96CV7580 (N. D. Ohio).

21. *Farm Labor Organizing Committee et al.,* v. *Ohio State Highway Patrol,* 991 F. Supp. 895 (N.D. Ohio, W. Div. 1997) (["A] The officers, agents, and employees of the Ohio State Highway Patrol are enjoined from questioning motorists about their immigration status [1] without reasonable suspicion based on articulable objective facts arising either [a] from the circumstances of the initial seizure of motorists or [b] other circumstances arising during such seizure that such motorists are in violation of federal law relating to immigration, or [2] uncoereced and otherwise lawful consent to such questioning; and [B] The officers, agents, and employees of the Ohio State Highway Patrol are enjoined from seizing immigration documents from motorists absent lawful cause for doing so and, if such seizure occurs, providing forthwith fully effective substitute documents").

22. *Farm Labor Organizing Committee et al.,* v. *Ohio State Highway Patrol et al.,* 184 F.R.D. 583 (N. D. Ohio, W. Div., 1998).

23. *Farm Labor Organizing Committee et al.,* v. *Ohio State Highway Patrol et al.,* 95 F. Supp. 2d 723 (N.D. Ohio, W. Div. 2000).

24. *U.S.* v. *Montero-Camargo,* 208 F. 3d 1122 (en banc) (9th Cir. 2000).

25. Ibid., 32.

26. ChorSwang Ngin, "Racism and Racialized Discourse on Asian Youth in Orange County; Cal. *Politics and Policy* 2 (1996): 3 (describing "model minority" Asian stereotype as based on a view of Asians as "quiet, hardworking, non-complaining" and "the accomplishments of many Asian students as holders of the prestigious Westinghouse Awards, the National Merit Scholarships and other accolades").

27. Ibid., 1; Davan Maharaj, "Rights Suit."

28. Daniel C. Tsang, "GREAT No More: But a New Gang Database Is Ready to Take Its Place," *OC Weekly,* 11 July 1997, 10 (discussing the Gang Reporting Evaluation and Tracking [GREAT] database, which stored all of the photos of the suspected gang members).

29. Daniel C. Tsang, "DWUS: Driving While a UCI Student," *OC Weekly,* 23 April 1999 (Irvine, California, police official called Hondas "notorious" for use by gang members).

30. ChorSwang Ngin, "Racism," 4.

31. Ibid.

32. Daniel C. Tsang, "GREAT No More."

33. Memorandum by Jim Armound, 12 August 1991, quoted in Daniel C. Tsang, "GREAT No More."

34. Davan Maharaj, "Rights Suit."

35. Daniel C. Tsang, "DWUS: Driving While a UCI Student."

36. Ricardo Alonso-Zaldivar and Eric Malnic, "Safety Checks of Wiring on Jets Are Urged," *Los Angeles Times,* 24 August 2000, A1 (the National Transportation Safety Board [NTSB] "formally concluded its investigation of the 1996 disaster, finding—as expected—that a short circuit in the plane's nearly 200 miles of wiring probably led to a fuel tank explosion that tore the aircraft apart about 13,800 feet above the Atlantic Ocean"); Don Phillips, "Probe of TWA Crash Concludes with a Warning"; NTSB Calls Attention to Risk of Fuel Tank Explosion Posed by Worn Wiring in Older Planes," *Washington Post,* 24 August 2000, A2 (while NTSB could not come to a definite conclusion about what caused the crash, "of the sources evaluated by the investigation, the most likely was a short circuit outside of the center wing tank that allowed explosive voltage to enter it through electrical wiring associated with the fuel quantity indication system").

37. Sandy Banks, "When Terrorism Strikes, People Often Fall Back on Stereotypes," *Los Angeles Times,* 15 May 2001, part 5, p. 1 (recalling early bulletins in wake of Oklahoma City bombing that police were looking for men of Middle Eastern appearance, and the detention of an Arab man as a suspect who was later released).

38. James Padgett, manager, Global Issues Division, Office of Civil Aviation Security and Intelligence, Federal Aviation Administration, interview by author, 24 August 2000 (recounting a story of an Arab American woman traveling through an airport in Texas who was told that she "fit a criminal profile"); Sam Husseini, "Profiles in Unfairness: What Happened to TWA 800 Is No Reason to Endanger Passengers' Civil Rights," *Washington Post,*

24 November 1996, C3 (under new FAA pilot program in wake of TWA 800 crash, "[I]f your 'profile' fits that of a terrorist, you will undergo more questions and searches than other passengers"); Michael Higgins, "Looking the Part: With Criminal Profiles Being Used More Widely to Spot Possible Terrorists and Drug Couriers, Claims of Bias Are Also on the Rise," *ABA Journal* 83 (November 1997): 48 (Arab American couple, both physicians, got extra personal scrutiny and had bags searched and visibly labeled because, as an airline employee told them, " 'Well, these are the guidelines and you fit the guidelines' ").

39. White House Commission on Aviation Safety and Security, Vice President Al Gore, chairman, *Final Report to President Clinton* (Washington, D.C.: GPO, 1997), 25 (recommendation 3.19, "Complement technology with automated passenger profiling").

40. James Padgett, interview.

41. Ibid.

42. Ibid.

43. Ibid.

44. Ibid.

45. Ibid.

Chapter Seven: MEETING THE CHALLENGE OF RACIAL PROFILING

1. Chief Charles Moose, interview by author, 7 August 2000.

2. Didi Nelson and Tom Hayes, interview by author, 8 August 2000.

3. Consent Decree, *U.S. v. New Jersey et al.,* Civ. No. 99-5970 (MLC), par. 26.

4. Ibid., par. 27 ("The State Police has adopted a protocol captioned 'F-55 [Motor Vehicle Stops],' dated December 14, 1999, which establishes criteria to be followed by state troopers in selecting which vehicles to stop for violation of state motor vehicle laws. This protocol includes the nondiscrimination requirements set forth in ¶ 26 and has been approved by the United States in so far as the protocol identifies practices and procedures required by the Decree").

5. Lorie Fridell, Robert Lunney, Drew Diamond, and Bruce Kubu, *Racially-Biased Policing: A Principled Response* (Washington, D.C.: Police Executive Research Forum, 2001), 52.

6. Consent Decree, *U.S. v. New Jersey,* par. 28 ("The State has adopted protocols [captioned F-55 Motor Vehicle Stops] dated 12/14/99; C-22 [Activity Reporting System], F-3 [Patrol Procedures], F-7 [Radio Procedures], F-19 [MVR equipment], F-31 [Consent Searches], and a Motor Vehicle Stop Search Report dated 12/21/99; and a Property Report [S.P. 131, Rev. 1/91]"). These policies reflect what is contained in the consent decree, but according to John Haggerty, a spokesman for the state police, the policies themselves are not available to the public. John Haggerty, telephone conversation with author, 12 December 2000.

7. Memorandum of Lt. Col. Stephen D. Madden, deputy director, Uniform Services Bureau, 2 August 1999, entitled "Consent Search Policy."

8. *Michigan Department of State Police Traffic Enforcement Summary, Third Quarter 2000.*

9. Brian Mackie, interview by author, 11 September 2000.

10. Brian Mackie, interview by author, 12 December 2000.

11. Brian Mackie, interview, 11 September 2000.

12. John Timoney, interview by author, 4 December 2000.

13. Preventing Biased Policing and the Perceptions of Biased Policing, Draft Model Policy, February 2001, B, Police Executives Research Forum, Washington, D.C.

14. John Farrell, interview by author, 11 September 2000.

15. Farrell concedes that there have, indeed, been other complaints against his department, especially on the use-of-force issue. At this writing, the U.S. Department of Justice is investigating the Prince Georges County Police for alleged violations of civil rights. See April Witt and Paul Schwartzman, "Pr. Georges Prosecutor Acts to Check Police Tactics," *Washington Post,* 7 June 2001, B1 ("In November, the U.S. Justice Department began an investigation of the Prince Georges County Police Department after a 15-month period in which officers shot twelve people, killing five of them. The federal probe is examining the agency's use of deadly force as well as alleged patterns of brutality, racial discrimination and abuses by the canine squad").

16. See *Report of the National Advisory Commission on Civil Disorders* (also known as the *Report of the Kerner Commission*) (New York: Pantheon Books, 1968).

17. Interview with Assistant Chief Steve Creighton, San Diego Police Department, interview by author, 14 November 2000.

18. Dean Esserman, interview by author, 16 August 2000.

19. The description of the training here comes from the author's observation of two training sessions conducted by Didi Nelson and Tom Hayes in July 2000. The rest of the quotes come from an interview with Nelson and Hayes on August 8, 2000.

20. Commander Jerry Clayton, interview by author, 6 October 2000.

21. Rose Ochi, interview by author, 30 January 2001.

22. Cecil Thomas, interview by author, 9 August 2000.

23. Ida Gillis, interview by author, 1 January 2001.

24. Robert Wasserman, interview by author, 29 December 2000.

25. *The Interactive Courtroom* (New York: Practising Law Institute CD-ROM Series, 2000).

26. Robert McNeilly, interview by author, 5 December 2000.

27. Deborah Ramirez, interview by author, 19 August 2000.

28. Ron Jornd, interview by author, 20 August 2000.

29. "Study Indicates Blacks Receive More Tickets," *Associated Press,* 4 October 2000 (study by *Dallas Morning News* revealing blacks in twenty-

eight mostly rural Texas counties received twice the number of tickets than the general driving population rejected by chair of the Department of Public Safety Board, saying study was flawed, so "I'm not going to start a massive investigation unless and until there is some indication that something is going on"); see also David A. Harris, "When Success Bleeds Attack: The Coming Backlash Against Racial Profiling Studies," Michigan, *Journal of Race and Law* 6 (2001) (arguing that police departments, which have resisted recognizing problems because of lack of sufficient data and then refuse to collect data because there is no problem, have an obligation as public institutions to collect the data in order to meet the important concerns of the public).

30. John Timoney, interview.

31. William Bratton, interview by author, 14 December 2000.

32. The author helped draft the original Conyers bill, H.R. 118, which was introduced in the 105th Congress in January 1997. The bill, and the idea of data collection as a way to begin to address racial profiling, were based on the author's 1997 article, " 'Driving While Black' and All Other Traffic Offenses: The Supreme Court and Pretextual Traffic Stops," *Journal of Criminal Law and Criminology* 87 (1997): 544.

33. H.R. 118 (105th Cong., 1st sess., 1997).

34. Adoption of policy prohibiting certain police actions; Data Collection and reporting. Conn. Gen. Stat. sec. 24-1m (2001).

35. Racial Profiling Revised Statutes of Missouri, sec. 590.650 (Bender 2001).

36. The monograph explains what police departments should include in their data-collection efforts. As a matter of routine, the authors say, the following data are almost always collected for every traffic stop under current systems:

1. Date, time, and location of the stop;
2. License number, state, and description of the vehicle;
3. Length of stop; and
4. Name and identification numbers of officers initiating or participating in the stop.

   If the foregoing pieces of information are not part of any system for recording data on traffic stops, whether used to study racial profiling or not, they should be. Then, in order to conduct a study of possible racial profiling, the following data should be collected in addition to the routine elements specified above.

5. Date of birth, since younger drivers, particularly African Americans, report a perception that police single them out for stops;
6. Gender, because black males report higher rates of stops than all whites and all black females;
7. Race or ethnicity, as perceived by the officer (see no. 10 below), using at least the following categories, with others to be added according to the racial and ethnic makeup of the locale:

- White
- Black
- Asian, Pacific Islander
- Native American
- Middle Eastern, East Indian
- Hispanic/Latino

8. Reason for the stop. The reasons should be broken down in ways that allow us to know whether the stop was the result of externally generated information, like a BOLO bulletin or 911 call, a high-danger, low-discretion traffic offense such as reckless driving, or a low-danger, high-discretion offense such as driving with a cracked taillight lens. Larger numbers of the latter type of stops could indicate a pattern of abuse of police discretion.

9. Disposition, or what happened as a result of each stop, such as the following:
   - Oral Warning
   - Written Warning
   - Arrest Made
   - Arrest By [Preexisting] Warrant
   - Criminal Citation
   - Traffic Citation—Hazardous
   - Traffic Citation—Nonhazardous
   - Courtesy Service/Citizen Assist
   - No Action Taken

10. Whether a search was conducted. This would be extremely valuable for determining not only whether certain racial or ethnic groups were targeted for this intrusive post-stop activity, but also for determining just how efficient and productive the department's searching activity is. Since a search is a relatively rare event, most of the time most officers would simply check "no search" at the top and would not need to fill out the rest of the information.

   This comprehensive list is not much longer than what police will already be collecting in states like Connecticut and Missouri, and it will ensure that the analysis that emerges from any data-collection effort can actually help all of the relevant questions. The extra time and effort invested would be minimal, and the benefit would be a complete picture unavailable with a more limited set of data.

37. Letter from Marc Thompson, village manager, Ottawa Hills, Ohio, to Rep. Peter Lawson Jones, Ohio House of Representatives, 12 January 2001 (copy on file with author).

38. John Lamberth, interview by author, 26 October 2000.

39. See, e.g., Tony Perry, "Police-Stop Data Suggest Imbalance; San Diego Chief Promises More Study to See If Blacks and Latinos Are Being Singled Out By Officers Because of Skin Color," *Los Angeles Times,* 29 Septem-

ber 2000, A1 (at release of first segment of data, which showed blacks and Latinos stopped disproportionately relative to population, chief of police was nonetheless "backed" by members of the minority community and the A.C.L.U., whom the chief had included in the study process, and leaders of both the Urban League and A.C.L.U. chapters praised the department's effort and leadership on the issue); Mark Arner and Joe Hughes, "Police Stop Blacks, Latinos More Often"; "Data from Profiling Report Echo Fears of S.D. Minorities," *S.D. Union Tribune,* 29 September 2000, at A1 (community leaders praised the police department for doing the study, despite results).

40. John Lamberth, interview by author, 26 October 2000.

41. Matthew Zingraff, interview by author, 1 February 2001.

42. Letter from Marc Thompson to Peter Lawson Jones, supra, showing rates of arrests, citations, and warnings of nonwhite drivers slightly higher than nonwhite driving populations in both 1999 and 2000.

43. Thomas Zolper, "Troopers in Racial Profiling Probe Appear in Court Plead Not Guilty in Patrol Records Case," *Bergen Record,* 28 May 1999, A1.

44. Adam Gelb and Tony Boyle, of PSComm, interview by author, 2 February 2001.

45. Jim Tomaino, interview by author, 11 September 2000.

46. Walter Bader, interview by author, 14 August 2000.

47. Rulette Armstead, interview by author, 25 August 2000.

48. Bill Lansdowne, interview by author, 4 August 2000; Rob Davis, interview by author, 8 August 2000.

49. David Linn, interview by author, August 2000.

50. National Public Radio broadcast, Brian Donohue of the Newark Star Ledger Discusses the Effect of In-Car Police Video Cameras on the Number of Traffic Stops Made in New Jersey, 17 February 2000.

51. Ibid.

52. Ron Jornd, interview by author, 20 August 2000.

53. Robert McNeilly, interview by author, 5 December 2000.

54. Samuel Walker and Geoffrey P. Alpert, "Police Accountability: Establishing an Early Warning System," IQ Service Report, vol. 32, no. 8, August 2000 (Washington, D.C.: International City/County Management Association, August 2000).

55. Ibid.

56. Ibid., 2, quoting Thomas Frazier, former director of the U.S. Department of Justice's Office of Community Oriented Policing Services and former police chief in Baltimore, Maryland.

57. Christopher Commission, *Report of the Independent Commission on the Los Angeles Police Department,* p. 35 (Los Angeles: The Commission 1991).

58. Don Terry, "Kansas City Police Go after Their 'Bad Boys,' *New York Times,* 10 September 1991, A1.

59. Sean P. Murphy, "Wave of Abuse Claims Laid to a Few Officers," *Boston Globe,* 4 October 1992.

60. Samuel Walker, "Traffic Stop Data Collection: Making Sense of the Data" (on file with the author), 2001.

61. Robert McNeilly, interview by author, 5 December 2000.

62. Chuck Bossetti, interview by author, 2 May 2001.

63. Robert Wasserman, interview by author, 29 December 2000.

64. 42 U.S.C. 14141 (a) (1994).

65. "Special Lititgation Section FAQ," 2 January 2001, at www.usdoj.gov/crt/split/faq.htm.

66. Ibid.

67. Ibid., 7, quoting *International Brotherhood of Teamsters* v. *U.S.,* 431 U.S. 324, 336 (1977).

68. Statement of Steven H. Rosenbaum, chief, Special Litigation Section, Civil Rights Division, U.S. Department of Justice, before the National Association of Police Organizations National Law Enforcement Rights Center Legal Rights and Legislative Seminar, Washington, D.C., 26 April 1999.

69. Consent Decree, *U.S.* v. *City of Los Angeles and the Los Angeles Police Department et al.,* Civ. No. 00-11769 GAF (N.D. Cal. 2001).

70. Consent Decree, *U.S.* v. *New Jersey et al.,* Civ. No. 99-5970(MLC) (D. N.J. 1999).

71. *U.S.* v. *Pittsburgh and Pittsburgh Police Bureau,* C.A. 97–354 (1997).

72. Consent Decree, *U.S.* v. *City of Steubenville et al.,* 2:97 CU 966 (E.D. Ohio 1997).

73. Memorandum of Agreement Between the U.S. Department of Justice, Montgomery County, Maryland, and the Montgomery County Department of Police and the Fraternal Order of Police, Montgomery County Lodge 35, Inc. (2000), IB. 14 January 2000.

74. "Ohio City's Police Union Fights U.S. in Brutality Case," *New York Times,* 26 November 1999, A41.

75. "Special Lititgation Section FAQ," at www.usdoj.gov/crt/split/faq.htm, 2 January 2001.

76. Remarks of Joseph Brann, former director of the U.S. Department of Justice Office of Community Oriented Policing Services, at event sponsored by Police Executives Research Forum at the annual meeting of the International Association of Chiefs of Police, San Diego, California, 13 November 2000.

77. The End Racial Profiling Act of 2001, H. O. 2074 (107th Congress).

78. Heather MacDonald, "Stop Persecuting the Police," *Wall Street Journal,* 7 February 2001.

79. Cal Code Ann., Civil Code, Div. 1, Section 52.3, "Action to obtain equitable and declaratory relief to eliminate pattern or practice by law enforcement officers depriving person of legal rights."

80. Scott Gold, "State Steps into Police Reform in Riverside," *Los Angeles Times,* 18 February 2001.

CHAPTER EIGHT: A CASE STUDY: HOW ONE POLICE AGENCY CHANGED FOR THE BETTER

1. Yvette Bradley, interview by author, 22 September 2000.

2. "Color Blind? Disproportionate Number of Black Women Are Strip-Searched by U.S. Customs Agents," *Dateline NBC* broadcast, 27 April 1999.

3. Testimony of Jenneral Denson, House Ways and Means Committee, Oversight Subcommittee, 20 May 1999.

4. Renee Ferguson, interview by author, 5 October 2000.

5. Ibid.

6. Buritica also testified in Congress. Testimony of Amanda Buritica, House Ways and Means Committee, Oversight Subcommittee, 20 May 1999.

7. Edward Fox, interview by author, 24 August 2000. Amanda Buritica had been represented by a San Francisco lawyer named Greg Fox.

8. Though it is difficult to estimate just what percentage of illegal narcotics enter the country this way, it is surely a substantial amount. For example, according to the office of National Drug Control Policy (ONDCP), law enforcement authorities only seize about 12 percent of all heroin imported into the United States at the border between 1995 and 1998. ONDCP, "What America's Users Spend on Illegal Drugs, 1998–1999" (ONDCP, December 2000 available at http://www.whitehousedrugpolicy.gov/drugfact/american_users_spend/section2.html), at table 18 and figure 5. The predicted price per gram of cocaine and heroin fell between 1981 and 1999 and the predicted price per gram of marijuana remained steady between 1981 and 1991 despite increased interdiction efforts at all importation points, implying that the effect of the efforts on supply have been ineffective at best. Ibid. at figures 9, 10, and 12. See also Ethan Nadelmann, "Drug Prohibition in the United States: Costs, Consequences and Alternatives," *Science* (September 1989): 939–947 (interdiction efforts "have met with scant success in the past and show few indications of succeeding in the future. . . . Interdiction efforts have shown little success in stemming the flow of cocaine and heroin into the United States"); U.S. Department of State, International Narcotics Control Strategy Report, March 1997, Executive Summary, Policy and Program Overview for 1996, available at http://www.usis.usemb.se/drugs/Exec/executiv.htm ("Despite the U.S. [Government]-led effort, in 1996 hundreds of tons of cocaine flowed not only to the United States and Western Europe, but to markets in Latin America, Asia, Africa, and countries of the former Soviet Union").

9. Testimony of Jenneral Denson and Amanda Buritica; testimony of Edward Fox, House Ways and Means Committee, Oversight Subcommittee, 20 May 1999.

10. Testimony of Ray Kelly, commissioner of the U.S. Customs Service, House Ways and Means Committee, Oversight Subcommittee, 20 May 1999.

11. "Color Blind?"; "Women Subject to Racial Profiling by U.S. Customs Officials Invited to Testify Before Congressional Committee," *Dateline NBC* broadcast, 30 May 1999.

12. General Accounting Office, U.S. Customs Service, "Better Targeting of Airline Passengers for Personal Searches Could Produce Better Results," report to the Honorable Richard J. Durbin, U.S. Senate, March 2000.

13. Ibid., 10 ("Generally, passengers of particular races and gender [*sic*] were more likely" to be subjected to intrusive personal searches).

14. Ibid.

15. Ibid., 12.

16. Ibid., p. 12, table 3.

17. Ibid., 12.

18. Ibid., 12, 14.

19. Ibid.

20. Ibid., 10.

21. Personal Search Review Commission, *Report on Personal Searches by the U.S. Customs Service* (copy on file with the author), 2000.

22. Michael Fletcher, "Customs Review Finds Flaws; Disproportionate Searching of Black Women Is Curtailed," *Washington Post,* 29 June 2000, A29.

23. Personal Search Review Commission, 6–7.

24. U.S. Treasury Department, Office of Professional Responsibility, *Report on Personal Searches by the U.S. Customs Service,* June 1999.

25. *Passenger Targeting Committee Report,* July 1999.

26. Ibid.

27. There is just one exception to this rule: a situation in which an agent suspected a person in front of him of being armed and dangerous. Under these facts, a pat-down search can proceed immediately, without a supervisor's approval.

28. U.S. Customs Service, *Personal Search Handbook* (Rev. 1999).

29. Ibid.

30. Ibid.

31. U.S. Customs Service internal memorandum (copy on file with the author).

32. "Changing Customs: Airport Drug Busts Plunge," *New York Post,* 24 November 1999, 8.

33. Sanford Cloud, Jr., Independent Advisor's Report to Commissioner Kelly on the U.S. Customs Service's Personal Search Review Commission's Findings and Recommendations, 21 June 2000, 18.

34. Ibid.

35. Michael Fletcher, "Customs Review Finds Flaws; Disproportionate Searching of Black Women Is Curtailed," *Washington Post,* 29 June 2000, A29.

CHAPTER NINE: RACIAL PROFILING AFTER SEPTEMBER 11, 2001: NEW REALITY, SAME PROBLEMS

1. Frank Newport, "Racial Profiling Seen as Widespread, Particularly Among Young Black Men," Gallup Poll, 9 December 1999.

2. Ibid.

3. Jeffrey M. Jones, "Americans Felt Uneasy Toward Arabs Even Before September 11," *Gallup Poll Monthly,* 28 September 2001 ("Nearly six in 10 Americans interviewed in a Setember 14–15 Gallup poll favored requiring people of Arab descent to undergo special, more intensive security checks when flying on American airplanes."); Kay Lazar, "Terrorism Ushers In New Racial Perspectives," *Boston Herald,* 28 October 2001 ("The increased suspicion of Arabs was highlighted in a September Gallup Poll that found nearly 60 percent of Americans surveyed favored requiring people of Arab descent to undergo special, more intensive security checks when flying on American airplanes."); Jonah Goldberg, "When Profiling Makes Sense," *Washington Times,* 29 October 2001 ("a Gallup poll finds that 74 percent [54 percent in a Zogby Poll] of African Americans want Arab-looking travelers to get extra scrutiny at airports.").

4. Kathleen Parker, "All Is Fair in This War Except for Insensitivity," *Chicago Tribune,* 26 September 2001.

5. Stanley Crouch, "U.S. Must Stay Tough About Sealing Borders," *New York Daily News,* 14 March 2002.

6. Stanley Crouch, "Wake Up: Arabs Should Be Profiled," *St. Louis Post-Dispatch,* 19 March 2002, B7.

7. Richard Zoglin and Sally B. Donnelly, "Welcome to America's Best-Run Airport, And Why It's Still Not Good Enough," *Time,* 15 July 2002, p. 22.

8. Ibid.

9. E.g., Remarks of the Honorable Norman Y. Mineta, U.S. Secretary of Transportation, at Arab Community Center for Economic and Social Services Gala Dinner, Cobo Hall Conference Center, Detroit, Michigan, 20 April 2002, p. 3 ("It is very tempting to take false comfort in the belief that we can spot the bad guy based on appearance alone. Some are yielding to that temptation in their arguments for racial profiling, but false comfort is a luxury we cannot afford."), available at http://www.dot.gov/affairs/042002sp.htm.

10. Ibid.

11. See Chapters Two and Three.

12. Kevin Johnson, "In the Heartland, A Call to Mobilize," *USA Today,* 25 March 2002.

13. Jonathan Peterson, "Response to Terror: Deportation Sweep Targets Middle Easterners," *Los Angeles Times,* 9 January 2002 at A5 (U.S. Department of Justice announces that it will only target 6,000 visa violators from Arab countries, even though most of the 300,000 visa violators in the U.S. are from Latin America); National Public Radio, "U.S. Government's

Obligation to Its Foreign Prisoners," 24 January 2002 ("We know that earlier this month the Justice Department identified approximately 6,000 men from the Middle East who had ignored deportation orders, and the government said, 'We're going to find them. We're going to deal with them.' Now people have said, 'Well, wait a minute. We're dealing with hundreds of thousands of people, you know, more than 300,000 that are from Latin America.' ").

14. E.g., Philip Shenon, "Justice Dept. Wants to Query More Foreigners," *The New York Times,* 21 March 2002 (announcing expansion of program of interviewing "young, mostly Muslim foreign men visiting the United States" to a total of eight thousand eighteen-to-thirty-three-year-old men who had recently entered the country on nonimmigrant visas, who were "selected for interviews because they fit the criteria of persons who might have knowledge of foreign-based terrorists" and are not themselves suspects).

15. Ibid.

16. Deputy Attorney General of the U.S., Memorandum for All United States Attorneys, All Members of the Anti-Terrorism Task Forces, 9 November 2001 (on file with author).

17. Ibid.

18. Ibid.

19. In fact, the airline security system in place on September 11, called CAPPS (Computer Assisted Passenger Prescreening System), works on exactly such a profile. According to published reports, CAPPS identified nine of the nineteen September 11 hijackers as security risks. Associated Press, "Airline Security Flagged Several Sept. 11 Hijackers Before Flights," *USA Today,* 4 March 2002.

20. Daniel Rubin and Michael Dorgan, "Terrorists' September 11 Plot a Many-Tentacled Creature," Knight-Ridder/Tribune News Service, September 9, 2002 ("Zacarias Moussaoui, a volatile French-Moroccan who has been called the 20th hijacker, was arrested in the United States in the month before the terror attacks when his flight inspectors in Minnesota began wondering why he wanted to learn to fly but not to take off or land."); Guy Taylor, "FBI Nets Suspects in Global Manhunt; Attacks Led to New Urgency to Find Al Qaeda Terrorists," *Washington Times,* September 9, 2002, at A1 ("FBI agents detained him August 26, 2001, after employees at a Minneapolis flight school reported him as a suspicious foreigner wanting to learn how to fly and steer an aircraft without learning takeoff and landing techniques.").

21. Dan Eggen, "Ashcroft: No Database for TIPs," *The Washington Post,* 26 July 2002, at A10 (Attorney General quoted as saying, "I believe that there are substantial numbers of individuals in this country who endorse the Al Qaeda agenda" and who should therefore be viewed as terrorists or aiders and abetters of terrorists).

22. Early on in the process, the Department of Justice began to refuse requests for the numbers of those detained. By July of 2002, some reports

indicated that the department had deported almost all of these detainees, leaving fewer than forty in custody. In early August 2002, U.S. District Judge Gladys Kessler ruled that the federal government must release the names of all of those it had detained; "secret arrests," Judge Kessler said, had no place in a democracy. *Center for National Security Studies* v. *U.S. Department of Justice,* Memorandum Opinion, C.A. No. 01-2500 (GK), Memorandum Opinion, 2 August 2002 (Kessler, U.S. Dist. Judge). And the Attorney General has also made wide use of the material witness statute to detain those he suspects of involvement in terrorist activity, but against whom the Department of Justice has no evidence. In two cases arising from post–September 11 material witness detentions, courts have split—one deciding that material witness detention for purposes of having the witness testify in front of a grand jury was not allowed, *U.S.* v. *Osama Awadallah,* 202 F. Supp. 2d 55 (S.D.N.Y., 30 April 2002), the other saying just the opposite. In regards to Application of the United States for a Material Witness Warrant, 2002 WL 1592739 (S.D.N.Y., 11 July 2002).

23. Adam Liptak, Neil A. Lewis, and Benjamin Weiser, "After September 11, a Legal Battle on the Limits of Civil Liberty," *The New York Times,* 4 August 2002, at A1.

24. Id. ("The roundup that followed the attacks, conducted with wartime urgency and uncommon secrecy, led to the detentions of more than 1,200 people. . . . The government's effort has produced few if any law enforcement coups."); Philip Shenon, "Lawyers for 9/11 Defendant Seek 2-Month Delay in Trial," *The New York Times,* 9 August 2002, at A13 (characterizing Zacarias Moussaoui, who was arrested weeks before September 11, 2001, as "the only person charged in the September 11 terror attacks.").

25. Federal News Service, Transcript of Press Conference with U.S. Attorney John Ashcroft, Alexandria, Va., 20 March 2002.

26. Id. When asked directly about the report issued at the press conference, which was heavily redacted, whether he was simply "asking the American people to trust the government that you got good leads here," Ashcroft refused to budge. "We are not going to disclose sensitive law-enforcement information . . . [O]ur intention is to give as much information as we can to the American people to tell them the kind of situation that brought us to the conclusion that this is a very productive way to operate. We are not going to disclose information which will impair our ability to keep America safe. So the word 'redacted' will appear whenever and as often as is necessary . . ." Id.

27. Brooke A. Masters and Cheryl W. Thompson, "U.S. Plans to Query More New Arrivals; 3,000 Foreign Nationals Added to List," *The Washington Post,* 21 March 2002, at A18.

28. Id.

29. E.g., Fox Butterfield, "Police Are Split on Questioning of Mideast Men," *The New York Times,* 22 November 2001.

30. Jim McGee, "Ex-FBI Officials Criticize Tactics on Terrorism," *The Washington Post,* 28 November 2001.

31. Bill Dedman, "Airport Security: Memo Warns Against Use of Profiling As Defense," *The Boston Globe,* 12 October 2001.

32. Ibid.

33. James Lange et al., "Final Speed Violation Survey of the New Jersey Turnpike," Public Service Research Institute (copy on file with author).

34. Ibid.

35. Letter from U.S. Department of Justice, Special Litigation Section of Civil Rights Division, to Public Service Research Institute (copy on file with author).

36. David Koncieniewski, "Troopers Seek Release of Race-Based Study," *The New York Times,* 22 March 2002, B5.

37. Heather MacDonald, "The Racial Profiling Myth Debunked," *City Journal,* Spring 2002.

38. Ibid.

39. See Chapter Two, pp. 30–33; see also David A. Harris, "Car Wars: The Fourth Amendment's Death on the Highway," 66 *George Washington Law Review* 556 (1998).

40. Id.

41. Jeff Brazil and Steve Berry, "Color of Driver Is Key Stops in I-95 Videos," *The Orlando Sentinel,* 23 August 1992, A1.

42. Email communication between Dr. John and the author, July 20, 2002 (copy on file with the author).

43. The U.S. Supreme Court issued yet another ruling affirming the law on consent searches in 2002. *U.S.* v. *Drayton,* No. 01-631, ___ U.S. ___, 122 S. Ct. 2105 (2002).

44. *State* v. *Carty,* 170 N.J. 632, 790 A.2d 903 (2002).

45. Summary of Troop D Consent Searches for 2000, document released by New Jersey State Police in April 2001 hearings.

46. "Moorestown Station Consent to Search Seizures for Whites, Blacks, and Hispanics," documents released by New Jersey State Police in April 2001 hearings.

47. Peter Verniero and Paul Zoubek, *Interim Report of the State Police Review Team Regarding Allegations of Racial Profiling,* 29 April 1999, p. 4.

48. Heather MacDonald, "The Myth of Racial Profiling," *City Journal,* Spring 2001.

49. David Kocieniewski, "New Jersey Troopers Avoid Jail in Case that Highlighted Profiling," *The New York Times,* 15 January 2002, A1.

CHAPTER TEN: CONCLUSION: THE SELF-FULFILLING PROPHECY AND THE FUTURE

1. Eric Schmitt, "U.S. Now More Diverse, Racially and Ethnically," *New York Times,* 1 April 2001, 1–20.

INDEX